ISBN 978-0-483-50971-9
PIBN 10501099

ON

DIFFERENT SUBJECTS,

LEFT FOR PUBLICATION

BY

JOHN TAYLOR, LL.D.

LATE PREBENDARY OF WESTMINSTER,

RECTOR OF BOSWORTH, LEICESTERSHIRE,

AND MINISTER OF ST. MARGARET'S, WESTMINSTER.

PUBLISHED BY

THE REV. SAMUEL HAYES, A.M.

USHER OF WESTMINSTER-SCHOOL.

TO WHICH IS ADDED,

A SERMON,

WRITTEN BY

SAMUEL JOHNSON, LL.D.

FOR THE FUNERAL OF HIS WIFE.

DUBLIN:

PRINTED BY P. BYRNE, GRAFTON-STREET.

M.DCC.XCIII.

TO

HIS GRACE

WILLIAM,

DUKE OF DEVONSHIRE.

MY LORD,

HAD Dr. Taylor been willing, in his life time, to have obliged the World with the following Diſcourſes, I am ſure he would have ſought no other Patronage than that of Your GRACE.

This was, of itſelf, a very ſtrong inducement to me to ſolicit the ſame honour. But, even without this incitement, the Virtues which Your GRACE ſo uniformly diſplays in private life, naturally point You out, as a Perſon to whom moral and religious inveſtigations may, with the greateſt propriety, be aſcribed. And I flatter myſelf that the following Diſcourſes will not be deemed unworthy of the honour which

I am,

MY LORD,

with the greateſt reſpect,

Your GRACE's moſt obliged,

and moſt humble Servant,

SAMUEL HAYES.

CONTENTS.

SERMON

SERMON

SERMON

SERMON

SERMONS, &c.

SERMON I.

The Second Chapter of Genesis, and the former part of the 24th Verse.

Therefore shall a man leave his Father and his Mother, and shall cleave unto his Wife.

THAT Society is necessary to the happiness of human Nature, that the gloom of solitude, and the stillness of retirement, however they may flatter at a distance, with pleasing views of independence and serenity, neither extinguish the Passions, nor enlighten the Understanding, that discontent will intrude upon privacy, and temptations follow us to the desert, every one may be easily convinced, either by his own experience, or that of others. That knowledge is advanced by an intercourse of

 sentiments,

ſentiments, and an exchange of obſervations, and that the boſom is diſburthened, by a communication of its cares, is too well known for proof or illuſtration. In ſolitude perplexity ſwells into diſtraction, and grief ſettles into melancholy; even the ſatisfactions and pleaſures, that may by chance be found, are but imperfectly enjoyed, when they are enjoyed without participation.

How high this diſpoſition may extend, and how far Society may contribute to the felicity of more exalted Natures, it is not eaſy to determine, nor neceſſary to enquire; it ſeems however probable, that this inclination is allotted to all rational Beings of limited excellence, and that it is the privilege only of the infinite Creator to derive all his happineſs from himſelf.

It is a proof of the regard of God for the happineſs of mankind, that the means by which it muſt be attained are obvious and evident; that we are not left to diſcover them, by difficult ſpeculations, intricate diſquiſitions, or long experience, but are led to them, equally by our paſſions and our reaſon, in proſperity and diſtreſs. Every man perceives his own inſufficiency to ſupply himſelf with what either neceſſity or convenience

venience require, and applies to others for assistance. Every one feels his satisfaction impaired by the suppression of pleasing emotions, and consequently endeavours to find an opportunity of diffusing his satisfaction.

As a general relation to the rest of the species is not sufficient to procure gratification for the private desires of particular persons; as closer ties of Union are necessary to promote the separate interests of Individuals; the great Society of the World is divided into different Communities, which are again subdivided into smaller Bodies, and more contracted Associations, which pursue, or ought to pursue, a particular interest, insubordination to the public good, and consistently with the general happiness of Mankind.

Each of these subdivisions produces new dependencies and relations, and every particular relation gives rise to a particular scheme of duties; duties which are of the utmost importance, and of the most sacred obligation, as the neglect of them would defeat all the blessings of Society, and cut off even the hope of happineſs; as it would poiſon the fountain from whence it muſt be drawn, and make thoſe Inſtitutions, which have been formed as neceſſary to peace and ſatisfaction, the means of diſquiet and miſery.

The loweſt ſubdiviſion of Society, is that by which it is broken into private families; nor do any duties demand more to be explained and enforced, than thoſe which this relation produces: becauſe none are more univerſally obligatory, and perhaps very few more frequently neglected.

The univerſality of theſe duties requires no other proof than may be received from the moſt curſory and ſuperficial obſervation of human life. Very few men have it in their power to injure Society in a large extent; the general happineſs of the world can be very little interrupted by the wickedneſs of any ſingle Man, and the number is not large of thoſe by whom the peace of any particular Nation can be diſturbed; but every Man may injure a family, and produce domeſtic diſorders and diſtreſſes; almoſt every one has opportunities and perhaps ſometimes temptations, to rebel as a wife, or tyrannize as a huſband; and therefore,

fore, to almoſt every one are thoſe admonitions neceſſary, that may aſſiſt in regulating the conduct, and impreſs juſt notions of the behaviour which theſe Relations exact.

Nor are theſe obligations more evident than the neglect of them; a neglect of which daily examples may be found, and from which daily calamities ariſe. Almoſt all the miſeries of life, almoſt all the wickedneſs that infeſts, and all the diſtreſſes that afflict Mankind, are the conſequences of ſome defect in theſe duties. It is therefore no objection to the propriety of diſcourſing upon them, that they are well known and generally acknowledged; for a very ſmall part of the diſorders of the World proceed from ignorance of the laws, by which life ought to be regulated; nor do many, even of thoſe whoſe hands are polluted with the fouleſt crimes, deny the reaſonableneſs of virtue, or attempt to juſtify their own actions. Men are not blindly betrayed into corruption, but abandon themſelves to their paſſions with their eyes open; and loſe the direction of Truth, becauſe they do not attend to her voice, not becauſe they do not hear, or do not underſtand it. It is there-

fore

fore no leſs uſeful to rouſe the thoughtleſs, than inſtruct the ignorant; to awaken the attention, than enlighten the underſtanding.

There is another reaſon, for which it may be proper to dwell long upon theſe Duties, and return frequently to them; that deep impreſſions of them may be formed and renewed, as often as time or temptation ſhall begin to eraſe them Offences againſt Society in its greater extent are cognizable by human laws. No Man can invade the property, or diſturb the quiet of his Neighbour, without ſubjecting himſelf to penalties, and ſuffering in proportion to the injuries he has offered. But cruelty and pride, oppreſſion and partiality, may tyrannize in private families without controul; Meekneſs may be trampled upon, and Piety inſulted, without any appeal, but to conſcience and to Heaven. A thouſand methods of torture may be invented, a thouſand acts of unkindneſs, or diſregard, may be committed; a thouſand innocent gratifications may be denied, and a thouſand hardſhips impoſed, without any violation of national laws. Life may be imbittered with hourly vexation; and weeks, months, and years, be lingered out in misery, without any legal cause of separation, or possibility of judicial redress. Perhaps no sharper anguish is felt, than that which cannot be complained of; nor any greater cruelties inflicted, than some which no human Authority can relieve.

That Marriage itself, an Institution designed only for the promotion of happiness, and for the relief of the disappointments, anxieties, and distresses to which we are subject in our present state, does not always produce the effects, for which it was appointed; that it sometimes condenses the gloom, which it was intended to dispel, and encreases the weight, which was expected to be made lighter by it, must, however unwillingly, be yet acknowledged.

It is to be considered to what causes effects, so unexpected and unpleasing, so contrary to the end of the Institution, and so unlikely to arise from it, are to be attributed; it is necessary to enquire, whether those that are thus unhappy, are to impute their misery to any other cause, than their

own

own folly, and to the neglect of those duties, which prudence and Religion equally require.

This Enquiry may not only be of use in stating and explaining the duties of the Marriage-state, but may contribute to free it from licentious misrepresentations, and weak objections; which indeed can have little force upon minds not already adapted to receive impressions from them, by habits of debauchery; but which when they co-operate with lewdness, intemperance and vanity; when they are proposed to an understanding naturally weak, and made yet weaker, by luxury and sloth, by an implicit resignation to reigning follies, and an habitual compliance with every appetite; may at least add strength to prejudices, to support an opinion already favoured, and perhaps hinder conviction, or at least retard it.

It may indeed be asserted to the honour of Marriage, that it has few adversaries among Men either distinguished for their abilities, or eminent for their virtue. Those who have assumed the province of attacking it, of overturning the constitution of the

the World, of encountering the authority of the wiſeſt Legiſlators, from whom it has received the higheſt ſanction of human wiſdom; and ſubverting the maxims of the moſt flouriſhing States, in which it has been dignified with honours, and promoted with immunities; thoſe who have undertaken the taſk of contending with reaſon and experience, with Earth and with Heaven, are Men who ſeem generally not ſelected by nature for great attempts, or difficult undertakings. They are, for the moſt part, ſuch as owe not their determinations to their arguments, but their arguments to their determinations; Diſputants animated not by a conſciouſneſs of truth, but by the numbers of their adherents; and heated, not with zeal for the right, but with the rage of licentiouſneſs and impatience of reſtraint. And perhaps to the ſober, the underſtanding, and the pious, it may be ſufficient to remark, that Religion and Marriage have the ſame Enemies.

There are indeed ſome in other Communions of the Chriſtian Church, who cenſure marriage upon different motives, and

prefer

prefer celibacy as a ſtate more immediately devoted to the honour of God, and the regular and aſſiduous practice of the duties of Religion; and have recommended vows of abſtinence, no where commanded in Scripture, and impoſed reſtraints upon lawful deſires; of which it is eaſy to judge how well they are adapted to the preſent ſtate of human nature, by the frequent violation of them, even in thoſe Societies where they are voluntarily incurred, and where no vigilance is omited to ſecure the obſervation of them.

But the Authors of theſe rigorous and unnatural ſchemes of life, though certainly miſled by falſe notions of holineſs, and perverted conceptions of the duties of our Religion, have at leaſt the merit of miſtaken endeavours to promote virtue, and muſt be allowed to have reaſoned at leaſt with ſome degree of probability, in vindication of their conduct. They were generally perſons of Piety, and ſometimes of Knowledge, and are therefore not to be confounded with the Fool, the Drunkard, and the Libertine. They who decline Marriage for the ſake of a more ſevere and morti-

fied

fied life, are ſurely to be diſtinguiſhed from thoſe, who condemn it as too rigorous a confinement, and wiſh the abolition of it, in favour of boundleſs voluptuouſneſs and licenſed debauchery.

Perhaps even the errors of miſtaken goodneſs may be rectified, and the prejudices ſurmounted by deliberate attention to the nature of the Inſtitution; and certainly the calumnies of wickedneſs may be, by the ſame means, confuted, though its clamours may not be ſilenced; ſince commonly in debates like this, confutation and conviction are very diſtant from each other. For that nothing but vice or folly obſtructs the happineſs of a married liſe may be made evident by examining.

First, The Nature and End of Marriage.

Secondly, The means by which that End is to be attained.

Firſt, The Nature and End of Marriage.

The Vow of Marriage which the wiſdom of moſt civilized Nations has enjoined, and which the rules of the Chriſtian Church enjoin, may be properly conſidered as a vow of perpetual and indiſſoluble Friendſhip; Friendſhip which no change of for-

tune

tune, nor any alteration of external circumſtances can be allowed to interrupt or weaken. After the commencement of this ſtate there remain no longer any ſeparate intereſts; the two Individuals become united, and are therefore to enjoy the ſame felicity, and ſuffer the ſame misfortunes; to have the ſame Friends and the ſame Enemies, the ſame ſucceſs and the ſame diſappointments. It is eaſy by purſuing the parallel between Friendſhip and Marriage, to ſhow how exact a conformity there is between them, to prove that all the precepts laid down with reſpect to the contraction, and the maxims advanced with regard to the effects, of Friendſhip, are true of Marriage in a more literal ſenſe, and a ſtricter acceptation.

It has been long obſerved that Friendſhip is to be confined to one; or that, to uſe the words of the Axiom, * *He that hath Friends, has no Friend.* That ardour of kindneſs, that unbounded confidence, that unſuſpecting ſecurity which friendſhip requires, cannot be extended beyond a ſingle

* ᾧ φίλοι οὐ φίλος.

object. A divided affection may be termed benevolence, but can hardly rise to Friendship; for the narrow limits of the human mind allow it not intensely to contemplate more than one idea. As we love one more, we must love another less; and however impartially we may, for a very short time, distribute our regards, the balance of affection will quickly incline, perhaps against our consent, to one side or the other. Besides, though we should love our Friends *equally*, which is perhaps *not* possible; and *each* according to their *Merit*, which is *very difficult;* what shall secure them from jealousy of each other? Will not each think highly of his own value, and imagine himself rated below his worth? Or what shall preserve their common Friend from the same jealousy, with regard to them? As he divides his affection and esteem between them, he can in return claim no more than a dividend of theirs: and as he regards them equally, they may justly rank some other in equality with him; and what then shall hinder an endless communication of confidence, which must certainly end in treachery at last? Let these reflections be applied to Marriage,

and

and perhaps Polygamy may loſe its vindicators.

It is remarked that * *Friendſhip amongſt equals is the moſt laſting*, and perhaps there are few cauſes to which more unhappy marriages are to be aſcribed than a diſproportion between the original condition of the two perſons. Difference of condition makes difference of education; and difference of education produces differences of habits, ſentiments, and inclinations. From thence ariſe contrary views, and oppoſite ſchemes, of which the frequent, though not neceſſary, conſequences, are debates, diſguſt, alienation, and ſettled hatred.

Strict friendſhip † *is to have the ſame deſires and the ſame averſions.* Whoever is to chuſe a Friend is to conſider firſt the reſemblance, or the diſſimilitude of tempers. How neceſſary this caution is to be urged as preparatory to Marriage, the miſery of thoſe who neglect it ſufficiently evinces. To enumerate all the varieties of diſpoſition, to which it may on this occaſion be convenient to attend, would be a tedious taſk;

* Amicitia inter Pares firmiſſima.

† An obſervation of Catiline in Salluſt.

but

but it is at leaſt proper to enforce one precept on this head, a precept which was never yet broken without fatal conſequences, *Let the Religion of the Man and Woman be the ſame.* The rancour and hatred, the rage and perſecution with which Religious diſputes have filled the World, need not be related; every Hiſtory can inform us, that no malice is ſo fierce, ſo cruel, and implacable, as that which is excited by religious diſcord. It is to no purpoſe that they ſtipulate for the free enjoyment of their own opinion; for how can he be happy, who ſees the perſon moſt dear to him in a ſtate of dangerous error, and ignorant of thoſe Sacred Truths, which are neceſſary to the approbation of God, and to future felicity? How can he engage not to endeavour to propagate truth, and promote the Salvation of thoſe he loves? or if he has been betrayed into ſuch engagements by an ungoverned paſſion, how can he vindicate himſelf in the obſervation of them? The education of Children will ſoon make it neceſſary to determine, which of the two opinions ſhall be tranſmitted to their poſterity; and how can either conſent to train up in error and deluſion those from whom they expect the highest satisfactions, and the only comforts of declining life?

On account of this conformity of notions it is, that equality of condition is chiefly eligible; for as *Friendship*, so Marriage, *either finds* or makes an equality. No disadvantage of birth or fortune ought to impede the exaltation of virtue and of wisdom; for with Marriage begins union, and union obliterates all distinctions. It may indeed become the person who received the benefit, to remember it, that gratitude may heighten affection; but the person that conferred it ought to forget it, because if it was deserved, it cannot be mentioned without injustice, nor if undeserved, without imprudence. All reproaches of this kind must be either retractions of a good action, or proclamations of our own weakness.

Friends, says the Proverbial observation, *have every thing in common.* This is likewise implied in the Marriage Covenant. Matrimony admits of no separate possessions, nor incommunicable interests. This rule, like all others, has been often broken by low views and sordid stipulations; but,

like

like all other precepts, founded on reaſon and in truth, it has received a new confirmation from almoſt every breach of it; and thoſe Parents, whoſe age had no better effects upon their underſtanding, than to fill them with avarice and ſtratagem, have brought miſery and ruin upon their Children, by the means which they weakly imagined conducive to their happineſs.

There is yet another precept equally relating to Friendſhip and to Marriage; a precept which, in either caſe, can never be too ſtrongly inculcated, or too ſcrupulouſly obſerved; *Contract Friendſhip only with the good.* Virtue is the firſt quality to be conſidered in the choice of a Friend, and yet more in a fixed and irrevocable choice. This maxim ſurely requires no comment, nor any vindication; it is equally clear and certain, obvious to the ſuperficial, and inconteſtable by the moſt accurate Examiner. To dwell upon it is therefore ſuperfluous; for, though often neglected, it never was denied. Every man will, without heſitation, confeſs, that it is abſurd to truſt a known deceiver, or voluntarily to depend for quiet and for happineſs upon inſolence, cruelty and oppreſſion. Thus Marriage appears to differ from Friendſhip chiefly in the degree of its efficacy, and the authority of its inſtituti on. It was appointed by God himſelf, as neceſſary to happineſs, even in a ſtate of innocence; and the relation prodced by it, was declared more powerful than that of Birth. *Therefore ſhall a man leave his father and his mother, and ſhall cleave unto his wife.* But as notwithſtanding its conformity to human nature, it ſometimes fails to produce the effects intended, it is neceſſary to enquire,

Secondly, by what means the end of Marriage is to be attained.

As it appears by examining the natural ſyſtem of the Univerſe, that the greateſt and ſmalleſt bodies are inveſted with the ſame properties, and moved by the ſame laws; ſo a ſurvey of the moral World will inform us, that greater or leſs Societies are to be made happy by the ſame means, and that however relations may be varied, or circumſtances changed, Virtue, and Virtue alone, is the parent of felicity. We can only, in whatſoever ſtate we may be placed, ſecure ourſelves from diſquiet and from miſery by a reſolute attention to truth and reaſon. Without this, it is in vain that a man chuſes a Friend, or cleaves to a Wife. If paſſion be ſuffered to prevail over right, and the duties of our ſtate be broken through, or neglected, for the ſake of gratifying our anger, our pride, or our revenge; the union of hearts will quickly be diſſolved, and kindneſs will give way to reſentment and averſion.

The Duties, by the practice of which a married life is to be made happy, are the ſame with thoſe of Friendſhip, but exalted to higher perfection. Love muſt be more ardent, and confidence without limits. It is therefore neceſſary on each part to deſerve that confidence by the moſt unſhaken fidelity, and to preſerve their love unextinguiſhed by continual acts of tenderneſs; not only to deteſt all real, but ſeeming offences; and to avoid ſuſpicion and guilt, with almoſt equal ſolicitude.

But ſince the frailty of our nature is ſuch that we cannot hope from each other an unvaried rectitude of conduct, or an uninterrupted courſe of wiſdom or virtue; as folly will ſometimes intrude upon an unguarded hour; aud temptations, by frequent attacks, will ſometimes prevail; one of the chief acts of love is readily to forgive errors, and overlook defects. Neglect is to be reclaimed by kindneſs, and perverſeneſs ſoftened by compliance. Sudden ſtarts of paſſion are patiently to be borne, and the calm moments of recollection ſilently expected. For if one offence be made a plea for another; if anger be to be oppoſed with anger, and reproach retorted for reproach; either the conteſt muſt be continued for ever, or one muſt at laſt be obliged by violence to do what might have been at firſt done, not only more gracefully, but with more advantage.

Marriage, however in general it reſembles Friendſhip, differs from it in this; that all its duties are not reciprocal. Friends are equal in every reſpect; but the relation of Marriage produces authority on one ſide, and exacts obedience on the other; obedience, an unpleaſing duty; which yet the nature of the ſtate makes indiſpenſable; for Friends may ſeparate when they can no longer reconcile the ſentiments, or approve the ſchemes of each other; but as marriage is indiſſoluble, either one muſt be content to ſubmit, when

conviction

conviction cannot be obtained; or life must be wasted in perpetual disputes.

But though obedience may be justly required, servility is not to be exacted; and though it may be lawful to exert authority, it must be remembered, that to govern and to tyrannize are very different, and that oppression will naturally provoke rebellion.

The great rule both of authority and obedience is the law of God; a law which is not to be broken for the promotion of any ends, or in compliance with any commands; and which indeed never can be violated without destroying that confidence, which is the great source of mutual happiness; for how can that person be trusted, whom no principles oblige to fidelity?

Thus Religion appears, in every state of life, to be the basis of happiness, and the operating power which makes every good institution valid and efficacious. And he that shall attempt to attain happiness by the means which God has ordained, and *shall leave his Father and his Mother, and shall cleave unto his Wife,* shall

ſhall ſurely find the higheſt degree of ſatisfaction that our preſent ſtate allows; if, in his choice, he pays the firſt regard to virtue, and regulates his conduct by the precepts of religion.

SERMON II.

ISAIAH, Chap. lv. Verse 7.

Let the wicked forsake his way, and the unrighteous Man his thoughts, and let him return unto the Lord, and he will have mercy upon him, and to our God, for he will abundantly pardon.

THAT God is a Being of infinite mercy; that he desires not the death of a Sinner, nor takes any pleasure in the misery of his Creatures; may not only be deduced from the consideration of his nature, and his attributes; but, for the sake of those that are incapable of philosophical enquiries, who make far the greatest part of Mankind, it is evidently revealed to us in the Scriptures, in which the Supreme Being, the source of life, the author of existence,

iſtence, who ſpake the word, and the World was made, who commanded, and it was created, is deſcribed as looking down from the height of infinite felicity, with tenderneſs and pity, upon the Sons of Men; inciting them, by ſoft impulſes, to perſeverance in virtue, and recalling them, by inſtruction and puniſhment, from error and from vice. He is repreſented as not more formidable for his power, than amiable for his mercy; and is introduced as expoſtulating with Mankind upon their obſtinacy in wickedneſs; and warning them, with the higheſt affection, to avoid thoſe puniſhments, which the laws of his government make it neceſſary to inflict upon the inflexible and diſobedient. *Return unto me, and I will return unto you, ſaith the Lord of Hoſts,* Mal. iii. 7. *Make you a new heart, and a new ſpirit, for why will ye die, O houſe of Iſrael?* Ezek. xviii. 31. His mercy is ever made the chief motive of obedience to him; and with the higheſt reaſon inculcated, as the attribute which may animate us moſt powerfully to an attention to our duty. *If thou, O Lord, wert extreme to mark what is done amiſs, O Lord, who ſhall abide it? But there is mercy*

with

with thee, therefore ſhalt thou be feared. If God were a Power unmerciful and ſevere, a rigid Exactor of unvaried regularity and unfailing virtue; if he were not to be pleaſed but with perfection, nor to be pacified after tranſgreſſions and offences: in vain would the beſt Men endeavour to recommend themſelves to his favour; in vain would the moſt circumſpect watch the motions of his own heart, and the moſt diligent apply himſelf to the exerciſe of virtue. They would only deſtroy their eaſe by ineffectual ſolicitude, confine their deſires with unneceſſary reſtraints, and weary out their lives in unavailing labours. God would not be to be ſerved, becauſe all ſervice would be rejected; it would be much more reaſonable to abſtract the mind from the contemplation of him, than to have him only before us, as an object of terror, as a Being too mighty to be reſiſted, and too cruel to be implored: a Being that created Men, only to be miſerable, and revealed himſelf to them, only to interrupt even the tranſient and imperfect enjoyments of this life, to aſtoniſh them with terror, and to overwhelm them with deſpair.

But

But there is mercy with him, therefore ſhall he be feared. It is reaſonable, that we ſhould endeavour to pleaſe him, becauſe we know that every ſincere endeavour will be rewarded by him; that we ſhould uſe all the means in our power, to enlighten our minds, and regulate our lives, becauſe our errors, if involuntary, will not be imputed to us; and our conduct, though not exactly agreeable to the divine ideas of rectitude, yet if approved, after honeſt and diligent enquiries, by our own conſciences, will not be condemned by that God, who judges of the heart, weighs every circumſtance of our lives, and admits every real extenuation of our failings and tranſgreſſions.

Were there not mercy with him, were he not to be reconciled after the commiſſion of a crime, what muſt be the ſtate of thoſe, who are conſcious of having once offended him? A ſtate of gloomy melancholy, or outrageous deſparation; a diſmal wearineſs of life, and inexpreſſible agonies at the thought of death; for what affright or affliction could equal the horrors of that mind, which expected every moment to

fall

fall into the hands of implacable Omnipotence?

But the mercy of God extends not only to thoſe that have made his will, in ſome degree, the rule of their actions, and have only deviated from it by inadvertency, ſurprize, inattention, or negligence, but even to thoſe that have polluted themſelves with ſtudied and premeditated wickedneſs; that have violated his commands in oppoſition to conviction, and gone on, from crime to crime, under a ſenſe of the divine diſapprobation.

Even theſe are not for ever excluded from his favour, but have in their hands means, appointed by himſelf, of reconciliation to him; means by which pardon may be obtained, and by which they may be reſtored to thoſe hopes of happineſs, from which they have fallen by their own fault.

The great duty, to the performance of which theſe benefits are promiſed, is Repentance; a duty, which it is of the utmoſt importance to every Man to underſtand and practiſe; and which it therefore may be neceſſary to explain and enforce, by ſhewing,

First, What is the true nature of Repentance.

Secondly, What are the obligations to an early Repentance.

First, What is the true nature of Repentance.

The duty of Repentance, like moſt other parts of Religion, has been miſrepreſented by the weakneſs of ſuperſtition, or the artifices of intereſt. The cleareſt precepts have been obſcured by falſe interpretations, and one error added to another, till the underſtanding of Men has been bewildered, and their morals depraved by a falſe appearance of Religion.

Repentance has been made, by ſome, to conſiſt in the outward expreſſions of ſorrow for ſin, in tears and ſighs, in dejection and lamentation.

It muſt be owned that where the crime is public, and where others may be in danger of corruption from the example, ſome public and open declarations of Repentance may be proper, if made with decency and propriety, which are neceſſary to preſerve the beſt actions from contempt and ridicule; but they are neceſſary only, for the ſake of deſtroying the influence of a bad example, and are no otherwiſe eſſential to this duty. No Man is obliged to accuſe himſelf of crimes, which are known to God alone; even the fear of hurting others ought often to reſtrain him from it, ſince to confeſs crimes may be, in ſome meaſure, to teach them, and thoſe may imitate him in wickedneſs, who will not follow him in his Repentance.

It ſeems here not impertinent to mention the practice of private confeſſion to the Prieſt, indiſpenſably enjoined by the Roman Church, as abſolutely neceſſary to true Repentance; but which is no where commanded in Scripture, or recommended otherwiſe, than as a method of diſburthening the conſcience, for the ſake of receiving comfort or inſtruction, and as ſuch, is directed by our own Liturgy.

Thus much, and no more, ſeems to be implied in the Apoſtles's precept, *of confeſſing our faults one to another*, a precept expreſſed with ſuch latitude, that it appears only to be one of thoſe which it may be often convenient to obſerve, but which is to be obſerved no further, than as it may be convenient. For we are left

entirely

entirely at liberty, what terms, whether general or particular, we ſhall uſe in our confeſſions. The precept, in a literal and rational ſenſe, can be ſaid to direct no more, than general acts of humiliation, and acknowledgements of our own depravity.

No Man ought to judge of the efficacy of his own Repentance, or the ſincerity of another's, by ſuch variable and uncertain tokens, as proceed more from the conſtitution of the body, than the diſpoſition of the mind, or more from ſudden paſſions and violent emotions, than from a fixed temper, or ſettled reſolutions. Tears are often to be found, where there is little ſorrow, and the deepeſt ſorrow without any tears. Even ſorrow itſelf is no other than an accidental, or a ſecondary, part of Repentance, which may, and indeed ought to ariſe from the conſciouſneſs of our own guilt; but which is merely a natural and neceſſary effect, in which choice has very little part, and which therefore is no virtue. He that feels no ſorrow for ſin, has indeed great reaſon to doubt of the ſincerity of his own Repentance, ſince he ſeems not to be truly ſenſible of his danger and his miſery;

but

but he that feels it in the higheſt degree is not to put confidence in it. He is only to expect mercy upon his reformation.

For reformation is the chief part of Repentance; not he that only bewails and confeſſes, but he that forſakes his ſins, repents acceptably to God, that God who *will have mercy, and not ſacrifice*; who will only accept a pure heart and real virtue, not outward forms of grief, or pompous ſolemnities of devotion. To conceive that any thing can be ſubſtituted in the place of reformation is a dangerous and fatal, though perhaps no uncommon, error; nor is it leſs erroneous, though leſs deſtructive, to ſuppoſe, that any thing can be added to the efficacy of a good life by a conformity to any extraordinary ceremonies or particular inſtitutions.

To falſe notions of Repentance many Nations owe the cuſtom, which prevails amongſt them, of retiring in the decline of life to ſolitudes and cloyſters, to atone for wickedneſs by penance and mortifications. It muſt indeed be confeſſed, that it may be prudent in a Man, long accuſtomed to yield to particular temptations, to remove himſelf from them as far as he can,

becauſe

becauſe every paſſion is more ſtrong or violent, as its particular object is more near. Thus it would be madneſs in a Man, long enſlaved by intemperance, to frequent revels and banquets with an intent to reform; nor can it be expected that cruelty and tyranny ſhould be corrected, by continuance in high authority.

That particular ſtate which contributes moſt to excite and ſtimulate our inordinate paſſions, may be changed with very good effect; but any retirement from the World does not neceſſarily precede or follow repentance, becauſe it is not requiſite to reformation. A Man whoſe conſcience accuſes him of having perverted others ſeems under ſome obligations to continue in the World, and to practiſe virtue in public, that thoſe who have been ſeduced by his example, may by his example be reclaimed.

For reformation includes, not only the forbearance of thoſe crimes of which we have been guilty, and the practice of thoſe duties which we have hitherto neglected, but a reparation, as far as we are able to make it, of all the injuries that we have done, either to Mankind in general, or to particular perſons. If we have been guilty of the open propagation of error, or the promulgation of ſalſehood, we muſt make our recantation no leſs openly; we muſt endeavour, without regard to the ſhame and reproach to which we may be expoſed, to undeceive thoſe whom we have formerly miſled. If we have deprived any Man of his right, wc muſt reſtore it to him; if we have aſperſed his reputation, we muſt retract our calumny. Whatever can be done to obviate the ill conſequences of our paſt miſconduct, muſt be diligently and ſteadily practiſed. Whoever has been made vicious or unhappy by our fault, muſt be reſtored to virtue and happineſs, ſo far as our counſel or fortune can contribute to it.

Let no Man imagine that he may indulge his malice, his avarice, or bis ambition, at the expence of others; that he may raiſe himſelf to wealth and honour by the breach of every law of Heaven and Earth, then retire laden with the plunder of the miſerable, ſpend his life in fantaſtic penances, or faiſe devotion, and by his compliance with the external duties of Religion, atone for with-holding what he has torn away from the lawful poſſeſſor by rapine and extortion. Let him not flatter himſelf with falſe perſuaſions that prayer and mortification can alter the great and invariable rules of reaſon and juſtice. Let him not think that he can acquire a right to keep what he had no right to take away, or that frequent proſtrations before God will juſtify his perſeverance in oppreſſing Men. Let him be aſſured that his preſence profanes the temple, and that his prayer will be turned into ſin.

A frequent and ſerious reflection upon the neceſſity of reparation and reſtitution, may be very effectual to reſtrain Men from injuſtice and defamation, from cruelty and extortion; for nothing is more certain, than that moſt propoſe to themſelves to die the death of the Righteous, and intend, however they may offend God in the purſuit of their intereſt, or the gratifications of their paſſions, to reconcile themſelves to him by Repentance. Would Men therefore deeply imprint upon their minds the true notions of Repentance in its whole extent, many temptations would loſe their force; for who would utter a falſehood, which he muſt ſhamefully retract; or take away, at the expence of his reputation

and

and his innocence, what, if he hopes for eternal happineſs, he muſt afterwards reſtore? Who would commit a crime, of which he muſt retain the guilt, but loſe the advantage?

There is indeed a partial reſtitution, with which many have attempted to quiet their conſciences, and have betrayed their own ſouls. When they are ſufficiently enriched by wicked practices, and leave off to rob from ſatiety of wealth, or are awaked to reflection upon their own lives by danger, adverſity, or ſickneſs, they then become deſirous to be at peace with God, and hope to obtain, by refunding part of their acquiſitions, a permiſſion to enjoy the reſt. In purſuance of this view, Churches are built, Schools endowed, the Poor clothed, and the Ignorant educated; works indeed highly pleaſing to God, when performed in concurrence with the other duties of Religion, but which will never atone for the violation of juſtice. To plunder one Man for the ſake of relieving another, is not charity; to build temples with the gains of wickedneſs, is to endeavour to bribe the Divinity. This ought ye to have done, and not left the other undone. Ye ought doubtlefs to be charitable, but ye ought firft to be juft.

There are others who confider God as a Judge ftill more eafily reconciled to crimes, and therefore perform their acts of atonement after death, and deftine their eftates to charity, when they can ferve the end of luxuryor vanity no longer. But whoever he be that has loaded his foul with the fpoils of the unhappy, and riots in affluence by cruelty and injuftice, let him not be deceived! God is not mocked. Reftitution muft be made to thofe who have been wronged, and whatever he with-holds from them, he with holds at the hazard of eternal happinefs.

An amendment of life is the chief and effential part of Repentance. He that has performed that great work, needs not difturb his confcience with fubtle fcruples, or nice diftinctions. He needs not recollect, whether he was awakened from the lethargy of fin, by the love of God, or the fear of punifhment. The Scripture applies to all our paffions; and eternal punifhments had been threatened to no purpofe, if thefe menaces were not intended to promote virtue.

But as this reformation is not to be accomplifhed by our own natural power, unaffifted by God, we muft, when we form our firft refolutions of a new life, apply ourfelves, with fervour and conftancy, to thofe means which God has prefcribed for obtaining his affiftance. We muft implore a bleffing by frequent prayer, and confirm our faith by the Holy Sacrament. We muft ufe all thofe inftitutions that contribute to the increafe of piety, and omit nothing that may either promote our progrefs in virtue, or prevent a relapfe into vice. It may be enquired, whether a Repentance begun in ficknefs, and prevented by death from exerting its influence upon the conduct, will avail in the fight of God. To this queftion it may be anfwered in general, that as all reformation is begun by a change of the temper and inclinations, which, when altered to a certain degree, neceffarily produce an alteration in the life and manners; if God who fees the heart, fees it rectified in fuch a manner as would confequently produce a good life, he will accept that Repentance.

But it is of the higheft importance to thofe who have fo long delayed to fecure

their

their ſalvation, that they loſe none of the moments which yet remain; that they omit no act of juſtice or mercy now in their power; that they ſummon all their diligence to improve the remains of life, and exert every virtue which they have opportunities to practiſe. And when they have done all that can poſſibly be done by them, they cannot yet be certain of acceptance, becauſe they cannot know, whether a repentance, proceeding wholly from the fear of death, would not languiſh and ceaſe to operate, if that fear was taken away.

Since therefore ſuch is the hazard and uncertain efficacy of Repentance long delayed, let us ſeriouſly reflect,

Secondly, upon the obligations to an early Repentance.

He is eſteemed by the prudent and the diligent to be no good regulator of his private affairs, who defers till to-morrow, what is neceſſary to be done, and what it is in his power to do, to-day. The obligation would ſtill be ſtronger, if we ſuppoſe that the preſent is the only day in which he knows it will be in his power. This is the caſe of every Man, who delays to reform his life, and lulls himſelf in the ſupineſs of iniquity. He knows not that the opportunities he now rejects will ever be again offered him, or that they will not be denied him becauſe he has rejected them. This he certainly knows, that life is continually ſtealing from him, and that every day cuts off ſome part of that time which is already perhaps almoſt at an end.

But the time not only grows every day ſhorter, but the work to be performed in it more difficult; every hour, in which Repentance is delayed, produces ſomething new to be repented of. Habits grow ſtronger by long continuance, and paſſions more violent by indulgence. Vice, by repeated acts, becomes almoſt natural; and pleaſures, by frequent enjoyment captivate the mind almoſt beyond reſiſtance.

If avarice has been the predominant paſſion, and wealth has been accumulated by extortion and rapacity, Repentance is not to be poſtponed. Acquiſitions, long enjoyed, are with great difficuly quitted, with ſo great difficulty, that we ſeldom, very ſeldom, meet with true Repentance in thoſe whom the deſire of riches has be-

trayed

trayed to wickedneſs. Men who could willingly reſign the luxuries and ſenſual pleaſures of a large fortune, cannot conſent to live without the grandeur and the homage. And they who would leave all, cannot bear the reproach, which they apprehend from ſuch an acknowledgment of wrong.

Thus are Men with-held from Repentance, and conſequently debarred from eternal felicity; but theſe reaſons, being founded in temporal intereſt, acquire every day greater ſtrength to miſlead us, though not greater efficacy to juſtify us. A Man may, by fondly indulging a falſe notion, voluntarily forget that it is falſe, but can never make it true. We muſt baniſh every falſe argument, every known deluſion from our minds, before our paſſions can operate in its favour; and forſake what we know muſt be forſaken, before we have endeared it to ourſelves by long poſſeſſion. Repentance is always difficult, and the difficulty grows ſtill greater by delay. But let thoſe who have hitherto neglected this great duty remember, that it is yet in their power, and that they cannot periſh everlaſtingly but by their own choice! Let them therefore endeavour to redeem the time loſt, and repair their negligence by vigilance and ardour! *Let the wicked forſake his way, and the unrighteous Man his thoughts; and let him return unto the Lord, and he will have mercy upon him, and to our God for he will abundantly pardon.*

SERMON III.

PROVERBS, Chap. xxviii. Verſe 14.

Happy is the Man that feareth alway: but he that hardeneth his heart, ſhall fall into miſchief.

THE great purpoſe of revealed Religion is to afford Man a clear repreſentation of his dependence on the Supreme Being, by teaching him to conſider God, as his Creator, and Governor, his Father and his Judge. Thoſe to whom Providence has granted the knowledge of the Holy Scriptures, have no need to perplex themſelves with difficult ſpeculations, to deduce their duty from remote principles, or to enforce it by doubtful motives. The Bible tells us, in plain and authoritative terms, that there is a way to life and a way to death; that there are acts which

God

God will reward, and acts that he will punish. That with soberness, righteousness, and godliness, God will be pleased; and that with intemperance, iniquity, and impiety, God will be offended; and that of those who are careful to please him, the reward will be such, as eye hath not seen, nor ear heard; and of those who, having offended him, die without Repentance, the punishment will be inconceivably severe, and dreadful.

In consequence of this general doctrine, the whole system of moral and religious duty is expressed, in the language of Scripture, by the *fear of God*. A good Man is characterised, as a Man that feareth God; and the fear of the Lord is said to be the beginning of wisdom; and the Text affirms, that happy is the Man that feareth always.

On the distinction of this fear, into servile and filial, or fear of punishment, or fear of offence, on which much has been superstructed by the casuistical Theology of the Romish Church, it is not necessary to dwell. It is sufficient to observe, that the Religion which makes fear the great principle of action, implicitly condemns all

self-

ſelf-confidence, all preſumptuous ſecurity; and enjoins a conſtant ſtate of vigilance and caution, a perpetual diſtruſt of our own hearts, a full conviction of our natural weakneſs, and an earneſt ſolicitude for Divine Aſſiſtance.

The Philoſophers of the Heathen World ſeemed to hope, that Man might be flattered into Virtue; and therefore told him much of his rank, and of the meaneſt of degeneracy; they aſſerted, indeed with truth, that all greatneſs was in the practice of Virtue; but of Virtue, their notions were narrow; and pride, which their doctrine made its chief ſupport, was not of power ſufficient to ſtruggle with ſenſe or paſſion.

Of that Religion, which has been taught from God, the baſis is Humility: a holy fear which attends good Men through the whole courſe of their lives; and keeps them always attentive to the motives and conſequences of every action; if always unſatisfied with their progreſs in Holineſs, always wiſhing to advance, and always afraid of falling away.

This Fear is of ſuch efficacy to the great purpoſe of our being, that the Wiſe Man has

has pronounced him happy that fears al-ways; and declares, that he who hardens his heart ſhall fall into miſchief. Let us therefore carefully conſider,

Firſt, What he is to fear, whoſe fear will make him happy.

Secondly, What is that hardneſs of heart which ends in miſchief.

Thirdly, How the heart is hardened. And

Fourthly, What is the conſequence of hardneſs of heart.

Firſt, We muſt enquire, what he is to fear, whoſe fear will make him happy.

The great and primary object of a good Man's fear, is ſin; and in proportion to the atrociouſneſs of the crime, he will ſhrink from it with more horror. When he medi-tates on the infinite perfection of his Maker and his Judge; when he conſiders that the Heavens are not pure in the ſight of God, and yet remembers, that he muſt in a ſhort time appear before him; he dreads the contaminations of evil, and endeavours to paſs through his appointed time, with ſuch cautions, as may keep him unſpotted from the world.

The dread of ſin neceſſarily produces the dread of temptation: he that wiſhes to eſcape the effects, flies likewiſe from the cauſe. The humility of a Man truly religious ſeldom ſuffers him to think himſelf able to reſiſt thoſe incitements to evil, which by the approach of immediate gratifications may be preſented to ſenſe or fancy; his care is not for victory, but ſafety; and when he can *eſcape* aſſaults, he does not willingly *encounter* them.

The continual occurrence of temptation, and that imbecillity of nature, which every Man ſees in others, and has experienced in himſelf, ſeems to have made many doubtful of the poſſibility of Salvation. In the common modes of life, they find that buſineſs enſnares, and that pleaſure ſeduces; that ſucceſs produces pride, and miſcarriage envy; that converſation conſiſts too often of cenſure or of flattery; and that even care for the intereſts of friends, or attention to the eſtabliſhment of a family, generates conteſt and competition, enmity and malevolence, and at laſt fills the mind with ſecular ſolicitude.

Under the terrors which this proſpect of the world has impreſſed upon them, many

many have endeavoured to ſecure their innocence, by excluding the poſſibility of crimes; and have fled for refuge, from vanity and ſin, to the ſolitude of deſerts; where they have paſſed their time in woods and caverns; and after a life of labour and maceration, prayer and penitence, died at laſt in ſecrecy and ſilence.

Many more of both ſexes, have withdrawn, and ſtill withdraw themſelves, from crowds and glitter, and pleaſure, to Monaſteries and Convents; where they engage themſelves, by irrevocable vows, in certain modes of life, more or leſs auſtere, according to the ſeveral inſtitutions; but all of them comprizing many poſitive hardſhips, and all prohibiting almoſt all ſenſual gratifications. The fundamental and general principle of all monaſtic communities, is Celibacy, Poverty, and Obedience to the Superior. In ſome, there is a perpetual abſtinence from all food that may join delight with nouriſhment; to which, in others, is added an obligation to ſilence and ſolitute;—to ſuffer, to watch, and to pray, is their whole employment.

Of theſe, it muſt be confeſſed, that they fear always, and that they eſcape many tempta-

temptations, to which all are expoſed, and by which many fall, who venture themſelves into the whirl of human affairs; they are exempt from avarice, and all its concomitants, and by allowing themſelves to poſſeſs nothing, they are free from thoſe conteſts for honour and power, which fill the open world with ſtratagems and violence. But ſurely it cannot be ſaid that they have reached the perfection of a religious Life; it cannot be allowed, that flight is victory; or that He fills his place in the Creation laudably, who does no ill, *only* becauſe he does *nothing*. Thoſe who live upon that which is produced by the labour of others, could not live, if there were none to labour; and if Celibacy could be univerſal, the race of Man muſt ſoon have an end.

Of theſe recluſes, it may without uncharitable cenſure be affirmed; that they have ſecured their innocence, by the loſs of their Virtue; that to avoid the commiſſion of ſome faults, they have made many duties impracticable; and that leſt they ſhould do what they ought *not* to do, they leave much *undone*, which they ought to *do*. They muſt however be allowed, to expreſs a just ſenſe of the dangers, with which we are ſurrounded; and a ſtrong conviction of the vigilance neceſſary to obtain ſalvation; and it is our buſineſs to avoid their errors, and imitate their piety.

He is happy that carries about with him in the world the temper of the cloiſter; and preſerves the fear of doing evil, while he ſuffers himſelf to be impelled by the zeal of doing good; who uſes the comforts and the conveniencies of his condition, as though he uſed them not, with that conſtant deſire of a better ſtate, which ſinks the value of earthly things; who can be rich or poor, without pride in riches, or diſcontent in poverty; who can manage the buſineſs of life, with ſuch indifference, as may ſhut out from his heart all incitements to fraud or injuſtice; who can partake the pleaſures of ſenſe with temperance, and enjoy the diſtinctions of honour with moderation; who can paſs undefiled through a polluted World; and, among all the viciſſitudes of good and evil, have his heart fixed only where true joys are to be found.

This can only be done, by fearing always, by preſerving in the mind a conſtant apprehenſion

prehension of the Divine Presence, and a constant dread of the Divine displeasure; impressions which the converse of mankind, and the solicitations of sense and fancy, are continually labouring to efface, and which we must therefore renew by all such practices as Religion prescribes; and which may be learned from the lives of them, who have been distinguished, as examples of piety, by the general approbation of the Christian World.

The great efficient of union between the soul and its Creator, is Prayer; of which the necessity is such that St. Paul directs us, to pray without ceasing; that is, to preserve in the mind such a constant dependence upon God, and such a constant desire of his assistance, as may be equivalent to constant prayer.

No man can pray, with ardour of devotion, but he must excite in himself a reverential idea of that Power, to whom he addresses his petitions; nor can he suddenly reconcile himself to an action, by which he shall displease him, to whom he has been returning thanks for his Creation and Preservation, and by whom he hopes to be still preserved. He therefore, who prays often, fortifies himſelf by a natural effect, and may hope to be preſerved in ſafety, by the ſtronger aid of Divine Protection.

Beſides the returns of daily and regular Prayer, it will be neceſſary for moſt men to aſſiſt themſelves, from time to time, by ſome particular and unaccuſtomed acts of Devotion. For this purpoſe, intervals of retirement may be properly recommended; in which the duſt of Life may be ſhaken off and in which the courſe of Life may be properly reviewed, and its future poſſibilities eſtimated. At ſuch times ſecular temptations are removed, and earthly cares are diſmiſſed; a vain tranſitory world may be contemplated in its true ſtate; paſt offences may obtain pardon by Repentance; new reſolutions may be formed, upon new convictions; the paſt may ſupply inſtruction to the preſent and to the future; and ſuch preparation may be made for thoſe events, which threaten ſpiritual danger, that temptation cannot eaſily come unexpected; and intereſt and pleaſure, whenever they renew their attacks, will find the ſoul upon its guard,

guard, with either caution to avoid, or vigour to repel them.

In theſe ſeaſons of retreat and recollection, what external helps ſhall be added muſt by every one be diſcreetly and ſoberly conſidered. Faſts and other auſterities, however they have been brought into diſrepute by wild Enthuſiaſm, have been always recommended, and always practiſed, by the ſincere Believers of reveal-Religion; and as they have a natural tendency to diſengage the mind from ſenſuality, they may be of great uſe, as awakeners of holy Fear; and they may aſſiſt our progreſs in a good life, while they are conſidered only as expreſſions of our love of God, and are not ſubſtituted for the love of our Neighbours.

As all thoſe duties are to be practiſed, leſt the heart ſhould be hardened, we are to conſider,

Secondly, What is meant by *hardneſs of heart.*

It is apparent from the Text, that the hardneſs of heart, which betrays to miſchief, is contrary to the fear which ſecures happineſs. The fear of God, is a certain tenderneſs of Spirit, which ſhrinks from

from evil, and the cauſes of evil; ſuch a ſenſe of God's Preſence, and ſuch perſuaſion of his Juſtice, as gives ſin the appearance of evil, and therefore excites every effort to combat and eſcape it.

Hardneſs of heart, therefore, is a thoughtleſs neglect of the Divine Law; ſuch an acquieſcence in the pleaſures of ſenſe, and ſuch delight in the pride of life, as leaves no place in the mind for meditation on higher things; ſuch an indifference about the laſt event of human actions, as never looks forward to a future ſtate, but ſuffers the paſſions to operate with their full force, without any other end, than the gratifications of the preſent world.

To Men of hearts thus hardened, Providence is ſeldom wholly inattentive; they are often called to the remembrance of their Creator, both by bleſſings and afflictions; by recoveries from ſickneſs, by deliverances from danger, by loſs of friends, and by miſcarriage of tranſactions. As theſe calls are neglected, the hardneſs is increaſed; and there is danger, leſt he, whom they have refuſed to hear, ſhould call them no more.

This ſtate of dereliction, is the higheſt degree of miſery; and ſince it is ſo much to be dreaded, all approaches to it are diligently to be avoided. It is therefore neceſſary to enquire,

Thirdly, How, or by what cauſes, the heart is hardened.

The moſt dangerous hardneſs of heart is that which proceeds from ſome enormous wickedneſs, of which the criminal dreads the recollection, becauſe he cannot prevail upon himſelf to repair the injury; or becauſe he dreads the irruption of thoſe images, by which guilt muſt always be accompanied; and, finding a temporal eaſe in negligence and forgetfulneſs, by degrees confirms himſelf in ſtubborn impenitence.

This is the moſt dreadful and deplorable ſtate of the heart; but this I hope is not very common. That which frequently occurs, though very dangerous, is not deſperate; ſince it conſiſts, not in the perverſion of the will, but in the alienation of the thought; by ſuch hearts God is not defied, he is only forgotten. Of this forgetfulneſs, the general cauſes are worldly cares and ſenſual pleaſures. If there is a

Man, of whoſe ſoul avarice or ambition have complete poſſeſſion, and who places his hope in riches or advancement, he will be employed in bargains, or in ſchemes, and make no excurſion into remote futurity, nor conſider the time, in which the rich and the poor ſhall lie down together; when all temporal advantages ſhall forſake him, and he ſhall appear before the ſupreme tribunal of Eternal Juſtice. The ſlave of pleaſure ſoon ſinks into a kind of voluptuous dotage; intoxicated with preſent delights, and careleſs of every thing elſe; his days and his nights glide away in luxury or in vice, and he has no cure, but to keep thought away; for thought is always troubleſome to *him*, who lives without his own approbation.

That ſuch men are not rouſed to the knowledge and the conſideration of their real ſtate, will appear leſs ſtrange; when it is obſerved, that they are almoſt always either ſtupidly, or profanely, negligent of thoſe external duties of Religion, which are inſtituted to excite and preſerve the fear of God. By perpetual abſence from public worſhip, they miſs all opportunities, which the pious wiſdom of Chriſtia-

nity

nity has afforded them, of comparing their lives with the rules, which the Scripture contains; and awakening their attention to the preſence of God, by hearing him invoked, and joining their own voices in the common ſupplication. That careleſſneſs of the world to come, which firſt ſuffered them to omit the duties of devotion, is, by that omiſſion, hourly encreaſed; and having firſt neglected the means of holineſs, they in time do not remember them.

A great part of them whoſe hearts are thus hardened, may juſtly impute that inſenſibility to the violation of the Sabbath. He that keeps one day in the week holy, has not time to become profligate, before the returning day of recollection reinſtates his principles, and renews his caution. This is the benefit of periodical worſhip. But he, to whom all days are alike, will find *no* day for prayer and repentance.

Many enjoyments, innocent in themſelves, may become dangerous by too much frequency; publick ſpectacles, convivial entertainments, domeſtick games, ſports of the field, or gay or ludicrous converſation, all of them harmleſs, and ſome of them uſeful, while they are regulated by religious prudence, may yet become pernicious, when they paſs their bounds, and uſurp too much of that time which is given us, that we may work out our Salvation.

And ſurely whatever may diminiſh the fear of God, or abate the tenderneſs of conſcience, muſt be diligently avoided by thoſe who remember what is to be explained.

Fourthly, The conſequence of Hardneſs of Heart.

He that hardeneth his heart ſhall fall into miſchief. Whether miſchief be conſidered, as immediately ſignifying wickedneſs, or miſery, the ſenſe is eventually the ſame. Miſery is the effect of wickedneſs, and wickedneſs is the cauſe of miſery; and he that hardeneth his heart ſhall be both wicked and miſerable. Wicked he will doubtleſs be, for he that has loſt the fear of God has nothing by which he can oppoſe temptation. He has a breaſt open and expoſed, of which intereſt or voluptuouſneſs take eaſy poſſeſſion. He is the ſlave of his own deſires, and the ſport of his own paſſions. He acts without a rule of action; and he determines without any true principle of judgement. If he who

fears

ſears always, who preſerves in his mind a conſtant ſenſe of the danger of ſin, is yet often aſſaulted, and ſometimes overpowered, by temptation, what can be hoped for him, that has the ſame temptation, without the ſame defence? He who hardens his heart will certainly be wicked, and it neceſſarily follows, that he will certainly be miſerable. The doom of the obſtinate and impenitent ſinner is plainly declared; it is a fearful thing to fall into the hands of the living God.

Let us all therefore watch our thoughts and actions; and that we may not, by hardneſs of heart, fall into miſchief, let us endeavour and pray, that we may be among them that feared always, and by that fear may be prepared for everlaſting Happineſs.

SERMON IV.

ISAIAH, Chap. lviii. Ver. 7, 8.

Is it not to deal thy bread to the hungry, and that thou bring the poor that are caſt out, to thy houſe? when thou ſeeſt the naked that thou cover him, and that thou hide not thyſelf from thine own fleſh?

Then ſhall thy light break forth as the morning, and thine health ſhall ſpring forth ſpeedily; and thy righteouſneſs ſhall go before thee, the glory of the Lord ſhall be thy rereward.

IF the neceſſity of every duty is to be eſtimated by the frequency with which it is inculcated, and the ſanctions by which it is enforced; if the great Lawgiver of the univerſe, whoſe will is immutable, and whoſe decrees are eſtabliſhed for ever, may be be ſuppoſed to regard, in a particular manner, the obſervation of thoſe commands, which ſeem to be repeated only that they may be ſtrongly impreſſed, and ſecured, by an habitual ſubmiſſion, from violation and neglect, there is ſcarcely any virtue, that we ought more diligently to exerciſe than that of compaſſion to the needy and diſtreſſed.

If we look into the ſtate of mankind, and endeavour to deduce the will of God from the viſible diſpoſition of things, we find no duty more neceſſary to the ſupport of order, and the happineſs of ſociety, nor any of which we are more often reminded, by opportunities of practiſing it, or which is more ſtrongly urged upon us, by importunate ſolicitations, and affecting objects.

If we enquire into the opinions of thoſe men, on whom God conferred ſuperior wiſdom, in the Heathen world, all their ſuffrages will be found united in this great point. Amidſt all their wild opinions, and chimerical ſyſtems, the ſallies of unguided imagination, and the errors of bewildered reaſon; they have all endeavoured to evince the neceſſity of beneficence, and agreed to aſſign the firſt rank of excellence to him, who moſt contributes to improve the happineſs, and to ſoften the miſeries of life.

But we, who are bleſſed with clearer light, and taught to know the will of our Maker, not from long deductions from variable appearances, or intricate diſquiſitions of fallible reaſon, but by meſſengers inſpired by himſelf, and enabled to prove their miſſion, by works above the power of created Beings, may ſpare ourſelves the labour of tedious enquiries. The Holy Scriptures are in our hands; the Scriptures, which are able to make us wiſe unto Salvation; and by them we may be ſufficiently informed of the extent and importance of this great duty; a duty enjoined, explained, and enforced, by Moſes and the Prophets, by the Evangeliſts and Apoſtles, by the precepts of Solomon and the Example of Chriſt.

From thoſe to whom large poſſeſſions have been tranſmitted by their anceſtors, or whoſe induſtry has been bleſſed with ſucceſs, God always requires the tribute of Charity; he commands that what he has given be enjoyed in imitating his bounty, in diſpenſing happineſs, and chearing poverty,

verty, in eaſing the pains of diſeaſe, and lightening the burden of oppreſſion; he commands that the ſuperfluity of bread be dealt to the hungry; and the raiment, which the poſſeſſor cannot uſe, be beſtowed upon the naked, and that no man turn away from his own fleſh.

This is a tribute, which it is difficult to imagine that any man can be unwilling to pay, as an acknowledgement of his dependence upon the univerſal Benefactor, and an humble teſtimony of his confidence in that protection, without which, the ſtrongeſt foundations of human power muſt fail, at the firſt ſhock of adverſity, and the higheſt fabricks of earthly greatneſs ſink into ruin; without which, wealth is only a floating vapour, and policy an empty ſound.

But ſuch is the prevalence of temptations, not early reſiſted; ſuch the depravity of minds, by which unlawful deſires have been long indulged, and falſe appearances of happineſs purſued with ardour and pertinacioufneſs; ſo much are we influenced by example, and ſo diligently do we labour to deceive ourſelves, that it is not uncommon to find the ſentiments of benevolence almoſt

almoſt extinguiſhed, and all regard to the welfare of others overborne by a perpetual attention to immediate advantage and contracted views of preſent intereſt.

When any man has ſunk into a ſtate of inſenſibility like this, when he has learned to act only by the impulſe of apparent profit, when he can look upon diſtreſs, without partaking it, and hear the cries of poverty and ſickneſs, without a wiſh to relieve them; when he has ſo far diſordered his ideas as to value wealth, without regard to its end, and to amaſs, with eagerneſs, what is of no uſe in his hands; he is indeed not eaſily to be reclaimed; his reaſon, as well as his paſſions, is in combination againſt his ſoul, and there is little hope, that either perſuaſion will ſoften, or arguments convince him. A man, once hardened in cruelty by inveterate avarice, is ſcarcely to be conſidered as any longer human; nor is it to be hoped, that any impreſſion can be made upon him, by methods applicable only to reaſonable Beings. Beneficence and compaſſion can be awakened in ſuch hearts only by the operation of Divine Grace, and muſt be the effect of a

 miracle,

miracle, like that which turned the dry rock into a ſpringing well.

Let every one, that conſiders this ſtate of obdurate wickedneſs, that is ſtruck with horror at the mention of a man void of pity, that feels reſentment at the name of oppreſſion, and melts with ſorrow at the voice of miſery, remember that thoſe, who have now loſt all theſe ſentiments, were originally formed with paſſions, and inſtincts, and reaſon, like his own: let him reflect, that he, who now ſtands moſt firmly, may fall by negligence, and that negligence ariſes from ſecurity. Let him therefore obſerve, by what gradations men ſink into perdition, by what inſenſible deviations they wander from the ways of virtue 'till they are at length ſcarce able to return; and let him be warned by their example, to avoid the original cauſes of depravity, and repel the firſt attacks of unreaſonable ſelf-love; let him meditate on the excellence of Charity, and improve thoſe ſeeds of benevolence, which are implanted in every mind, but which will not produce fruit, without care and cultivation.

Such meditations are always neceſſary for the promotion of Virtue; for a careleſs and inattentive mind eaſily forgets its importance, and it will be practiſed only with a degree of ardour, proportioned to the ſenſe of our obligations to it.

To aſſiſt ſuch reflections, to confirm the benevolence of the liberal, and to ſhow thoſe who have lived without regard to the neceſſities of others, the abſurdity of their conduct, I ſhall enquire,

Firſt, Into the nature of Charity; and

Secondly, Into the advantages ariſing from the exerciſe of it.

Firſt, I ſhall enquire into the nature of Charity.

By Charity, is to be underſtood, every aſſiſtance of weakneſs, or ſupply of wants, produced by a deſire of benefiting others, and of pleaſing God. Not every act of liberality, every increaſe of the wealth of another, not every flow of negligent profuſions, or thoughtleſs ſtart of ſudden munificence, is to be dignified with this venerable name. There are many motives to the appearance of bounty, very different from thoſe of true Charity, and which, with whatever ſucceſs they may be impoſed upon Mankind, will be diſtinguiſhed at the laſt day by Him to whom all hearts are open. It is not impoſſible, that Men whoſe chief deſire is eſteem and applauſe, who court the favour of the multitude, and think fame the great end of action, may ſquander their wealth in ſuch a manner, that ſome part of it may benefit the virtuous or the miſerable; but as the Guilt, ſo the Virtue, of every action, ariſes from deſign; and thoſe bleſſings which are beſtowed by chance, will be of very little advantage to him that ſcattered them, with no other proſpect, than that of hearing his own praiſes; praiſes, of which he will not be often diſappointed, but of which our Lord has determined, that they ſhall be his reward. If any Man, in the diſtribution of his favours, finds the deſire of engaging gratitude, or gaining affection, to predominate in his mind; if he finds his benevolence weakened, by obſerving that his favours are forgotten, and that thoſe whom he has moſt ſtudiouſly benefited, are often leaſt zealous for his ſervice; he ought to remember, that he is not acting upon the proper motives of Charity. For true Charity ariſes from faith in the promiſes of God, and expects rewards only in a future ſtate. To hope for our recompence in this life, is not beneficence, but uſury.

And ſurely Charity may eaſily ſubſiſt, without temporal motives, when it is conſidered, that it is by the exerciſe of Charity alone, that we are enabled to receive any ſolid advantage from preſent proſperity, and to appropriate to ourſelves any poſſeſſion, beyond the poſſibility of loſing it. Of the uncertainty of ſucceſs, and the inſtability of greatneſs, we have examples every day before us. Scarcely can any Man turn his eyes upon the World, without obſerving the ſudden rotations of affairs, the ruin of the affluent, and the downfal of the high; and it may reaſonably be hoped, that no Man, to whom opportunities of ſuch obſervations occur, can forbear applying them to his own condition, and reflecting, that what he now contemplates in another, he may, in a few days, experience himſelf.

By theſe reflections, he muſt be naturally led to enquire, how he may fix ſuch fugitive advantages; how he ſhall hinder his wealth from flying away, and leaving him nothing, but melancholy, diſappointment, and remorse. This he can effect only, by the practice of Charity, by dealing his bread to the hungry, and bringing the poor that is cast out, to his house. By these means only he can lay up for himself treasures in Heaven, *where neither rust nor moth doth corrupt, and where Thieves do not break through and steal.* By a liberal distribution of his riches, he can place them above the reach of the spoiler, and exempt them from accident and danger; can purchase to himself that satisfaction which no power on earth can take away; and make them the means of happiness, when they are no longer in his hands. He may procure, by this use of his wealth, what he will find to be obtained by no other method of applying it, an alleviation of the sorrows of age, of the pains of sickness, and of the agonies of death.

To enforce the duty of Charity, it is so far from being necessary to produce any arguments, drawn from the narrow view of our condition, a view restrained to this world, that the chief reason for which it is to be practised, is the shortness and uncertainty of life. To a man who considers, for what purpose he was created, and why

he

he was placed in his preſent ſtate, how ſhort a time, at moſt, is allotted to his earthly duration, and how much of that time may be cut off; how can any thing give real ſatisfaction, that terminates in this life? How can he imagine, that any acquiſition can deſerve his labour, which has no tendency to the perfection of his mind? Or how can any enjoyment engage his deſires, but that of a pure conſcience, and reaſonable expectations of a more happy and permanent exiſtence? Whatever ſuperiority may diſtinguiſh us, and whatever plenty may ſurround us, we know, that they can be poſſeſſed but a ſhort time, and that the manner in which we employ them muſt determine our eternal ſtate; and what need can there be of any other argument for the uſe of them, agreeable to the command of him that beſtowed them? What ſtronger incitement can any man require to a due conſideration of the poor and needy, than that the Lord will deliver him in the day of trouble; in that day, when the ſhadow of death ſhall compaſs him about, and all the vanities of the world ſhall fade away; when all the comforts of this life ſhall forſake him, when pleaſure ſhall no longer delight, nor power protect

protect him? In that dreadful hour ſhall the man, whoſe care has been extended to the general happineſs of mankind, whoſe Charity has reſcued ſickneſs from the grave, and poverty from the dungeon, who has heard the groans of the aged, ſtruggling with misfortunes, and the cries of infants languiſhing with hunger, find favour in the ſight of the great Author of ſociety, and his recompence ſhall flow upon him, from the fountain of mercy; he ſhall ſtand without fear, on the brink of life, and paſs into eternity, with an humble confidence of finding that mercy which he has never denied. His Righteouſneſs ſhall go before him, and the Glory of the Lord ſhall be his rere-ward.

Theſe bleſſings, and theſe rewards, are to be gained by the due uſe of riches; but they are not confined to the rich, or unattainable by thoſe whom Providence has placed in lower ſtations. Charity is an univerſal duty, which it is in every man's power ſometimes to practice; ſince every degree of aſſiſtance given to another, upon proper motives, is an act of charity; and there is ſcarcely any man, in ſuch a ſtate of imbecillity, as that he may not, on

ſome

ſome occaſions, benefit his neighbour. He that cannot relieve the poor, may inſtruct the ignorant; and he that cannot attend the ſick, may reclaim the vicious. He that can give little aſſiſtance himſelf, may yet perform the duty of Charity, by inflaming the ardour of others, and recommending the petitions, which he cannot grant, to thoſe who have more to beſtow. The widow that ſhall give her mite to the treaſury, the poor man who ſhall bring to the thirſty a cup of cold water, ſhall not loſe their reward.

And that this reward is not without reaſon decreed to the beneficent, and that the duty of Charity is not exalted above its natural dignity and importance, will appear, by conſidering,

Secondly, The benefits ariſing from the exerciſe of Charity.

The chief advantage which is received, by mankind from the practice of Charity, is the promotion of Virtue, amongſt thoſe who are moſt expoſed to ſuch temptations as it is not eaſy to ſurmount; temptations, of which no man can ſay, that he ſhould be able to reſiſt them, and of which it is not eaſy for any one that has not known them

them, to eſtimate the force, and repreſent the danger.

We ſee, every day, men bleſſed with abundance, and revelling in delight, yet overborne by ungovernable deſires of increaſing their acquiſitions; and breaking through the boundaries of Religion, to pile heaps on heaps, and add one ſuperfluity to another, to obtain only nominal advantages, and imaginary pleaſures.

For theſe we ſee Friendſhips broken, Juſtice violated, and Nature forgotten; we ſee crimes committed, without the proſpect of obtaining any poſitive pleaſure, or removing any real pain. We ſee men toiling through meanneſs and guilt, to obtain that which they can enjoy only in idea, and which will ſupply them with nothing real, which they do not already abundantly poſſeſs.

If men formed by education and enlightened by experience, men whoſe obſervations of the world cannot but have ſhown them the neceſſity of Virtue, and who are able to diſcover the enormity of wickedneſs, by tracing its original, and purſuing its conſequences, can fall before ſuch temptations, and, in oppoſition to knowledge

and

and conviction, prefer to the happineſs of pleaſing God, the flatteries of dependants, or the ſmiles of power; what may not be expected from him, who is puſhed forward into ſin by the impulſe of poverty, who lives in continual want of what he ſees waſted by thouſands in negligent extravagance, and whoſe pain is every moment aggravated by the contempt of thoſe whom nature has ſubjected to the ſame neceſſities with himſelf, and who are only his ſuperior by that wealth which they know not how to poſſeſs with moderation or decency?

How ſtrongly may ſuch a man be tempted to declare war upon the proſperous and the great! With what obſtinacy and fury may he ruſh on from one outrage to another, impelled on one part, by the preſſure of neceſſity, and attracted on the other, by the proſpect of happineſs: of happineſs, which he ſees ſufficient to elevate thoſe that poſſeſs it above the conſideration of their own nature, and to turn them away from their own fleſh; that happineſs, which appears greater, by being compared with his own miſery, and which he admires the more, becauſe he cannot approach

approach it. He that finds in himſelf every natural power of enjoyment, will envy the tables of the luxurious, and the ſplendour of the proud; he who feels the cold of nakedneſs, and the faintneſs of hunger, cannot but be provoked to ſnatch that bread which is devoured by exceſs, and that raiment which is only worn as the decoration of vanity. Reſentment may eaſily combine with want, and incite him to return neglect with violence.

Such are the temptations of poverty; and who is there that can ſay, that he has not ſometimes forſaken virtue upon weaker motives? Let any man reflect upon the ſnares to which Poverty expoſes virtue, and remember, how certainly one crime makes way for another, till at laſt all diſtinction of good and evil is obliterated; and he will eaſily diſcover the neceſſity of Charity, to preſerve a great part of mankind from the moſt atrocious wickedneſs.

The great rule of action, by which we are directed to do to others whatever we would that others ſhould do to us, may be extended to God himſelf; whatever we aſk of God, we ought to be ready to be-

ſtow

ſtow on our neighbour; if we pray to be forgiven, we muſt forgive thoſe that treſpaſs againſt us; and is it not equally reaſonable, when we implore from Providence our daily bread, that we deal our bread to the hungry; and that we reſcue others from being betrayed by want into ſin, when we pray, that we may not ourſelves be led into temptation?

Poverty, for the greateſt part, produces ignorance, and ignorance facilitates the attack of temptation. For how ſhould any man reſiſt the ſolicitations of appetite, or the influence of paſſion, without any ſenſe of their guilt, or dread of the puniſhment? How ſhould he avoid the paths of vice, who never was directed to the way of virtue?

For this reaſon, no method of charity is more efficacious than that which at once enlightens ignorance and relieves poverty, that implants virtue in the mind, and wards off the blaſts of indigence that might deſtroy it in the bloom. Such is the charity of which an opportunity is now offered; charity by which thoſe, who would probably, without aſſiſtance, be the burdens or terrors of the community by growing up in idleneſs and vice, are enabled to ſupport

port themſelves by uſeful employments, and glorify God by reaſonable ſervice.

Such are the general motives which the Religion of Jeſus affords to the general exercise of charity, and ſuch are the particular motives for our laying hold of the opportunity, which Providence has this day put into our power for the practice of it; motives no leſs than the hope of everlaſting happineſs, and the fear of puniſhment which ſhall never end. Such incitements are ſurely ſufficient to quicken the ſloweſt, and animate the coldeſt; and if there can be imagined any place in which they muſt be more eminently prevalent, it muſt be the * place where we now reſide. The numerous Frequenters of this place conſtitute a mixed aſſemblage of the happy and the miſerable. Part of this audience has reſorted hither, to alleviate the miſeries of ſickneſs, and part, to divert the ſatiety of pleaſure; part, becauſe they are diſabled, by diſeaſes, to proſecute the employment of their ſtation; and part, becauſe their ſtation has allotted them, in their own opinion, no other buſineſs than to purſue their pleaſures. Part have exhauſted the medicines,

* Bath.

and part have worn out the delights of every other place; and theſe contrary conditions are ſo mingled together, that in few places are the miſeries of life ſo ſeverely felt, or its pleaſures more luxuriouſly enjoyed.

To each of theſe ſtates of life may the precepts of Charity be enforced with eminent propriety, and unanſwerable arguments. Thoſe, whoſe only complaint is a forfeit of felicity, and whoſe fearleſs and confident gaiety brings them hither, rather to waſte health than to repair it, cannot ſurely be ſo intent upon the conſtant ſucceſſion of amuſements which vanity and affluence have provided, as not ſometimes to turn their thoughts upon thoſe whom poverty and ignorance have cut off from enjoyment, and conſigned a prey to wickedneſs, to miſery, and to want. If their amuſements afford them the ſatisfaction which the eager repetition of them ſeems to declare, they muſt certainly pity thoſe who live in ſight of ſo much happineſs, which they can only view from a diſtance, but can never reach; and thoſe whom they pity, they cannot ſurely hear the promiſes made to charity without endeavouring

ing to relieve. But if, as the wiseſt among the votaries of pleaſure have confeſſed, they feel themſelves unſatisfied and deluded; if, as they own, their ardour is kept up by diſſimulation, and they lay aſide their appearance of felicity, when they retire from the eyes of thoſe among whom they deſire to propagate the deceit; if they feel that they have waſted life without poſſeſſing it; and know that they ſhall riſe to-morrow, to chaſe an empty good which they have often graſped at, but could never hold: they may ſurely ſpare ſomething for the purchaſe of ſolid ſatisfaction, and cut off part of that expence, by which nothing is procured, for the ſake of giving to others thoſe neceſſaries which the common wants of our Being demand, and by the diſtribution of which they may lay up ſome treaſures of happineſs againſt that day which is ſtealing upon them, the day of age, of ſickneſs and of death, in which they ſhall be able to reflect with pleaſure on no other part of their time paſt here, but that which was ſpent in the duties of Charity. But if theſe ſhall harden their diſpoſitions, if theſe ſhall with-hold their hands, let them not amuſe themſelves with the

the general excuſes ; or dream that any plea of inability will be accepted from thoſe who ſquander wealth upon trifles, and truſt ſums, that might relieve the wants of multitudes, to the ſkill of play, and the uncertainties of chance.

To thoſe to whom languiſhment and ſickneſs have ſhewn the inſtability of all human happineſs, I hope it will not be requiſite to enforce the neceſſity of ſecuring to themſelves a ſtate of unſhaken ſecurity, and unchangeable enjoyment. To inculcate the ſhortneſs of life to thoſe who feei hourly decays ; or to expatiate on the miſeries of diſeaſe and poverty to them, whom pain perhaps, at this inſtant, is dragging to the grave, would be a needleſs waſte of that time which their condition admoniſhes them to ſpend, not in hearing, but in practiſing their duty. And of ſickneſs, Charity ſeems the peculiar employment, becauſe it is an act of piety which can be practiſed with ſuch ſlight and tranſient attention as pain and faintneſs may allow. To the ſick therefore I may be allowed to pronounce the laſt ſummons to this mighty work, which perhaps the Divine Providence will allow them to hear. Remember thou ! that now fainteſt under the weight of long-continued maladies, that to thee, more emphatically, the night cometh in which no man can work ; and therefore ſay not to him that aſketh thee, " Go away now, and to-morrow I will give ;" To-morrow ? To-morrow is to *all* uncertain, to *thee* almoſt hopeleſs ; to-*day* if thou wilt hear the voice of God calling thee to repentance, and by repentance to charity ; harden not thy heart, but what thou knoweſt that in thy laſt moment thou ſhalt wiſh done, make haſte to do, leſt thy laſt moment be now upon thee.

And let us all, at all times, and in all places, remember, that they who have given food to the hungry, raiment to the naked, and inſtruction to the ignorant, ſhall be numbered by the Son of God, amongſt the Bleſſed of the Father.

SERMON V.

NEHEMIAH, Chap. ix. Verſe 33.

Howbeit thou art juſt in all that is brought upon us, for thou haſt done right, but we have done wickedly.

THERE is nothing upon which more Writers, in all ages, have laid out their abilities, than the miſeries of life; and it affords no pleaſing reflections to diſcover that a ſubject ſo little agreeable is not yet exhauſted.

Some have endeavoured to engage us in the contemplation of the evils of life for a very wiſe and good end. They have propoſed, by laying before us the uncertainty of proſperity, the vanity of pleaſure, and the inquietudes of power, the difficult attainment of moſt earthly bleſſings, and the ſhort duration of them all, to divert our thoughts from the glittering follies and tempting delufions that furround us, to an enquiry after more certain and permanent felicity; felicity not fubject to be interrupted by fudden viciffitudes, or impaired by the malice of the revengeful, the caprice of the inconftant, or the envy of the ambitious. They have endeavoured to demonftrate, and have in reality demonftrated to all thofe who will fteal a few moments from noife and fhow, and luxury, to attend to reafon and to truth, that nothing is worthy of our ardent wifhes, or intenfe folicitude, that terminates in this ftate of exiftence, and that thofe only make the true ufe of life, that employ it in obtaining the favour of God, and feeuring everlafting happinefs.

Others have taken occafion from the dangers that furround, and the troubles that perplex us, to difpute the wifdom or juftice of the Governor of the world, or to murmur at the laws of Divine Providence; as the prefent ftate of the world, the diforder and confufion of every thing about us, the cafual and certain evils to which we are expofed, and the difquiet and difguft which either accompany, or follow, thofe thoſe few pleaſures that are within our reach, ſeem, in their opinion, to carry no marks of infinite benignity. This has been the reaſoning by which the wicked and profligate, in all ages, have attempted to harden their hearts againſt the reproaches of conſcience, and delude others into a parcipitation of their crimes. By this argument weak minds have been betrayed into doubts and diſtruſt, and decoyed by degrees into a dangerous ſtate of ſuſpence, though perhaps never betrayed to abſolute infidelity. For few men have been made infidels by argument and reflection; their actions are not generally the reſult of their reaſonings, but their reaſonings of their actions. Yet theſe reaſonings, though they are not ſtrong enough to pervert a good mind, may yet, when they coincide with intereſt, and are aſſiſted by prejudice, contribute to confirm a man, already corrupted, in his impieties, and at leaſt retard his reformation, if not entirely obſtruct it.

Beſides, notions, thus derogatory from the providence of God, tend, even in the beſt men, if not timely eradicated, to weaken thoſe impreſſions of reverence and gratitude, which are neceſſary to add warmth to his devotions, and vigour to his virtue; for as the force of corporeal motion is weakened by every obſtruction, though it may not be entirely overcome by it, ſo the operations of the mind are by every falſe notion impeded and embarraſſed, and though they are not wholly diverted or ſuppreſſed, proceed at leaſt with leſs regularity, and with leſs celerity.

But theſe doubts may eaſily be removed and theſe arguments confuted, by a calm and impartial attention to Religion and to reaſon; it will appear upon examination, that though the world be full of miſery and diſorder, yet God is not to be charged with diſregard of his creation; that, if we ſuffer, we ſuffer by our own fault, and that *he has done right, but we have done wickedly.*

We are informed by the Scriptures, that God is not the Author of our preſent ſtate, that when he created man, he created him for happineſs; happineſs indeed dependant upon his own choice, and to be preſerved by his own conduct; for ſuch muſt neceſſarily be the happineſs of every reaſonable Being: that this happineſs was forfeited by a breach of the conditions to which it was annexed, and that the poſterity

rity of him that broke the covenant were involved in the consequences of his fault. Thus Religion shews us that physical and moral evil entered the world together; and reason and experience assure us, that they continue for the most part so closely united, that, to avoid misery, we must avoid sin, and that while it is in our power to be virtuous, it is in our power to be happy, at least to be happy to such a degree as may have little room for murmur and complaints.

Complaints are doubtless irrational in themselves, and unjust with respect to God, if the remedies of the evils we lament are in our hands; for what more can be expected from the beneficence of our Creator, than that he should place good and evil before us, and then direct us in our choice?

That God has not been sparing of his bounties to mankind, or left them, even since the original transgression of his command, in a state so calamitous as discontent and melancholy have represented it, will evidently appear, if we reflect,

First, How few of the evils of life can justly be ascribed to God.

Secondly, How far a general Piety might exempt any Community from thole evils.

Thirdly, How much, in the preſent corrupt ſtate of the world, particular men may by the practice of the duties of Religion, promote their own happineſs.

Firſt, How few of the evils of life can juſtly be aſcribed to God.

In examining what part of our preſent miſery is to be imputed to God, we muſt carefully diſtinguiſh that which is actually appointed by him, from that which is ouly permitted, or that which is the conſequence of ſomething done by ourſelves, and could not be prevented, but by the interruption of thoſe general and ſettled laws, which we term the courſe of nature, or the eſtabliſhed order of the univerſe. Thus it is decreed by God, that all men ſhould die; and therefore the death of each man may juſtly be aſcribed to God; but the circumſtances and time of his death are very much in his own power, or in the power of others. When a good man falls by the hand of an aſſaſſin, or is condemned by the teſtimony of falſe witneſſes, or the ſentence of a corrupt judge; his death

may,

may, in ſome meaſure, be called the work of God, but his murder is the action of men. That he was mortal is the effect of the divine decree; but that he was deprived of life unjuſtly, is the crime of his enemies.

If we examine all the afflictions of mind, body, and eſtate, by this rule, we ſhall find God not otherwiſe acceſſary to them, than as he works no miracles to prevent them, as he ſuffers men to be maſters of themſelves, and reſtrains them only by coercions applied to their reaſon. If God ſhould by a particular exertion of his Omnipotence, hinder murder or oppreſſion, no man could then be a murderer or an oppreſſor, becauſe he would be with-held from it by an irreſiſtible power; but then that power, which prevented crimes, would deſtroy Virtue; for Virtue is the conſequence of choice. Men would be no longer rational, or would be rational to no purpoſe, becauſe their actions would not be the reſult of free-will, determined by moral motives; but the ſettled and predeſtined motions of a machine impelled by neceſſity.

Thus it appears, that God would not act as the Governor of rational and moral

agents,

agents, if he ſhould lay any other reſtraints upon them, than the hope of rewards, or fear of puniſhments; and that to deſtroy, or obviate the conſequences of human actions, would be to deſtroy the preſent conſtitution of the world.

When therefore any man ſuffers pain from an injury offered him, that pain is not the act of God, but the effect of a crime, to which his enemy was determined by his own choice. He was created ſuſceptible of pain, but not neceſſarily ſubjected to that particular injury which he now feels, and he is therefore not to charge God with his afflictions. The materials for building are naturally combuſtible; but when a city is fired by incendiaries, God is not the author of its deſtruction.

God may indeed, by ſpecial acts of Providence, ſometimes hinder the deſigns of bad men from being ſucceſsfully executed, or the execution of them from producing ſuch conſequences as it naturally tends to; but this, whenever it is done, is a real, though not always a viſible miracle, and is not to be expected in the ordinary occurrences of life, or the common tranſactions of the world.

In making an eſtimate therefore of the miſeries that ariſe from the diſorders of the body, we muſt conſider how many diſeaſes proceed from our own lazineſs, intemperance, or negligence ; how many the vices or follies of our anceſtors have tranſmitted to us, and beware of imputing to God the conſequences of luxury, riot, and debauchery.

There are indeed diſtempers, which no caution can ſecure us from, and which appear to be more immediately the ſtrokes of Heaven ; but theſe are not of the moſt painful or lingering kind, they are for the moſt part acute and violent, and quickly terminate, either in recovery, or death ; and it is always to be remembered, that nothing but wickedneſs makes death an evil.

Nor are the diſquietudes of the mind leſs frequently excited by ourſelves. Pride is the general ſource of our infelicity. A man that has an high opinion of his own merits, of the extent of his capacity, of the depth of his penetration, and the force of his eloquence, naturally forms ſchemes of employment, and promotion, adequate to thoſe abilities he conceives himſelf poſſeſ-

ſed

ſed of; he exacts from others the ſame eſteem which he pays to himſelf, and imagines his deſerts diſregarded, if they are not rewarded to the extent of his wiſhes. He claims more than he has a right to hope for, finds his exorbitant demands rejected, retires to obſcurity and melancholy, and charges Heaven with his diſappointments.

Men are very ſeldom diſappointed, except when their deſires are immoderate, or when they ſuffer their paſſions to overpower their reaſon, and dwell upon delightful ſcenes of future honours, power, or riches, till they miſtake probabilities for certainties, or wild wiſhes for rational expectations. If ſuch men, when they awake from theſe voluntary dreams, find the pleaſing phanton vaniſh away; what can they blame but their own folly?

With no greater reaſon can we impute to Providence the fears and anxieties that harraſs and diſtract us; for they ariſe from too cloſe an adherence to thoſe things, from which we are commanded to diſengage our affections. We fail of being happy, becauſe we determine to obtain felicity by means different from thoſe which God hath appointed. We are forbidden to be

too

too ſolicitous about future events; and is the Author of that prohibition to be accuſed, becauſe men make themſelves miſerable by diſregarding it?

Poverty indeed is not always the effect of wickedneſs, it may often be the conſequence of Virtue; but it is not certain that poverty is an evil. If we exempt the poor man from all the miſeries to which his condition expoſes him from the wickedneſs of others, if we ſecure him from the cruelty of oppreſſion, and the contumelies of pride; if we ſuppoſe him to rate no enjoyment of this life, beyond its real and intrinſic value, and to indulge no deſire more than reaſon and religion allow; the inferiority of his ſtation will very little diminiſh his happineſs; and therefore the poverty of the virtuous reflects no reproach upon Providence. But poverty, like many other miſeries of life, is often little more than an imaginary calamity. Men often call themſelves poor, not becauſe they want neceſſaries, but becauſe they have not more than they want. This indeed is not always the caſe, nor ought we ever to harden our hearts againſt the cries of thoſe who implore our aſſiſtance, by

ſuppoſing

ſuppoſing that they feel leſs than they expreſs; but let us all relieve the neceſſitous according to our abilities, and real poverty will ſoon be baniſhed out of the world.

To theſe general heads may be reduced almoſt all the calamities that imbitter the life of man. To enumerate particular evils would be of little uſe. It is evident that moſt of our miſeries are, either imaginary, or the conſequences, either of our own faults, or the faults of others; and that it is therefore worthy of enquiry.

Secondly, How far a general piety might exempt any community from thoſe evils.

It is an obſervation very frequently made, that there is more tranquillity and ſatisfaction diffuſed through the inhabitants of uncultivated and ſavage countries, than is to be met with in nations filled with wealth and plenty, poliſhed with civility, and governed by laws. It is found happy to be free from contention, though that exemption be obtained by having nothing to contend for; and an equality of condition, though that condition be far from eligible, conduces more to the peace of ſociety, than an eſtabliſhed and legal ſubordination; in which every man is perpetually

tually endeavouring to exalt himſelf to the rank above him, though by degrading others already in poſſeſſion of it; and every man exerting his efforts, to hinder his inferiors from riſing to the level with himſelf. It appears that it is better to have no property, than to be in perpetual apprehenſions of fraudulent artifices, or open invaſions; and that the ſecurity ariſing from a regular adminiſtration of government, is not equal to that which is produced by the abſence of ambition, envy, or diſcontent.

Thus pleaſing is the proſpect of ſavage countries, merely from the ignorance of Vice, even without the knowledge of Virtue; thus happy are they, amidſt all the hardſhips and diſtreſſes that attend a ſtate of nature, becauſe they are in a great meaſure free from thoſe which men bring upon one another.

But a community, in which Virtue ſhould generally prevail, of which every member ſhould fear God with his whole heart, and love his neighbour as himſelf, where every man ſhould labour to make himſelf *perfect, even as his Father which is in Heaven is perfect*, and endeavour with his

his utmoſt diligence to imitate the divine juſtice and benevolence, would have no reaſon to envy thoſe nations, whoſe quiet is the effect of their ignorance.

If we conſider it with regard to public happineſs, it would be opulent without luxury, and powerful without faction; its counſels would be ſteady, becauſe they would be juſt; and its efforts vigorous becauſe they would be united. The governors would have nothing to fear from the turbulence of the people, nor the people any thing to apprehend from the ambition of their governors. The encroachments of foreign enemies, they could not always avoid, but would certainly repulſe, for ſcarcely any civilized nation has been ever enſlaved, till it was firſt corrupted.

With regard to private men, not only that happineſs, which neceſſarily deſcends to particulars from the public proſperity, would be enjoyed; but even thoſe bleſſings, which conſtitute the felicity of domeſtic life, and are leſs cloſely connected with the general good. Every man would be induſtrious to improve his property, becauſe he would be in no danger of ſeeing his improvements torn from him.

Every

Every man would aſſiſt his neighbour, becauſe he would be certain of receiving aſſiſtance, if he ſhould himſelf be attacked by neceſſity. Every man would endeavour after merit, becauſe merit would always be rewarded. Every tie of friendſhip and relation would add to happineſs, becauſe it would not be ſubject to be broken by envy, rivalſhip, or ſuſpicion. Children would honour their parents, becauſe all parents would be virtuous; all parents would love their children, becauſe all children would be obedient. The grief which we naturally feel at the death of thoſe that are dear to us, could not perhaps be wholly prevented, but would be much more moderate than in the preſent ſtate of things, becauſe no man could ever want a friend, and his loſs would therefore be leſs, becauſe his grief, like his other paſſions, would be regulated by his duty. Even the relations of ſubjection would produce no uneaſineſs, becauſe inſolence would be ſeparated from power and diſcontent from inferiority. Difference of opinions would never diſturb this community, becauſe every man would diſpute for truth alone, look upon the ignorance of others with compaſſion, and reclaim them from their errors with tenderneſs and modeſty. Perſecution would not be heard of among them, becauſe there would be no pride on one ſide, nor obſtinacy on the other. Diſputes about property would ſeldom happen, becauſe no man would grow rich by injuring another; and, when they did happen, they would be quickly terminated, becauſe each party would be equally deſirous of a juſt ſentence. All care and ſolicitude would be almoſt baniſhed from this happy region, becauſe no man would either have falſe friends, or public enemies. The immoderate deſire of riches would be extinguiſhed, where there was no vanity to be gratified. The fear of poverty would be diſpelled, where there was no man ſuffered to want what was neceſſary to his ſupport, or proportioned to his deſerts. Such would be the ſtate of a community generally virtuous, and this happineſs would probably be derived to future generations; ſince the earlieſt impreſſions would be in favour of virtue, ſince thoſe, to whom the care of education ſhould be committed, would make themſelves venerable by the obſervation of their own precepts, and the minds of the young and unexperienced

experienced would not be tainted with falſe notions, nor their conduct influenced by bad examples.

Such is the ſtate at which any community may arrive by the general practice of the duties of Religion. And can Providence be accuſed of cruelty or negligence, when ſuch happineſs as this is within our power? Can man be ſaid to have received his exiſtence as a puniſhment, or a curſe, when he may attain ſuch a ſtate as this; when even this is only preparatory to geater happineſs, and the ſame courſe of life will ſecure him from miſery, both in this world and in a future ſtate?

Let no man charge this proſpect of things with being a train of airy phantoms; a viſionary ſcene, with which a gay imagination may be amuſed in ſolitude and eaſe, but which the firſt ſurvey of the world will ſhew him to be nothing more than a pleaſing deluſion. Nothing has been mentioned which would not certainly be produced in any nation by a general piety. To effect all this, no miracle is required; men need only unite their endeavours, and exert thoſe abilities which God has conferred upon them, in conformity to the laws of Religion.

To general happineſs, indeed, is requir-ed a general concurrence in virtue; but we are not to delay the amendment of our own lives, in expectation of this favourable juncture. An univerſal reformation muſt be begun ſomewhere, and every man ought to be ambitious of being the firſt. He that does not promote it, retards it; for every man muſt, by his converſation, do either good or hurt. Let every man, therefore, endeavour to make the world happy, by a ſtrict performance of his duty to God and man, and the mighty work will ſoon be accompliſhed.

Governors have yet a harder taſk; they have not only their own actions, but thoſe of others, to regulate, and are not only chargeable with their own faults, but with all thoſe which they neglect to prevent or puniſh. As they are intruſted with the government for the ſake of the people, they are under the ſtrongeſt obligations to advance their happineſs, which they can only do by the encouragement of virtue.

But ſince the care of governors may be fruſtrated, ſince public happineſs, which muſt

muſt be the reſult of public virtue, ſeems to be at a great diſtance from us, let us conſider,

Thirdly, How much in the preſent corrupt ſtate of the world, particular men may by the practice of the duties of Religion, promote their own happineſs.

He is very ignorant of the nature of happineſs, who imagines it to conſiſt wholly in the outward circumſtances of life, which being in themſelves tranſient and variable, and generally dependant upon the will of others, can never be the true baſis of a ſolid ſatisfaction. To be wealthy, to be honoured, to be loved, or to be feared, is not always to be happy. The man who conſiders himſelf as a Being accountable to God, as a Being ſent into the world only to ſecure immortal happineſs by his obedience to thoſe laws which he has received from his Creator, will not be very ſolicitous about his preſent condition, which will ſoon give way to a ſtate permanent and unchangeable, in which nothing will avail him but his innocence, or diſturb him but his crimes. While this reflection is predominant in the mind, all the good and evil of life ſinks into nothing. While

he

he preſſes forward towards eternal felicity, honours and reproaches are equally contemptible. If he be injured, he will ſoon ceaſe to feel the wrong ; if he be calumniated, the day is coming in which all the nations of the earth, and all the Hoſt of Heaven, ſhall be witneſſes of his juſtification. If his friends forſake, or betray him, he alleviates his concern, by conſidering that the divine promiſes are never broken, and that the favour of God can only be forfeited by his own fault. In all his calamities he remembers, that it is in his own power to make them ſubſervient to his own advantage, and that patience is one of thoſe virtues which he is commanded to practiſe, and which God has determined to reward. That man can never be miſerable to whom perſecution is a bleſſing ; nor can his tranquillity be interrupted, who places all his happineſs in his proſpect of eternity.

Thus it appears, that by the practice of our duty, even our preſent ſtate may be made pleaſing and deſirable ; and that if we languiſh under calamities, they are brought upon us, not by the immediate hand of Providence, but by our own folly and diſobedience ; that happineſs will be diffuſed, as virtue prevails ; and *that God has done right, but we have done wickedly.*

SERMON VI.

PROVERBS, Chap. xii. Verſe 2.

When Pride cometh, then cometh Shame, but with the Lowly is Wiſdom.

THE writings of Solomon are filled with ſuch obſervations upon the nature and life of man, as were the reſult of long experience, aſſiſted with every advantage of mind and fortune, an experience that had made him acquainted with the actions, paſſions, virtues, and vices of all ranks, ages, and denominations of mankind, and enabled him, with the divine aſſiſtance, to leave to ſucceeding ages a collection of precepts

precepts that, if diligently attended to, will conduct us safe in the paths of life.

Of the ancient sages of the Heathen world, so often talked of, and so loudly applauded, there is recorded little more than single maxims, which they comprized in few words, and often inculcated; for these they were honoured by their contemporaries, and still continue reverenced and admired; nor would it either be justice or gratitude to depreciate their characters, since every discoverer, or propagator, of truth, is undoubtedly a benefactor to the world. But surely if single sentences could procure them the epithet of *wise*, Solomon may, for this collection of important counsels, *justly claim the title of the wisest amongst the sons of men.*

Among all the vices against which he has cautioned us (and he has scarcely left one untouched), there is none upon which he animadverts with more severity, or to which he more frequently recalls our attention, by reiterated reflections, than the vice of *pride*; for which there may be many reasons assigned, but, more particularly, two seem to deserve our consideration; the first drawn from the extensiveness of the

the ſin ; the other from the circumſtances of the Preacher.

The firſt is the extenſiveneſs of the ſin.

Pride is a corruption that ſeems almoſt originally engrafted in our nature ; it exerts itſelf in our firſt years, and, without continual endeavours to ſuppreſs it, influences our laſt. Other vices tyrannize over particular ages, and triumph in particular countries. Rage is the failing of youth, and avarice of age ; revenge is the predominant paſſion of one country, and inconſtancy the characteriſtic of another ; but pride is the native of every country, infects every climate, and corrupts every nation. It ranges equally through the gardens of the eaſt, and the deſerts of the ſouth, and reigns no leſs in the cavern of the ſavage, than in the palace of the Epicure. It mingles with all our other vices, and without the moſt conſtant and anxious care will mingle alſo with our virtues. It is no wonder, therefore, that Solomon ſo frequently directs us to avoid this fault, to which we are all ſo liable, ſince nothing is more agreeable to reaſon, than that precepts of the moſt general uſe ſhould be moſt frequently inculcated.

The

The ſecond reaſon may be drawn from the circumſtances of the Preacher.

Pride was probably a crime to which Solomon himſelf was moſt violently tempted; and indeed it might have been much more eaſily imagined, that he would have fallen into this ſin, than into ſome others, of which he was guilty, ſince he was placed in every circumſtance that could expoſe him to it. He was a king abſolute and independent, and by conſequence ſurrounded with ſycophants ready to ſecond the firſt motions of ſelf-love, and blow the ſparks of vanity; to echo all the applauſes, and ſuppreſs all the murmurs of the people to comply with every propoſal, and flatter every failing. Theſe are the tempters to which kings have been always expoſed, and whoſe ſnares few kings have been able to overcome.

But Solomon had not only the pride of royalty to ſuppreſs, but the pride of proſperity, of knowledge, and of wealth; each of them able to ſubdue the virtue of moſt men, to intoxicate their minds, and hold their reaſon in captivity. Well might Solomon more diligently warn us againſt a ſin which had aſſaulted him, in ſo many different

different forms. Could any ſuperiority to the reſt of the world make pride excuſable, it might have been pardoned in Solomon; but he has been ſo far from allowing it either in himſelf or others, that he has left a perpetual atteſtation in favour of humility, *that where Pride cometh, there cometh Shame, but with the lowly is wiſdom.*

This aſſertion I ſhall endeavour to explain and confirm,

Firſt, by conſidering the nature of pride in general, with its attendants and conſequences.

Secondly, by examining ſome of the uſual motives to pride; and ſhewing how little can be pleaded in excuſe of it.

Thirdly, by ſhewing the amiableneſs and excellence of humility.

Firſt, by conſidering in general the nature of pride, with its attendants and conſequences.

Pride, ſimply conſidered, is an immoderate degree of ſelf-eſteem, or an over-value ſet upon a man by himſelf, and, like moſt other vices, is founded originally on an intellectual falſhood. But this definition ſets this vice in the faireſt light, and ſeparates it from all its conſequences, by

conſidering

confidering man without relation to ſocie-ty, and independent of all outward cir-cumſtances. Pride, thus defined, is only the ſeed of that complicated ſin againſt which we are cautioned in the text. It is the pride of a ſolitary being, and the ſub-ject of ſcholaſtic diſquiſitions, not of a practical diſcourſe

In ſpeculation, pride may be confidered as ending where it began, and exerting no influence beyond the boſom in which it dwells; but in real life and the courſe of affairs, pride will always be attended with kindred paſſions, and produce effects equal-ly injurious to others, and deſtructive to itſelf.

He that overvalues himſelf will under-value others, and he that undervalues others will oppreſs them. To this fancied ſuperiority it is owing, that tyrants have ſquandered the lives of millions, and look-ed unconcerned on the miſeries of war. It is indeed ſcarcely credible, it would with-out experience be abſolutely incredible, that a man ſhould carry deſtruction and ſlaughter round the world, lay cities in aſhes, and put nations to the ſword, with-out one pang or one tear; that we ſhould feel no reluctance at ſeizing the poſſeſſions of another, at robbing parents of their children, and ſhortening or embittering innumerable lives. Yet this fatal, this dreadful effect, has pride been able to produce. Pride has been able to harden the heart againſt compaſſion, and ſtop the ears againſt the cries of miſery.

In this manner does pride operate, when unhappily united with power and dominion; and has in the lower ranks of mankind, ſimilar, though not equal effects. It makes maſters cruel and imperious, and magiſtrates inſolent and partial. It produces contempt and injuries, and diſſolves the bond of ſociety.

Nor is this ſpecies of pride more hurtful to the world, than deſtructive to itſelf. The oppreſſor unites Heaven and Earth againſt him; if a private man, he at length becomes the object of univerſal hatred and reproach; and if a prince, the neighbouring monarchs combine to his ruin. So that *when pride cometh, then cometh ſhame: but with the lowly is wiſdom.*

He that ſets too high a value upon his own merits, will of courſe think them ill rewarded with his preſent condition. He

will

will endeavour to exalt his fortune, and his rank above others, in proportion as his deserts are superior to theirs. He will conceive his virtues obscured by his fortune, lament that his great abilities lie useless and unobserved for want of a sphere of action, in which he might exert them in their full extent. Once fired with these notions, he will attempt to increase his fortune and enlarge his sphere; and how few there are that prosecute such attempts with innocence, a very transient observation will sufficiently inform us.

Every man has remarked the indirect methods made use of in the pursuit of wealth; a pursuit for the most part prompted by pride; for to what end is an ample fortune generally coveted? Not that the possessor may have it in his power to relieve distess, or recompense virtue; but that he may distinguish himself from the herd of mankind by expensive vices, foreign luxuries, and a pompous equipage. To pride therefore must be ascribed most of the fraud, injustice, violence, and extortion, by which wealth is frequently acquired.

Another

Another concomitant of pride is envy, or the desire of debasing others. A proud man is uneasy and dissatisfied, while any of those applauses are bestowed on another which he is desirous of himself. On this account he never fails of exerting all his art to destroy, or obstruct, a rising character. His inferiors he endeavours to depress, lest they should become his equals; and his equals, not only because they are so, but lest they should in time become his superiors. For this end he circulates the whisper of malevolence, aggravates the tale of calumny, and assists the clamour of defamation; opposes in public the justest designs, and in private depreciates the most uncontested virtues.

Another consequence of immoderate self esteem is an insatiable desire of propagating in others the favourable opinion he entertains of himself. No proud man is satisfied with being singly his own admirer; his excellences must receive the honour of the public suffrage. He therefore tortures his invention for means to make himself conspicuous, and to draw the eyes of the world upon him. It is impossible, and would be here improper, to enumerate all the fictitious qualities, all the petty emulations, and laborious trifles, to which this appetite, this eagerneſs of diſtinction, has given birth in men of narrow views, and mean attainments. But who can without horror think on thoſe wretches who attempt to raiſe a character by ſuperiority of guilt? who endeavour to excel in vice and outvie each other in debauchery? Yet thus far can pride infatuate the mind, and extinguiſh the light of reaſon.

But for the moſt part it is ordered by Providence, that the ſchemes of the ambitious are diſappointed, the calumnies of the envious detected, and falſe pretences to reputation ridiculed and expoſed, ſo that ſtill *when pride cometh, then cometh ſhame; but with the lowly is wiſdom.*

I am now to conſider, in the ſecond place, ſome of the uſual motives to pride, and ſhew how little they can be pleaded in excuſe of it.

A ſuperior Being that ſhould look down upon the diſorder, confuſion, and corruption of our world, that ſhould obſerve the ſhortneſs of our lives, the weakneſs of our bodies, the continual accidents, or injuries to which we are ſubject; the violence of

our

our paſſions, the irregularity of our conduct, and the tranſitory ſtate of every thing about us, would hardly believe there could be among us ſuch a vice as pride, or that any human Being ſhould need to be cautioued againſt being too much elated with his preſent ſtate. Yet ſo it is, that, however weak or wicked we may be, we fix our eyes on ſome other that is repreſented by our ſelf-love to be weaker, or more wicked, than ourſelves, and grow proud upon the compariſon. Thus in the midſt of danger and uncertainty, we ſee many intoxicated with the pride of proſperity; a proſperity that is hourly expoſed to be diſturbed, a proſperity that lies often at the mercy of a treacherous friend, or unfaithful ſervant, a proſperity which certainly cannot laſt long, but muſt ſoon be ended by the hand of death.

To conſider this motive to pride more attentively, let us examine what it is to be proſperous. To be proſperous, in the common acceptation, is to have a large or an increaſing, fortune, great numbers of friends and dependants, and to be high in the eſteem of the World in general. But do theſe things conſtitute the happineſs of a man? of a Being accountable to his Creator for his conduct, and, according to the account he ſhall give, deſigned to exiſt eternally in a future ſtate of happineſs, or miſery? What is the proſperity of ſuch a ſtate, but the approbation of that God, on whoſe ſentence futurity depends? But neither wealth, friendſhips, or honours, are proofs of that approbation, or means neceſſary to procure it. They often endanger, but ſeldom promote, the future happineſs of thoſe that poſſeſs them. And can pride be inſpired by ſuch proſperity as this?

Even with regard to the preſent life, pride is a very dangerous aſſociate to greatneſs. A proud man is oppoſed in his riſe, hated in his elevation, and inſulted in his fall. He may have dependants, but can have no friends; and paraſites, but no ingenuous companions.

Another common motive to pride is knowledge, a motive equally weak, vain, and idle, with the former. Learning, indeed, imperfect as it is, may contribute to many great and noble ends, and may be called in to the aſſiſtance of religion; as it is too often perverſely employed againſt it, it is of uſe to diſplay the greatneſs, and vindicate the juſtice, of the Almighty; to explain the difficulties, and enforce the proofs of Religion. And the ſmall advances that may be made in ſcience are of themſelves ſome proof of a future ſtate, ſince they ſhew that God, who can be ſuppoſed to make nothing in vain, has given us faculties evidently ſuperior to the buſineſs of this preſent world. And this is perhaps one reaſon, why our intellectual powers are in this life of ſo great extent as they are.

But how little reaſon have we to boaſt of our knowledge, when we only gaze and wonder at the ſurfaces of things! when the wiſeſt and moſt arrogant Philoſopher knows not how a grain of corn is generated, or why a ſtone falls to the ground! But were our knowledge far greater than it is, let us yet remember that goodneſs, not knowledge, is the happineſs of man! The day will come, it will come quickly, when it ſhall profit us more to have ſubdued one proud thought, than to have numbered the Hoſt of Heaven.

There is another more dangerous ſpecies of pride, ariſing from a conſciouſneſs of virtue, ſo watchful is the enemy of our

ſouls,

ſouls, and ſo deceitful are our own hearts, that too often a victory over one ſinful inclination expoſes us to be conquered by another. Spiritual pride repreſents a man to himſelf beloved by his Creator in a particular degree, and of conſequence, inclines him to think others not ſo high in his favour as himſelf. This is an error, into which weak minds are ſometimes apt to fall, not ſo much from the aſſurance that they have been ſteady in the practice of juſtice, righteouſneſs, and mercy, as that they have been punctually obſervant of ſome external acts of devotion. This kind of pride is generally accompanied with great uncharitableneſs, and ſevere cenſures of others, and may obſtruct the great duty of Repentance. But it may be hoped, that a ſufficient remedy againſt this ſin may be eaſily found, by reminding thoſe who are infected with it, that the Blood of Chriſt was poured out upon the Croſs to make their beſt endeavours acceptable to God. And that they, whoſe ſins require ſuch an expiation, have little reaſon to boaſt of their virtue.

Having thus proved the unreaſonableneſs, folly, and odious nature, of pride, I am, in the laſt place, to ſhew the amiableneſs and excellence of humility.

Upon this head I need not be long, ſince every argument againſt any vice is equally an argument in favour of the contrary virtue; and whoever proves the folly of being proud, ſhews, at the ſame time, *that with the lowly there is wiſdom* But to evince beyond oppoſition the excellence of this virtue, we may in few words obſerve, that the life of our Lord was one continued exerciſe of humility. The Son of God condeſcended to take our nature upon him, to become ſubject to pain, to bear, from his birth, the inconveniencies of poverty and to wander from city to city, amidſt oppoſition, reproach, and calumny. He diſdained not to converſe with publicans and ſinners, to miniſter to his own Diſciples, and to weep at the miſeries of his own creatures. He ſubmitted to inſults and revilings, and, being led like a lamb to the ſlaughter, opened not his mouth. At length, having borne all the cruel treatment that malice could ſuggeſt, or power inflict, he ſuffered the moſt lingering and ignominious death.

God of his infinite mercy grant, that, by imitating his humility, we may be made partakers

partakers of his merits! To whom, with the Father and the Holy Ghoſt, be aſcribed, as is moſt due, all honour, adoration, and praiſe, now and ever! Amen.

SERMON VII.

JEREMIAH, Chap. vi. Verse 16.

Thus saith the Lord, stand ye in the ways and see, and ask for the old paths, where is the good way, and walk therein, and ye shall find rest for your Souls. But they said, we will not walk therein.

THAT almost every age, from the beginning of the world, has been eminently marked out, and distinguished from the rest, by some peculiar character, by particular modes of thinking, or methods of acting, then almost universally prevalent, is is evident from the hiſtories of all nations. At one time, the whole world has bowed, without repining, to deſpotic power, and abſolute dominion; at another, not only the licentious and oppreſſive tyranny of governors has been reſtrained, but juſt and lawful authority trampled upon, and inſulted; at one time, all regard for private intereſt has been abſorded and loſt, in the concern for the welfare of the public; to which virtue itſelf has been made a ſacrifice; at another, every heart has been engroſſed by low views, and every ſentiment of the mind has been contracted into the narrow compaſs of ſelf-love. Thus have vice and virtue, wiſdom and folly, or perhaps only different follies and oppoſite vices, alternately prevailed; thus have mankind ruſhed from one error to another, and ſuffered equally by both extremes.

Theſe changes of conduct or opinion may be conſidered as the revolutions of human nature, often neceſſary, but always dangerous; neceſſary, when ſome favourite vice has generally infected the world, or ſome error, long eſtabliſhed, begins to tyrannize, to demand implicit faith,

and

and refuſe examination; but dangerous, leſt the mind, incenſed by oppreſſion, heated by conteſt, and elated by victory, ſhould be too far tranſported to attend to truth, and, out of zeal to ſecure her conqueſt, ſet up one error, to depreſs another.

That no change in Religion has been made with that calmneſs, caution, and moderation, which Religion itſelf requires, and which common prudence ſhews to be neceſſary in the tranſaction of any important affair, every nation of the earth can ſufficiently atteſt. Rage has been called in to the aſſiſtance of zeal, and deſtruction joined with reformation. Reſolved not to ſtop ſhort, men have generally gone too far, and, in lopping ſuperfluities, have wounded eſſentials.

This conduct when we conſider the weakneſs of human nature, and the circumſtances of moſt of thoſe by whom ſuch changes have been effected, is entitled at leaſt to compaſſion, if not to excuſe; nor can it be doubted, that our great Creator looks down with tenderneſs and compaſſion upon the irregular ſtarts and tempeſtuous agitations of a mind, moved by a zeal for

his

his honour, and a love of truth. Had al ler. ror and misconduct such a plea as this, they might indeed be lamented, and pray. ed against as weaknesses, but could hardly be censured, or condemned as crimes.

But more slow and silent transitions from one extreme to another are very frequent. Men not impelled by the vehemence of opposition, but seduced by inclinations less violent, too often deviate from the paths of truth, and persuade others to follow them. The pride of singularity influences the teacher, and a love of novelty corrupts the follower, till the delusion, extending itself by degrees, becomes at length general, and overspreads a people.

The prevailing spirit of the present age seems to be the spirit of scepticism and captiousness, of suspicion and distrust, a contempt of all authority, and a presumptious confidence in private judgment; a dislike of all established forms, merely because they are established, and of old paths, because they are old.

Into this temper have men been insensibly led by a warm assertion of the right of judging for themselves, a right not to be called in question, since God himself gave us a claim to it, in making us reaſonable Beings ; and the Apoſtle doubtleſs admits it, when he directs us to give the reaſon of our faith to any that ſhall demand it.

But this privilege, ill underſtood, has been, and always may be, the occaſion of very dangerous and pernicious miſtakes ; it may be exerciſed without knowledge or diſcretion, till error be entangled with error, till diviſions be multiplied by endleſs ſubdiviſions, till the bond of peace be entirely broken, and the Church become a ſcene of confuſion, a chaos of diſcordant forms of worſhip, and inconſiſtent ſyſtems of faith.

There are ſome men, we now find, to whom ſeparation and diſagreement appear not ſuch formidable evils, as they are generally repreſented ; who can look, with the utmoſt calmneſs and unconcern, at a riſing ſchiſm, and ſurvey, without any perturbation, the ſpeedy progreſs of an encreaſing hereſy. Let every man, ſay they, enjoy his opinions, ſince *he* only is anſwerable for them.

There are men, who for the moſt part value themſelves, and are ſometimes valued by others, for their enlarged views and generous

nerous ſentiments; who pretend to look with uncommon penetration into the cauſes of human actions, and the ſecret motions of the mind; but perhaps this opinion is no proof that their pretenſions are well grounded, or that they are better acquainted with human nature, than thoſe whom they affect to ridicule and inſult.

If it be granted that it is the duty of every man to publiſh, profeſs, and defend any important truth, and the truths of Religion, be allowed important; it will follow, that diverſity of ſentiments muſt naturally produce controverſies and altercations. And how few there are capable of managing debates without unbecoming heat, or diſhoneſt artifices, how ſoon zeal is kindled into fury, and how ſoon a concern for reputation mingles with a concern for truth, how readily the antagoniſts deviate into perſonal invectives, and, inſtead of confuting the arguments, defame the lives of thoſe whoſe doctrine they diſapprove, and how often diſputes terminate in uproar, riot, and perſecution, every one is convinced, and too many have experienced. That diverſity of opinions, which is the original and ſource of ſuch evils as

theſe,

these, cannot therefore be too diligently obviated; nor can too many endeavours be used to check the growth of new doctrines, and reclaim those that propagate them, before sects are formed, or schism established.

This is not to be done by denying, or disputing, the right of private judgement; but by exhorting all men to exercise it in a proper manner, according to each man's measure of knowledge, abilities, and opportunities; and by endeavouring to remove all those difficulties, which may obstruct the discovery of truth, and exposing the unreasonableness of such prejudices as may perplex or mislead the enquirer.

The prejudice to which many of the disorders of the present age, in which infidelity, superstition, and enthusiasm, seem contending for empire over us, may be justly ascribed, is an over-fondness for novelty, a desire of striking out new paths to peace and happiness, and a neglect of following the precept in the text, of asking for the old paths, where is the good way, and walking therein; a precept I shall therefore endeavour to illustrate,

First,

First, By laying before you the dangers of judging of Religion, without long and diligent examination.

Secondly, By evincing the reaſonableneſs of ſearching into antiquity, or of aſking for the old paths. And,

Thirdly, By ſhewing the happineſs which attends a well-grounded belief, and ſteady practice of Religion.

First, I propoſe to lay before you the dangers of judging of Religion, without a long and diligent examination.

There is no topic more the favourite of the preſent age, than the innocence of error accompanied with ſincerity. This doctrine has been cultivated with the utmoſt diligence, enforced with all the arts of argument, and embelliſhed with all the ornaments of eloquence, but perhaps not bounded, with equal care, by proper limitations, nor preſerved by juſt explication, from being a ſnare to pride, and a ſtumbling block to weakneſs.

That the judge of all the earth will do right, that he will require in proportion to what he has given, and puniſh men for the miſapplication or neglect of talents, not for the want of them, that he condemns

demns no man for not ſeeing what he has hid from him, or for not attending to what he could never hear, ſeems to be the neceſſary, the inevitable conſequence of his own attributes.

That error therefore may be innocent will not be denied, becauſe it undoubtedly may be ſincere; but this conceſſion will give very little countenance to the ſecurity and ſupineneſs, the coldneſs and indifference, of the preſent generation, if we conſider deliberately how much is required to conſtitute that ſincerity, which ſhall avert the wrath of God, and reconcile him to error.

Sincerity is not barely a full perſuaſion of the truth of our aſſertions, a perſuaſion too often grounded upon a high opinion of our own ſagacity, and confirmed perhaps by frequent triumphs over weak opponents, continually gaining new ſtrength by a neglect of re-examination, which perhaps we decline, by induſtriouſly diverting our attention from any objections that ariſe in our thoughts, and ſuppreſſing any ſuſpicion of a fallacy before the mind has time to connect its ideas, to form arguments, and draw concluſions. Sincerity is not a heat of the heart kept up by eager contentions or warm profeſſions, nor a tranquillity produced by confidence, and continued by indolence. There may be zeal without ſincerity, and ſecurity without innocence. If we forbear to enquire through lazineſs or pride, or enquire with partiality, paſſion, or precipitancy ; if we do not watch over the moſt hidden motions of our hearts, and endeavour, with our utmoſt efforts, to baniſh all thoſe ſecret tendencies, and all thoſe lurking inclinations, which operate very frequently without being attended to, even by ourſelves ; if we do not carry on our ſearch without regard to the reputation of our teachers, our followers, or ourſelves, and labour after truth with equal induſtry and caution, let us not preſume to put any truſt in our ſincerity.

Such is the preſent weakneſs and corruption of human nature, that ſincerity, real ſincerity, is rarely to be found ; but till it be found, it is the laſt degree of folly to repreſent error as innocent. By a God infinitely merciful, and propitiated by the death of our Bleſſed Saviour, it may indeed

deed be pardoned, but it cannot be justified.

But the greatest part of those that declaim with most vehemence in defence of their darling notions, seem to have very little claim even to pardon on account of their sincerity. It is difficult to conceive what time is allotted to religious questions and controversies by a man whose life is engrossed by the hurries of business, and whose thoughts are continually upon the stretch, to form plans for the improvement of his fortune, or the gratification of his ambition. Nor is it very probable, that such subjects are more seriously considered by men abandoned to pleasure, men who sit down to eat, and rise up to play, whose life is a circle of successive amusements and whose hours are distinguished only by vicissitudes of pleasure. And yet the questions which these frequently decide, and decide without the least suspicion of their own qualifications, are often of a very intricate and complicated kind, which must be disentangled by a long and continued attention, and resolved with many restrictions and great caution. Not only knowledge, judgement, and experience, but uninterrupted leiſure and retirement are neceſſary, that the chain of reaſoning may be preſerved unbroken, and the mind perform its operations without any hindrance from foreign objects.

To this end, men have formerly retreated to ſolitudes and cloiſters, and excluded all the cares and pleaſures of the world; and when they have ſpent a great part of their lives in ſtudy and meditation, at laſt, perhaps deliver their opinions, as learned men will generally do, with diffidence and fear.

Happy would it be for the preſent age if men were now thus diſtruſtful of their own abilities. They would not then adopt opinions, merely becauſe they wiſh them to be true, then defend what they have once adopted, warm themſelves into confidence, and then reſt ſatisfied with the pleaſing conſciouſneſs of their own ſincerity. We ſhould not then ſee men, not eminent for any ſuperior giſts of nature, or extraordinary attainments, endeavouring to form new ſects, and to draw the *world after them.* They may indeed act with an honeſt intention, and ſo far with ſincerity, but certainly without that caution which their

inexperience

inexperience ought to ſuggeſt, and that reverence for their ſuperiors which reaſon, as well as the laws of ſociety, requires. They ſeem, even when conſidered with the utmoſt candor, to have rather conſulted their own imaginations, than to have aſked for the old paths, where is the good way. It is therefore proper in this place that I ſhould endeavour,

Secondly, to evince the reaſonableneſs of ſearching into antiquity, or of aſking for the *Old paths*.

A contempt of the monuments, and the wiſdom of antiquity, may juſtly be reckoned one of the reigning follies of theſe days, to which pride and idleneſs have equally contributed. The ſtudy of antiquity is laborious; and to deſpiſe what we cannot, or will not underſtand, is a much more expeditious way to reputation. Part of the diſeſteem into which their writings are now fallen may indeed be aſcribed to that exorbitant degree of veneration in which they were once held by blindneſs and ſuperſtition. But there is a mean betwixt idolatry and inſult, between weak credulity and total diſbelief. The Ancients are not infallible, nor are their deciſions to be received without examination; but they are

at

at leaſt the determinations of men equally deſirous with ourſelves of diſcovering truth, and who had, in ſome caſes, better opportunities than we now have.

With regard to the order and government of the Primitive Church, we may doubtleſs follow their authority with perfect ſecurity; they could not poſſibly be ignorant of laws executed, and cuſtoms practiſed, by themſelves; nor would they, even ſuppoſing them corrupt, ſerve any intereſts of their own, by handing down falſe accounts to poſterity. We are therefore to enquire from them the different orders eſtabliſhed in the miniſtry from the Apoſtolic ages, the different employments of each, and their ſeveral ranks, ſubordinations, and degrees of authority. From their writings we are to vindicate the eſtabliſhment of our church; and by the ſame writings are thoſe who differ from us, in theſe particulars, to defend their conduct.

Nor is this the only, though perhaps the chief uſe of theſe writers; for, in matters of faith, and points of doctrine, thoſe, at leaſt, who lived in the ages neareſt to the times of the Apoſtles undoubtedly deſerve to be conſulted. The oral doctrines and occaſional explications of the Apoſtles would not be immediately forgotten, in the churches to which they had preached, and which had attended to them with the diligence and reverence which their miſſion and character demanded. Their ſolutions of difficulties and determinations of doubtful queſtions, muſt have been treaſured up in the memory of their audiences, and tranſmitted, for ſome time, from father to ſon. Every thing, at leaſt, that was declared by the inſpired teachers to be neceſſary to ſalvation, muſt have been carefully recorded ; and therefore what we find no traces of in the ſcripture, or the early fathers, as moſt of the peculiar tenets of the Romiſh Church, muſt certainly be concluded to be not neceſſary. Thus, by conſulting firſt the holy ſcriptures, and next the writers of the primitive church, we ſhall make ourſelves acquainted with the will of God ; thus ſhall we diſcover the good way, and find that reſt for our ſouls which will amply recompence our ſtudies and enquiries, as I ſhall attempt to prove,

Thirdly, By ſhewing the happineſs which attends a well-grounded belief and ſteady practice of religion.

The ſerenity and ſatisfaction at which we arrive by a firm and ſettled perſuaſion of the fundamental articles of our religion, is very juſtly repreſented by the expreſſion of finding reſt for the ſoul. A mind reſtleſs and undetermined, continually fluctuating betwixt various opinions, always in purſuit of ſome better ſcheme of duties, and more eligible ſyſtem of faith, eager to embrace every new doctrine, and adopt the notions of every pretender to extraordinary light, can never be ſufficiently calm and unruffled, to attend to thoſe duties which procure that peace of God which paſſeth all underſtanding.

Suſpence and uncertainty diſtract the ſoul, diſturb its motions, and retard its operations; while we doubt in what manner to worſhip God, there is great danger leſt we ſhould neglect to worſhip him at all. A man, conſcious of having long neglected to worſhip God, can ſcarcely place any confidence in his mercy; or hope, in the moſt preſſing exigencies, for his protection. And how miſerable is that man, who, on the bed of ſickneſs, or in the hour of death, is without truſt in the goodneſs

of

of his Creator ! This ſtate, dreadful as it appears, may be juſly apprehended by thoſe who ſpend their lives in roving from one new way to another, and are ſo far from aſking for the old paths, where is the good way, that when they are ſhewn it, they ſay, we will not walk therein.

There is a much cloſer connection between practice and ſpeculation than is generally imagined. A man, diſquieted with ſcruples concerning any important article of religion, will for the moſt part, find himſelf indifferent and cold, even to thoſe duties which he practiced before with the moſt active diligence and ardent ſatisfaction. Let him then aſk for the old paths, where is the good way, and he ſhall find reſt for his ſoul. His mind once ſet at eaſe from perplexity, and perpetual agitation, will return with more vigour to the exerciſes of piety. An uniform perſeverance in theſe holy practices will produce a ſteady confidence in the divine favour, and that confidence will compleat his happineſs. To which that we may all attain, God of his infinite mercy grant, for the merits of Jeſus

Chriſt,

Chriſt, our Saviour, to whom, with the Father and the Holy Ghoſt, be aſcribed, as is moſt due, all honour, adoration, and praiſe, now and ever! Amen.

SERMON VIII.

ROMANS xii, the latter part of the 16th verse.

Be not wise in your own conceits.

IT has been obferved by thofe who have employed themfelves in confidering the methods of Providence, and the government of the world, that good and evil are diftributed, through all ftates of life, if not in equal proportions, yet in fuch degrees as leave very little room for thofe murmurs and complaints which are frequently produced by fuperficial enquiries, negligent furveys, and impatient comparifons.

Every condition has, with regard to this life, its inconveniences, and every condition has likewife its advantages; though its pofition to the eye of the beholder may be fo varied, as that at fome times the mifery may be concealed, and at other times the happinefs;

happineſs; but to judge only by the eye, is not the way to diſcover truth. We may paſs by men, without being able to diſtinguiſh whether they are to be numbered among thoſe whoſe felicities, or whoſe ſorrows, preponderate; as we may walk over the ground, without knowing, whether its entrails contain mines of gold, or beds of ſand.

Nor is it leſs certain, that, with reſpect to the more important proſpects of a future ſtate, the ſame impartiality of diſtribution may be generally remarked; every condition of humanity, being expoſed on one ſide, and guarded on the other; ſo that every man is burthened, though none are overwhelmed; every Man is obliged to vigilance, but none are haraſſed beyond their ſtrength. The great buſineſs therefore of every man is to look diligently round him, that he may note the approaches of the enemy; and to bar the avenues of temptation, which the particular circumſtances of his life are moſt likely to lay open; and to keep his heart in perpetual alarm againſt thoſe ſins which conſtantly beſiege him. If he be rich, let him beware, leſt when he is *full he deny God*, and ſay, *who is the Lord?* If he be poor, let him cautiously avoid to *steal*, and *take the name* of his *God in vain.*

There are some conditions of humanity which are made particularly dangerous by an uncommon degree of seeming security; conditions, in which we appear so compleatly fortified, that we have little to dread, and therefore give ourselves up too readily to negligence and supineness; and are destroyed without precaution, because we flattered ourselves that destruction could not approach us. This fatal slumber of treacherous tranquillity may be produced and prolonged by many causes, by causes as various as the situations of life. Our condition may be such, as may place us out of the reach of those general admonitions, by which the rest of mankind are reminded of their errors, and awakened to their duty; it may remove us to a great distance from the common incitements to common wickedness, and therefore may superinduce a forgetfulness of our natural frailties, and suppress all suspicions of the encroachments of sin—And the sin to which we are particularly tempted may be of that insidious and seductive kind, as, that without alarming

ing us by the horrors of its appearance, and ſhocking us with the enormity of any ſingle acts, may, by ſlow advances, poſſeſs the ſoul, and in deſtroying us differ only from the atrociouſneſs of more apparent wickedneſs, as a lingering poiſon differs from the ſword ; more difficultly avoided, and more certainly fatal.

To temptations of this ſubtle, inſinuating kind, the life of men of learning ſeems above all others to be expoſed. As they are themſelves appointed the teachers of others, they very rarely have the dangers of their own ſtate ſet before them ; as they are, by their abſtraction and retirement, ſecluded from the gaieties, the luxuries and the pageantries of life, they are willingly perſuaded to believe, that becauſe they are at a great diſtance from the rocks on which conſcience is moſt frequently wrecked, that therefore they ſail with ſafety, and may give themſelves to the wind without a compaſs. The crimes, from which they are in danger, are not thoſe from which the mind has been taught to ſhrink away with horror, or againſt which the invectives of Moral or Theological writers have generally been directed ; and therefore they are ſuffered to approach unregarded, to gain ground imperceptibly upon minds directed to different views ; and to fix themſelves at leiſure in the heart, where perhaps they are ſcarcely diſcovered till they are paſt eradication.

To theſe cauſes, or to ſome of theſe, it muſt ſurely be imputed, that learning is found ſo frequently to fail in the direction of life ; and to operate ſo faintly and uncertainly in the regulation of *their* conduct, who are moſt celebrated for their application and proficiency. They have been betrayed, by ſome falſe ſecurity, to withhold their attention from their own lives ; they have grown knowing, without growing virtuous ; and have failed of the wiſdom which is the gift of the Father of lights, becauſe they have thought it unneceſſary to ſeek it with that anxiety and importunity to which only it is granted ; they have truſted to their own powers, and were *wiſe in their own conceits*.

There is perhaps no claſs of Men, to whom the precept, given by the Apoſtle to his converts againſt too great confidence in their underſtandings, may be more properly inculcated, than thoſe who are dedi-

cated

cated to the profeſſion of literature, and are therefore neceſſarily advanced to degrees of knowledge above them who are diſperſed among manual occupations, and the vulgar parts of life; whoſe attention is confined within the narrow limits of their own employments, and who have not often leiſure to think of more than the means of relieving their own wants, by ſupplying the demands of others.

With theſe, and ſuch as theſe, placed ſometimes, by whatever means, in much higher ſtations, a man of learning has ſuch frequent opportunities of comparing himſelf; and is ſo ſtrongly incited by that compariſon, to indulge the contemplation of his own ſuperiority; that it is not to be conſidered as wonderful, that vanity creeps in upon him; that he does not willingly withdraw his imagination from objects that ſo much flatter his paſſions, that he purſues the train of thought, from one reflection to another, places himſelf and others, in every ſituation, in which he can appear with advantage in his own eyes; riſes to compariſons with ſtill higher characters, and ſtill retains the habit of giving himſelf the preference; and in all diſputable

ble caſes turns the balance in his own fa-vour, by ſuper-adding from his own con-ceit, that wiſdom, which by nature he does not poſſeſs, or by induſtry he has not ac-quired.

This wiſdom in his own conceit is very eaſily at firſt miſtaken for qualities, not in themſelves criminal, nor in themſelves dangerous; nor is it eaſy to fix the limits, in ſpeculation, between a reſolute adher-ence to that which appears truth, and an obſtinate obtruſion of peculiar notions up-on the underſtanding of others; between the pleaſure that naturally ariſes from the enlargement of the mind, and increaſe of knowledge, and that which proceeds from a contempt of others, and the inſolent tri-umphs of intellectual ſuperiority. Yet though the confines of theſe qualities are nearly alike, their extremes are widely dif-ferent; and it will ſoon be diſcovered, how much evil is avoided by repreſſing that opinion of ourſelves, which vanity ſug-geſts; and that confidence, which is gain-ed only *by meaſuring ourſelves by ourſelves*, dwelling on our own excellence, and flat-tering ourſelves with ſecret panegyrics.

As this falſe claim to wiſdom is the

ſource of many faults, as well as miſeries, to men of learning, it ſeems of the utmoſt importance to obviate it in the young, who may be imagined to be very little tainted, and ſuppreſs it in others, whoſe greater advances, and more extenſive reputation, have more endangered them ; nor can any man think himſelf ſo innocent of this fault, or ſo ſecure from it, as that it ſhould be unneceſſary for him to conſider,

Firſt, The dangers, which men of learning incur, by being wiſe in their own conceits.

Secondly, The proper means, by which that pernicious conceit of wiſdom may be avoided or ſuppreſſed.

In order to ſtate with more accuracy the dangers which men, dedicated to learning, may be reaſonably imagined to incur, by being wiſe in their own conceits ; it is neceſſary to diſtinguiſh the different periods of their lives ; and to examine, whether this diſpoſition is not in its tendency equally oppoſite to our duty, and, by inevitable conſequence in its effects, equally deſtructive of our happineſs in every ſtate.

The buſineſs of the life of a ſcholar is to accumulate, and to diffuſe, knowledge ; to learn,

learn, in order that he may teach. The first part of his time is assigned to study, and the acquisition of learning; the latter, to the practice of those arts which he has acquired, and to the instruction of others who have had less time, or opportunities, or abilities, for improvement. In the state therefore of a learner, or of a teacher, the man of letters is always to be considered; and if it shall appear that, on whatever part of his task he is employed, a false opinion of his own excellence will naturally and certainly defeat his endeavours; it may be hoped, that there will be found sufficient reason, why no man should *be wise in his own conceit.*

Since no Man can teach what he has never learned, the value and usefulness of the latter part of his life must depend in a great measure upon the proper application of the earlier years; and he that neglects the improvement of his own mind, will never be enabled to instruct others. Light must strike on the body, by which light can be reflected. The disposition therefore, which best befits a young man, about to engage in a life of study, is patience in enquiry; eagerness of knowledge; and willingneſs to be inſtructed; a due ſubmiſſion to greater abilities and longer experience; and a ready obedience to thoſe, from whom he is to expect the removal of his ignorance, and the reſolution of his doubts.

How unlikely any one, wiſe in his own conceit, is to excite, or promote in himſelf ſuch inclinations, may be eaſily determined. It is well known that ſtudy is not diligently proſecuted, but at the expence of many pleaſures and amuſements; which no young man will be perſuaded to forbear, but upon the moſt cogent motives, and the ſtrongeſt conviction. He that is to draw truth from the depths of obſcurity, muſt be fully informed of its value, and the neceſſity of finding it; he that engages in a ſtate, oppoſite to the pleaſures of ſenſe, and the gratification of every higher paſſion, muſt have ſome principle within, ſtrongly implanted, which may enforce induſtry, and repel temptation. But how ſhall he, who is already *wiſe in his own conceit*, ſubmit to ſuch tedious and laborious methods of inſtruction? Why ſhould he toil for that, which, in his own opinion, he poſſeſſes; and drudge for the ſupply of wants, which he does not feel? He has already ſuch degrees of knowledge, as, magnified by his own imagination, exalt him above the reſt of mankind; and to climb higher, would be to labour without advantage.

He already has a wide extent of ſcience within his view, and his willingneſs to be pleaſed with himſelf does not ſuffer him to think, or to dwell on the thought of any thing beyond; and who that ſees all, would wiſh to ſee farther? That ſubmiſſion to authority, and that reverence for inſtruction, which ſo well becomes every man at his firſt entrance upon new regions of learning, where all is novelty, confuſion and darkneſs, and no way is to be found through the intricacies of oppoſite ſyſtems, but by tracing the ſteps of thoſe that have gone before; that willingneſs to receive implicitly what farther advances only can enable him to prove, which initiation always ſuppoſes; are very little to be expected from him, who looks down with ſcorn upon his teacher, and is more ready to cenſure the obſcurity of precepts, than to ſuſpect the force of his own underſtanding. Knowledge is to be attained by ſlow and gradual acquiſitions, by a careful review of our ideas, and a regular ſuperſtructure

ſtructure of one propoſition on another; and is therefore the reward only of diligence and patience. But patience is the effect of modeſty; pride graſps at the whole, and what it cannot hold, it affects to deſpiſe; it is rather ſolicitous to diſplay, than increaſe, its acquiſitions; and rather endeavours, by fame, to ſupply the want of knowledge, than by knowledge to arrive at fame.

That theſe are not imaginary repreſentations, but true copies of real life, moſt of thoſe, to whom the inſtruction of young men is intruſted, will be ready to confeſs; ſince they have often the diſſatisfaction of finding that, in proportion as greater advances have been made in the firſt period of life, there is leſs diligence in the ſecond. And that, as it was ſaid of the ancient Gauls, that they were more than men in the onſet, and leſs than women in the ſhock; it may be ſaid in our literary contentions, that many, who were men at ſchool, are boys at the college.

Their ardour remits, their diligence relaxes; and they give themſelves to a lazy contemplation of comparative excellence, without conſidering that the compariſon is hourly growing lefs advantageous, and that the acquifitions which they boaft are mouldering away.

Such is the danger to a learner, of too early an opinion of his own importance; but if we fuppofe him to have efcaped in his firft years this fatal confidence, and to be betrayed into it by a longer feries of fuccefsful application, its effects will then be equally dangerous; and as it hinders a young man from receiving inftruction, it will obftruct an older ftudent in conveying it.

There is no employment in which men are more eafily betrayed to indecency and impatience, than in that of teaching; in which they neceffarily converfe with thofe, who are their inferiors, in the relation by which they are connected, and whom it may be fometimes proper to treat with that dignity which too often fwells into arrogance; and to reftrain with fuch authority as not every man has learned to feparate from tyranny. In this ftate of temporary honour, a proud man is too willing to exert his prorogative; and too ready to forget that he is dictating to thofe, who may one day dictate to him. He is inclined

clined to wonder that what he comprehends himſelf is not equally clear to others; and often reproaches the intellects of his auditors, when he ought to blame the confuſion of his own ideas, and the improprieties of his own language. He reiterates therefore his poſitions without elucidation, and enforces his aſſertion by his frown, when he finds arguments leſs eaſy to be ſupplied. Thus forgetting that he had to do with men, whoſe paſſions are perhaps equally turbulent with his own, he transfers by degrees to his inſtruction the prejudices which are firſt raiſed by his behaviour; and having forced upon his pupils an hatred of their teacher, he ſees it quickly terminate in a contempt of the precept.

But inſtruction extends farther than to ſeminaries of ſtudents, or the narrow auditories of ſequeſtered literature. The end of learning, is to teach the public, to ſuperintend the conduct, watch over the morals and regulate the opinions, of pariſhes, dioceſes, and provinces, to check vices in their firſt eruption, and ſuppreſs hereſies in the whiſpers of their riſe. And ſurely this awful, this arduous taſk, requires qualities, which a man, *wiſe in his own conceit*, cannot

not

not eaſily attain; that mildneſs of addreſs, that patience of attention, that calmneſs of diſputation, that ſelection of times, and places, and circumſtances, which the vehemence of pride will not regard. And, in reality, it will generally be found, that the firſt objection and the laſt to an unacceptable paſtor, is, that he is proud, that he is too wiſe for familiarity, and will not deſcend to the level with common underſtandings.

Such is the conſequence of too high an eſteem of our own powers and knowledge; it makes us in youth negligent, and in age uſeleſs; it teaches us too ſoon to be ſatisfied with our attainments; or it makes our attainments unpleaſing, unpopular, and ineffectual; it neither ſuffers us to learn, nor to teach, but with-holds us from thoſe by whom we might be inſtructed, and drives thoſe from us whom we might inſtruct. It is therefore neceſſary to obviate theſe evils, by enquiring,

Secondly, By what means this pernicious conceit of wiſdom may be avoided or ſuppreſſed.

It might be imagined, if daily experience did not ſhew us how vainly judgments are formed of real life, from ſpeculative

lative principles, that it might be eaſy for any man to extirpate a high conceit of human learning from his own heart, or that of another; ſince one great purpoſe of knowledge is to ſhew us our own defects, follies, and miſeries; yet, whatever be the reaſon, we find none more ſubject to this fault, than thoſe whoſe courſe of life ought more particularly to exempt them from it.

For the ſuppreſſion of this vain conceit, ſo injurious to the profeſſors of learning, many conſiderations might be added to thoſe, which have already been drawn from its effects. The reaſons, indeed, why every man ſhould be humble, are inſeparably connected with human nature; for what can any man ſee, either within or without himſelf, that does not afford him ſome reaſon to remark his own ignorance, imbecillity, and meanneſs? But on theſe reflections it is leſs proper to inſiſt, becauſe they have been explained already by almoſt every writer upon moral and religious duties, and becauſe, in reality, the pride which requires our chief caution is not ſo much abſolute, as comparative. No man ſo much values himſelf upon the general prerogatives of human nature, as upon his

own

own peculiar ſuperiority to other men; nor will he therefore be humbled, by being told of the ignorance, the weakneſs, and wickedneſs of humanity; for he is ſatisfied with being accounted one of the moſt knowing, among the ignorant; the moſt able, among the weak; and the moſt virtuous, among the wicked.

The pride of the learned therefore can only be repreſſed by ſhewing, what indeed might eaſily be ſhewn, that it is not juſtifiable, even upon compariſon with the reſt of men; for, without urging any thing in derogation from the dignity and importance of learning in general, which muſt always, either immediately, or by the intervention of others, govern the world, it will be found, that they who are moſt diſpoſed to be ſwelled to haughtineſs by their own attainments, are generally ſo far from having any juſt claim to the ſuperiority which they exert, that they are betrayed to vanity by ignorance; and are pleaſed with themſelves, as a Hind with his cottage, not becauſe, upon enquiry, they are convinced of the reaſonableneſs of the preference; but becauſe they overvalue the little they poſſeſs, for want of knowing its

littleneſs;

littleneſs; and are contented with their own ſtate, as a blind man feels no loſs from the abſence of beauty. Nor needs there any other proof of the origin of literary pride, than that it is chiefly to be found amongſt thoſe, who have ſecluded themſelves from the world, in purſuit of petty enquiries, and trivial ſtudies.

To ſuch men it ſhould be recommended, that, before they ſuffer themſelves to fix the rule of their own accompliſhments, and look down on others with contempt, they ſhould enjoin themſelves to ſpend ſome time in enquiring into their own pretenſions; and conſider who they are whom they deſpiſe, and for what reaſon they ſuffer themſelves to indulge the arrogance of contempt. Such an examination will ſoon drive back the pedant to his college, with juſter conceptions, and with humbler ſentiments; for he will find that thoſe, whom he imagined ſo much below his own exaltation, often flouriſh in the eſteem of the world, while he himſelf is unknown; and teaching thoſe arts, by which ſociety is ſupported, and on which the happineſs of the world depends; while he is pleaſing himſeif with idle amuſements, and wasting his life upon questions, of which very few desire the solution.

But if this method of obtaining humility be ineffectual, he may however establish it, upon more strong and lasting principles, by applying himself to the duties of Religion, and the word of God.

That sacred and inscrutable word, which will shew him the inefficacy of all other knowledge, and those duties which will imprint upon his mind, that he best understands the sacred writings who most carefully obeys them. Thus will humility fix a firm and lasting basis, by annihilation of all empty distinctions and petty competitions, by shewing, that *one thing only is necessary*, and that *God is all in all.*

SERMON

SERMON IX.

1 CORINTHIANS, Chap. 11. Verſe 28.

But let a man examine himſelf, and ſo let him eat of that bread, and drink of that cup.

NOTHING is more frequently injurious to Religion, or more dangerous to Mankind, than the practice of adding to the divine inſtitutions, and of teaching for doctrines the commandments of men. The doctrines of the bleſſed ſacrament, which, as they are expreſſed in the holy ſcriptures, do not ſeem to be very dark or difficult, yet have been ſo perverted and miſrepreſented, as to occaſion many diſputes among men of learning, and many diviſions in the Chriſtian world. In our own church, many religious minds have been filled with groundleſs

groundleſs apprehenſions, and diſtracted with unneceſſary inquietudes, by miſtaken notions of the Lord's Supper. Many have forborne to partake of it, becauſe they have not, in their own opinion, arrived at that degree of holineſs, required to it which they erroneouſly conceive to be ſuch, as indeed no mere man ever can attain ; a holineſs, which conſiſts in little leſs, than a compleat exemption from ſin, and an uniform, and uninterrupted obſervance of every precept of Religion. They find themſelves unable to perform this duty without imperfections, and therefore they entirely neglect it ; not conſidering, that the ſame reaſon is of equal force for the neglect of every duty ; ſince none can be performed by us, in this frail ſtate, without lapſes, negligences, and failings ; and that God will except unfeigned repentance, ſincere intentions, and earneſt endeavours, though entangled with many frailties. They do not conſider, that the participation of the ſacrament is a duty enjoined all Chriſtians, though all do not riſe to equal degrees of virtue ; and, by conſequence, that many muſt be admitted to the holy table, who have not reached the utmoſt heights of religious

gious excellence. Heaven itſelf will be acceſſible to many, who died in their ſtruggles with ſin, in their endeavours after virtue, and the beginning of a new life. And ſurely, they are not to be excluded from commemorating the ſufferings of our Saviour, in a Chriſtian congregation, who would not be ſhut from Heaven, from the aſſemblies of Saints, and the choirs of Angels.

There are ſome who neglect this duty, as they omit others, not from ſcruples of melancholy piety, or miſtaken ſeverity, but from ſupineneſs and careleſſneſs, or an opinion, that this precept is leſs neceſſary to be obſerved, than ſome others delivered by the ſame authority.

Many other notions, not well-grounded, or capable of proof, are entertained of this inſtitution; which I ſhall endeavour, without giving a particular account of them, to obviate and ſuppreſs, by ſhewing,

Firſt, What is the nature and end of this inſtitution according to the Scriptures.

Secondly, What are the obligations which enforce the duty of Communion. And,

Thirdly, what things are required of them that come to the Lord's Supper.

First, I propose to lay before you the nature and end of this institution according to the scriptures.

The account of the first institution of this sacrament is thus delivered by the Evangelist (Luke, chap. xxii. v. 19.) And he took bread and gave thanks, and brake it, and gave it unto them, saying, *This is my Body which is given for you ; This do in remembrance of Me.* Likewise also the Cup after supper, saying, *This Cup is the New Testament in my blood which is shed for you.* This narration is repeated in the Epistle to the Corinthians, with this comment or explanation : *As often as ye eat this Bread, or drink this Cup, ye do shew the Lord's death till He come.* From these passages compared then it appears, that this sacrament is a representation of the death of our Saviour, appointed by himself, to be celebrated by all his followers, in all ages ; to the end that, by commemorating his sufferings in a solemn and public manner, they might declare their confidence in his merits, their belief of his mission, and their adherence to his Religion.

It has likewise a tendency to increase this confidence, confirm this belief, and

establish

eſtabliſh this adherence, not only by the new ſtrength which every idea acquires by a new impreſſion, and which every perſuaſion attains by new recollection, approbation, and meditation, but likewiſe by the ſupernatural and extraordinary influences of Grace, and thoſe bleſſings which God has annexed to the due uſe of means appointed by himſelf.

By commemorating the death of Chriſt, as the Redeemer of the world, we confeſs our belief in him ; for why elſe ſhould we perform ſo ſolemn a rite in commemoration of him ? To confeſs our belief in him, is to declare ourſelves his followers. We enter into an obligation to perform thoſe conditions upon which he has admitted us to follow him, and to practice all the duties of that Religion which he has taught us.

This is implied in the word ſacrament, which, being originally uſed to ſignify an oath of fidelity taken by the Soldiers to their leaders, is now made uſe of by the Church, to import a ſolemn vow, of unſhaken adherence to the faith of Chriſt.

Thus the ſacrament is a kind of repetition of baptiſm, the means whereby we are readmitted into the communion of the church of Chriſt, when we have, by ſin, been ſeparated from it; for every ſin, and much more any habit or courſe of ſin long continued, is, according to the different degrees of guilt, an apoſtacy or defection from our Saviour; as it is a breach of thoſe conditions upon which we became his followers; and he that breaks the condition of a covenant, diſſolves it on his ſide. Having therefore broken the covenant between us and our Redeemer, we loſe the benefits of his death; nor can we have any hopes of obtaining them, while we remain in this ſtate of ſeparation from him.

But vain had been the ſufferings of our Saviour, had there not been left means of reconciliation to him; ſince every man falls away from him occaſionally by ſins of negligence at leaſt, and perhaps by known, deliberate, premeditated offences. So that ſome method of renewing the covenant between God and man was neceſſary; and for this purpoſe this ſacrament was inſtituted; which is therefore a renewal of our broken vows, a re-entrance into the ſociety of the church, and the act by which we are reſtored to the benefits of our Saviour's death,

death, upon performance of the terms preſcribed by him.

So that this ſacrament is a ſolemn rati-
fication of a covenant renewed ; by which, after having alienated ourſelves from Chriſt by ſin, we are reſtored, upon our repentance and reformation, to pardon and favour, and the certain hopes of everlaſting life.

When we thus enter upon a new life by a ſolemn, deliberate, and ſerious dedica-
tion of ourſelves to a more exact and vigi-
lant ſervice of God, and oblige ourſelves to the duties of piety by this ſacrament, we may hope to obtain, by fervent and humble prayer, ſuch aſſiſtances from God as may enable us to perform thoſe engagements, which we have entered into by his command, and in the manner appointed by him ; always remembering, that we muſt uſe our own endeavours, and exert our ut-
moſt natural powers, for God only co-ope-
rates with the diligent and the watchful. We muſt avoid ſin, by avoiding thoſe occaſions which betray us to it, and as we pray that we may not be led, we muſt be cautious of leading ourſelves into temptation.

All

All ſin that is committed by Chriſtians is committed either through an abſolute forgetfulneſs of God, for the time in which the inordinate paſſion, of whatever kind it be, predominates and prevails; or because, if the ideas of God and Religion were preſent to our minds, they were not ſtrong enough to overcome and ſuppreſs the deſires excited by ſome pleaſing, or the apprehenſions raiſed by ſome terrible, object. So that either the love or fear of temporal good or evil were more powerful than the love or fear of God.

All ideas influence our conduct with more or leſs force, as they are more or leſs ſtrongly impreſſed upon the mind; and they are impreſſed more ſtrongly, as they are more frequently recollected or renewed. For every idea, whether of love, fear, grief, or any other paſſion, loſes its force by time; and, unleſs revived by accident, or voluntary meditation, will at laſt vaniſh. But by dwelling upon, and indulging any idea, we may increaſe its efficacy and force, make it by degrees predominant in the ſoul, and raiſe it to an aſcendant over our paſſions, ſo that it ſhall eaſily over-rule

thoſe

those affections or appetites which formerly tyrannized within us.

Thus, by a neglect of God's worship and sacraments, a man may lose almost all distinction whatsoever of good and evil, and, having no awe of the divine power to oppose his inclinations to wickedness, may go forward from crime to crime without remorse. And he that struggles against vice, and is often overcome by powerful temptations, if, instead of giving way to idleness and despair, he continues his resistance; and, by a diligent attendance upon the service and sacraments of church, together with a regular practice of private devotion, endeavours to strengthen his faith, and imprint upon himself an habitual attention to the laws of God, and a constant sense of his presence; he will soon find himself able to avoid the snares of sin, or, if he fall into them by inadvertency, to break them. He will find the fear of God grow superior to the desires of wealth, or the love of pleasure; and, by persisting to frequent the church and sacraments, and thereby to preserve those notions of piety from being effaced or weakened, he will be able to persevere in

a steady

a ſteady practice of virtue, and enjoy the unſpeakable pleaſures of a quiet conſcience.

Thus it appears, that the bleſſed ſacrament is a commemoration of the death of our Lord ; conſequently, a declaration of our faith ; and both naturally, and by the co-operation of God, the means of increaſing that faith. And it appears alſo that it is a renewal of our baptiſmal vow, after we have broken it by ſin ; and a renovation of that covenant by which we are adopted the followers of Jeſus, and made partakers of his merits, and the benefits of his death.

This account has almoſt anticipated what I profeſſed to treat of,

Secondly, the obligations which enforce the Duty of Communion.

For the obligations to any duty muſt bear proportion to the importance of it ; and the importance of a duty muſt be rated by the effect which it produces or promotes ; and, therefore, as the benefits which we receive from this ſacrament have been already ſhewn, the neceſſity of it is ſufficiently apparent.

But we may farther enforce this practice

upon

upon ourſelves and others, by conſidering, firſt, that it is a poſitive injunction of our bleſſed Saviour, which, therefore, all thoſe who believe in him are bound to obey. That to diſpute the uſefulneſs, or call in queſtion the neceſſity of it, is to reform his religion, and to ſet up our own wiſdom in oppoſition to his commands; and that to refuſe the means of grace, is to place our confidence in our own ſtrength, and to neglect the aſſiſtance of that Comforter, who came down from Heaven according to the moſt true promiſe of our bleſſed Saviour, to lead the Apoſtles out of darkneſs and error, and to guide them and us into the clear light and certain knowledge of God, and of his Son Jeſus Chriſt.

If we conſider this ſacrament as a renewal of the vow of baptiſm, and the means of reconciling us to God, and reſtoring us to a participation of the merits of our Saviour, which we had forfeited by ſin, we ſhall need no perſuaſions to a frequent communion. For certainly nothing can be more dreadful than to live under the diſpleaſure of God, in conſtant danger of appearing before him, while he is yet unappeaſed, and of loſing the benefits of

our

our redemption. Whoever he be, whom ſin has deluded and led away, let him not delay to return to his duty, leſt ſome ſudden diſeaſe ſeize upon him, and the hand of death cut him off for ever from any poſſibility of reformation, while he is indolent and voluptuous, irreligious and profane. It will be too late to bewail his ſupineneſs, and lament his folly, when the dreadful and irrevocable ſentence is paſt, and the gates of hell are cloſed upon him. "Seek ye the Lord while he may be found; "call ye on him while he is near! Let the "wicked forſake his way, and the unrighte-"ous man his thoughts; and let him re-"turn unto the Lord, and he will have "mercy on him, and to our God, for he "will abundantly pardon."

But leſt, inſtead of obtaining pardon, we aggravate our ſins, by coming unprepared to the holy table, let us conſider,

Thirdly, What is required of them that come to the Lord's Supper.

With reſpect to the preparatory duties requiſite to a worthy reception of the ſacrament, Saint Paul has left this precept; "Let a man examine himſelf, and ſo let "him eat of that bread." Which will be

eaſily

eaſily explained, by recurring to what has been already ſaid of the nature of the ſacrament.

By partaking of the communion, we declare, in the moſt ſolemn manner, in the preſence of God and man, that we hold the faith of Jeſus; that we are his followers, who expect eternal ſalvation from his merits; and, therefore, that we engage ourſelves to that obedience to his commands, and that ſtrictneſs and regularity of life, which he requires from thoſe who place their confidence in his mediation. We profeſs, likewiſe, that we ſincerely and humbly repent of thoſe offences by which we have ſeparated ourſelves from him; and that, in conſequence of this profeſſion, we unite ourſelves again to the communion of the church.

Nothing can be more reaſonable before this ſolemn profeſſion, than that a man examine himſelf, whether it be true; whether he really and unfeignedly reſolves to accept the conditions of ſalvation offered to him, and to perform his part of the covenant which he comes to ratify; or, whether he is not about to mock God; to profeſs a faith which he does hold, and a purity a purity which he does not intend to aim at.

The terms, upon which we are to hope for any benefits from the merits of Chriſt, are faith, repentance, and ſubſequent obedience. Theſe are therefore the three chief and general heads of examination. We cannot receive the ſacrament, unleſs we believe in Chriſt, because by receiving it we declare our belief in him, and a lying tongue is an abomination to the Lord. We cannot receive it without repentance, becauſe repentance is the means by which, after ſin, we are reconciled to God; and we cannot, without dreadful wickedneſs, by partaking of the outward tokens of reconciliation, declare that we believe God at peace with our ſouls, when we know, that by the omiſſion of repentance we are yet in a ſtate of voluntary alienation from him. We cannot receive it, without a ſincere intention of obedience; becauſe, by declaring ourſelves his followers, we enter into obligations to obey his commandments. We are therefore not tranſiently and careleſsly, but frequently and ſeriouſly to aſk ourſelves, whether we firmly believe the promiſes of our Saviour; whether we

repent

repent of our ſins, and reſolve, for the future, to avoid all thoſe things which God has forbidden, and practiſe all thoſe which he has commanded. And when any man is convinced, that he has formed real reſolutions of a new life, let him pray for ſtrength and conſtancy to perſevere in them, and then let him come joyfully to the holy table, in ſure confidence of pardon, reconciliation, and life everlaſting.

Which that we may all obtain, God of his infinite mercy grant, for the merits of Jeſus Chriſt, our Saviour; to whom with the Father and the Holy Spirit, three Perſons and one God, be aſcribed all honour, adoration, and praiſe, now and for ever! Amen.

SERMON X.

GALATIANS, Chap. vi. Verſe 7.

Be not deceived, God is not mocked; for whatſoever a man ſoweth, that ſhall he reap.

ONE of the mighty bleſſings, beſtowed upon us by the Chriſtian Revolution, is, that we have now a certain knowledge of a future ſtate, and of the rewards and puniſhments that await us after death, and will be adjuſted according to our conduct in this world. We on whom the light of the Goſpel ſhines, walk no longer in darkneſs, doubtful of the benefit of *good*, or the danger of *bad* actions; we know, that we live and act under the eye of our Father and our Judge, by whom nothing is overlooked or forgotten, and who, though to

try

try our obedience he ſuffers, in the preſent ſtate of things, the ſame events to happen to the good and to the evil, will at laſt certainly diſtinguiſh them, by allotting them different conditions beyond the grave; when it will appear, in the ſight of men and of angels, how amiable is godlineſs, and how odious is ſin, by the final ſentence, which ſhall bring upon man the conſequences of his own actions, ſo as that *whatſoever a man ſhall ſow, that ſhall he reap.*

The ancient Heathens, with whoſe notions we are acquainted, how far ſoever they might have carried their ſpeculations of moral or civil wiſdom, had no conception of a future ſtate, except idle fictions, which thoſe who conſidered them treated as ridiculous; or dark conjectures, formed by men of deep thoughts and great enquiry, but neither, in themſelves, capable of compelling conviction, nor brought at all to the knowledge of the groſs of mankind, of thoſe who lived in pleaſure and idleneſs, or in ſolitude and labour; they were confined to the cloſet of the ſtudent, or the ſchool of the lecturer, and were very little diffuſed among the buſy or the vulgar.

There

There is no reaſon to wonder, that many enormities ſhould prevail, where there was nothing to oppoſe them. When we conſider the various and perpetual temptations of appetite within, and intereſt without; when we ſee, that on every ſide there is ſomething that ſolicits the deſires, and which cannot be innocently obtained; what can we then expect, but that, notwithſtanding all the ſecurities of law, and all the vigilance of magiſtrates, thoſe that know of no other world will eagerly make the moſt of this, and pleaſe themſelves whenever they can, with very little regard to the right of others?

As the ſtate of the Heathens was a ſtate of darkneſs, it muſt have been a ſtate, likewiſe, of diſorder; a ſtate of perpetual conteſt for the goods of this life, and by conſequence of perpetual danger to thoſe who *abounded*, and of temptation to thoſe that were in *want*.

The Jews enjoyed a very ample communication of the Divine will, and had a religion which an inſpired Legiſlator had preſcribed. But even to this nation, the only nation free from idolatry, and acquainted with the perfections of the *true* God, was the doctrine of a future ſtate ſo obſcurely revealed, that it was not *neceſſarily* conſequential to the reception, or obſervation, of their *practical* religion. The Sadducees, who *acknowledged* the authority of the Moſaical law, yet *denied* the ſeparate exiſtence of the ſoul, had no expectation of a future ſtate. They held that there was no reſurrection, neither Angel nor Spirit.

This was not in thoſe times the *general* ſtate of the Jewiſh nation; the Phariſees held the reſurrection, and with them probably far the greater part of the people; but that any man could be a Jew, and yet deny a future ſtate, is a ſufficient proof that it had not yet been *clearly revealed*, and that it was reſerved for the Preachers of Chriſtianity to bring life and immortality to light. In ſuch a degree of light they are now placed, that they can be denied or doubted no longer, but as the *Goſpel*, that ſhews them, is doubted or denied. It is now certain that we are *here*, not in our *total*, nor in our *ultimate exiſtence*, but in a ſtate of exerciſe and probation, commanded to qualify ourſelves, by pure hearts and virtuous actions, for the enjoyment of future felicity in the preſence of God; and prohibited

prohibited to break the laws which his wiſdom has given us, under the penal ſanction of baniſhment from *heaven* into *regions of miſery.*

Yet notwithſtanding the expreſs declaration of our Saviour, and the conſtant reference of our actions and duties to a future ſtate, throughout the whole volume of the New Teſtament ; there are yet, as in the Apoſtles time, men who are deceived, who act as if they thought God would be mocked or deluded, and who appear to forget, that *whatſoever a man ſows, that ſhall he reap.*

From this important caution, given by the Apoſtle immediately to thoſe whom he was then directing, and conſequently to all profeſſors of the religion of Chriſt, occaſion may be taken to conſider,

Firſt, How ſinners *are deceived.*

Secondly, How certain it is, that *God is not mocked.*

Thirdly, In what ſenſe it is to be underſtood, that whatſoever a man ſows, that ſhall he reap.

In examining, firſt, how ſinners are deceived, it will immediately occur to us that no man is deceived to his damnation, but by the devil himſelf. The ſubtilties of the devil are undoubtedly many ; he has probably the power of preſenting opportunities of ſin, and at the ſame time of inflaming the paſſions, of ſuggeſting evil deſires, and interrupting holy meditations; but his power is ſo limited by the Governor of the Univerſe, that he cannot hurt us without our own conſent; his power is but like that of a wicked companion, who may ſolicit us to crimes or follies, but with whom we feel no neceſſity of complying ; he therefore that yields to temptation, has the greater part in his own deſtruction ; he has been warned of his danger, he has been taught his duty ; and, if theſe warnings and inſtructions have had no effect, he may be ſaid voluntarily to deſert the right way, and not ſo much to be deceived by another, as to deceive himſelf.

Of ſelf-deceit, in the great buſineſs of our lives, there are various modes. The far greater part of mankind deceive themſelves by willing negligence, by refuſing to think on their real ſtate, leſt ſuch thoughts ſhould trouble their quiet, or interrupt their purſuits. To live religiouſly, is to walk, not by ſight, but by faith ; to act in confidence of things unſeen, in hope of future recompenſe, and in fear of future puniſhment. To abſtract the thoughts from things ſpiritual is not difficult; things future do not obtrude themſelves upon the ſenſes, and therefore eaſily give way to external objects. He that is willing to forget Religion, may quickly loſe it; and that moſt men are willing to forget it, experience informs us. If we look into the gay, or the buſy world, we ſee every eye directed towards pleaſure or advantage, and every hour filled with expectation or occupied by employment, and day paſſed after day in the enjoyment of ſucceſs, or the vexation of diſappointment.

Nor is it true only of men, who are engaged in enterprizes of hazard, which reſtrain the faculties to the utmo ſt,and keep attention always upon the ſtretch. Religion is not only neglected by the projector and adventurer, by men who ſuſpend their happineſs on the ſlender thread of artifice, or ſtand tottering upon the point of chance. For if we viſit the moſt cool and regular parts of the community, if we turn our eye to the farm, or to the ſhop, where one year glides uniformly after another, and nothing

nothing new or important is either expected or dreaded; yet ftill the fame indifference about eternity will be found. There is no intereft fo fmall, nor engagement fo flight, but that, if it be followed and expanded, it may be fufficient to keep religion out of the thoughts. Many men may be obferved, not agitated by very violent paffions, nor overborne by any powerful habits, nor depraved by any great degrees of wickednefs; men who are honeft dealers, faithful friends, and inoffenfive neighbours, who yet have no vital principle of Religion; who live wholly without felf-examination; and indulge any defire that happens to arife, with very little refiftance, or compunction; who hardly know what it is to combat a temptation, or to repent of a fault; but go on, neither felf-approved, nor felf-condemned; not endeavouring after any excellence, nor reforming any vicious practice, or irregular defire. They have no care of futurity, neither is God in all their thoughts; they direct none of their actions to his glory, they do nothing with the hope of pleafing, they avoid nothing for the fear of offending him. Thofe men want not much of being religious,

religious, they have nothing more than casual views to reform, and, from being peaceable and temperate Heathens, might, if they would once awaken to their eternal interest, become pious and exemplary Christians. But let them not be deceived, they cannot suppose that God will accept him, who never wished to be accepted by him, or made his will the rule of action.

Others there are, who, without attending to the written revelation of God's will, form to themselves a scheme of conduct, in which vice is mingled with virtue, and who cover from themselves, and hope to cover from God, the indulgence of some criminal desire, or the continuance of some vicious habit, by a few splendid instances of public spirit, or some few effusions of occasional bounty. But to these men it may, with emphatical propriety, be urged, that God is not mocked; he will not be worshipped nor obeyed, but according to his own laws.

The mode of self-deception which prevails most in the world, and by which the greatest number of souls is at least betrayed to destruction, is the art, which we are all too apt to practise, of putting far from us the evil day, of ſetting the hour of death, and the day of account, at a great diſtance.

That death is certain, every one knows: nor is it leſs known, that life is deſtroyed at all ages by a thouſand cauſes; that the ſtrong and the vigorous are liable to diſeaſes, and that caution and temperance afford no ſecurity againſt the final ſtroke. Yet as the thought of diſſolution is dreadful, we do not willingly admit it; the deſire of life is connected with animation; every living being ſhrinks from his deſtruction; to wiſh, and to hope, are never far aſunder; as we wiſh for long life, we hope that our wiſhes will be granted, and what we hope we either believe, or do not examine. So tenaciouſly does our credulity lay hold of life, that it is rare to find any man ſo old, as not to expect an addition to his years, or ſo far waſted and enfeebled with diſeaſe, as not to flatter himſelf with hopes of recovery.

To thoſe, who procraſtinate amendment, in hopes of better opportunities in future time, it is too often vainly urged by the preacher, and vainly ſuggeſted by a thouſand examples, that the hour of death is

uncertain,

uncertain. This, which ought to be the cauſe of their terror, is the ground of their hope; that as death is uncertain, it may be diſtant. This uncertainty is, in effect, the great ſupport of the whole ſyſtem of life. The man who died yeſterday had purchaſed an eſtate, to which he intended ſome time to retire; or built a houſe, which he was hereafter to inhabit; and planted gardens and groves, that, in a certain number of years, were to ſupply delicacies to his feaſts, and ſhades to his meditations. He is ſnatched away, and has left his deſigns and his labours to others.

As men pleaſe themſelves with felicities to be enjoyed in the days of leiſure and retreat; ſo among theſe felicities, it is not uncommon to deſign a reformation of life, and a courſe of piety. Among the more enlightened and judicious part of mankind, there are many who live in a continual diſapprobation of their own conduct, who know that they do every day what they ought to leave undone, and every day leave undone what they ought to do; and who therefore conſider themſelves as living under the divine diſpleaſure, in a ſtate in which it would be very dangerous to die.

Such

Such men anſwer the reproaches of conſcience with promiſes of amendment, promiſes made with ſincerity and intention of performance, but which they conſider as debts to be diſcharged at ſome remote time. They neither ſin with ſtupid negligence, nor with impious defiance, of the divine laws; they fear the puniſhments denounced againſt ſin, but pacify their anxiety with poſſibilities of repentance, and with a plan of life to be led according to the ſtrict precepts of Religion, and to be cloſed at laſt by a death ſoftened by holy conſolations. Projects of future piety are perhaps not leſs common than of future pleaſure, and are, as there is reaſon to fear, not leſs commonly interrupted; with this dreadful difference, that he who miſſes his intended pleaſure, eſcapes a diſappointment, but he who is cut off before the ſeaſon of repentance, is expoſed to the vengeance of an angry God.

Whoever has been deluded by this infatuation, and has hitherto neglected thoſe duties which he intends ſome time to perform, is admoniſhed, by all the principles of prudence, and all the courſe of nature, to conſider how much he ventures, and with how little probability in his favour. The continuance of life, though, like all other things, adjuſted by Providence, may be properly conſidered by us caſual; and wiſdom always directs us, not to leave that to chance which may be made certain, and not to venture any thing upon chance which it will much hurt us to loſe.

He who, accuſed by his conſcience of habitual diſobedience, defers his reformation, apparently leaves his ſoul in the power of chance. We are in full poſſeſſion of the *preſent* moment; let the *preſent* moment be improved; let that, which muſt neceſſarily be done ſome time, be no longer neglected. Let us remember, that if our lot ſhould fall otherwiſe than we ſuppoſe; if we are of the number of them, to whom length of life is not granted; we loſe, what can never be recovered, and what will never be recompenſed, the mercy of God, and the joys of futurity.

That long life is not commonly granted, is ſufficienty apparent; for life is called long, not as being, at its greateſt length, of much duration, but as being longer than common. Since therefore the common condition of man is not to live long, we

have

have no reafon to conclude, that what happens to few will happen to us.

But to abate our confidence in our own refolutions, it is to be remembered, that though we fhould arrive at the great year deftined for the change of life, it is by no means certain, that we fhall effect what we have purpofed. Age is fhackled with infirmity and difeafes. Immediate pain and prefent vexation will then do what amufement and gaity did before, will enchain the attention, and occupy the thoughts, and leave little vacancy for the paft or future. Whoever fuffers great pain has no other care than to obtain eafe; and, if eafe is for a time obtained, he values it too much, to leffen it by painful reflections.

Neither is an efficacious repentance fo eafy a work, as that we may be fure of performing it at the time appointed by ourfelves. The longer habits have been indulged, the more imperious they become; it is not by bidding them to be gone, that we can at once difmifs them; they may be fuppreffed and lie dormant for a time, and refume their force at an unexpected moment, by fome fudden temptation; they

can

can be ſubdued only by continued caution and repeated conflicts.

The longer ſin has been indulged, the more irkſome will be the retroſpect of life. So much uneaſineſs will be ſuffered, at the review of years ſpent in vicious enjoyment, that there is reaſon to fear, leſt that delay, which began in the love of pleaſure, will be continued for fear of pain.

Neither is it certain, that the grace, without which no man can correct his own corruption, when it has been offered and refuſed, will be offered again; or that he who ſtopped his ears againſt the firſt call, will be vouchſafed a ſecond. *He* cannot expect to be received among the ſervants of God, who will obey him only at his own time; for ſuch preſumption is, in ſome degree, a mockery of God, and we are to conſider, ſecondly, how certain it is, that God is not mocked.

God is not mocked in any ſenſe. He will not be mocked with counterfeit piety, he will not be mocked with idle reſolutions; but the ſenſe in which the text declares, that God is not mocked, ſeems to be, that God will not ſuffer his decrees to

be

be invalidated ; he will not leave his promiſes unfulfilled ; nor his threats unexecuted. And this will eaſily appear, if we conſider, that promiſes and threats can only become ineffectual by change of mind, or want of power. God cannot change his will, *he is not a man that he ſhould repent* ; what he has ſpoken will ſurely come to paſs. Neither can he want power to execute his purpoſes ; he who ſpoke, and the world was made, can ſpeak again, and it will periſh. God's *arm is not ſhortened, that he cannot ſave* ; neither is it ſhortened, that he cannot puniſh ; and that he will do to every man according to his works will be ſhown, when we have conſidered,

Thirdly, in what ſenſe it is to be underſtood, that whatſoever a man ſows, that ſhall he reap.

To ſow and to reap are figurative terms. To ſow ſignifies to act ; and to reap, is to receive the product of our actions. As no man can ſow one ſort of grain, and reap another, in the ordinary proceſs of nature ; as no man gathers grapes of thorns or figs of thiſtles, or, when he ſcatters tares in the furrows, gathers wheat into his garners ; ſo, in the final diſpenſations of Providence,

the

the ſame correſpondence ſhall be found in the moral ſyſtem ; every action ſhall at laſt be followed by its due conſequences ; we ſhall be treated according to our obedience or tranſgreſſions ; the good ſhall not miſs their reward, nor the wicked eſcape their puniſhment ; but, when men ſhall give account of their own works, they that have done good ſhall paſs into everlaſting life, and they that have done evil into everlaſting fire.

Let us therefore at this, and at all times, moſt heartily and fervently beſeech Almighty God to give us faithful and ſincere repentance, to pardon and forgive us all our ſins, to endue us with the grace of his Holy Spirit, and to amend our lives according to his holy will and commandments.

SERMON XI.

1 PETER, Chap. iii. Ver. 8.

Finally be ye all of one mind, having compaſſion one of another, love as brethren, be faithful, be courteous.

THE Apoſtle, directing this Epiſtle to the new converts, ſcattered over the provinces of Aſia, having laid before them the great advantage of the Religion which they had embraced, no leſs than the ſalvation of their ſouls, and the high price for which they were redeemed, the precious Blood of Chriſt, proceeds to explain to them what is required by their *new* profeſſion. He reminds them, that they live among the Heathen, of whom it muſt neceſſarily be ſuppoſed, that every one watched their conduct with suspicious vigilance; and that it is *their* duty to recommend *right Belief* by *virtuous Practice*; that their *example*, as well as their *arguments*, may propagate the truth.

In this course of instruction, the first mentions the civil relation of governors and subjects; and enjoins them to honour the supreme Magistrate, and to respect all subordinate authority, which is established for the preservation of order, and the administration of justice. He then descends to domestic connections, and recommends to servants obedience and patience, and to husbands and wives their relative and respective duties; to husbands tenderness, and to wives obedience, modesty and gentleness; that the husband, who is not yet converted by the power of exortation, may be drawn to the religion of his wife, by perceiving its good effects upon her conversation and behaviour.

He then extends his precepts to greater generality, and lays down a short system of domestic virtue to be universally adopted, directing the new Christians,

First, to be all of one mind.

By

By the union of minds which the Apoſtle recommends, it muſt be ſuppoſed that he means not ſpeculative, but practical union; not ſimilitude of opinions, but ſimilitude of virtues. In religious opinions, if there was then any diſagreement, they had then living authority, to which they might have recourſe: and their buſineſs was probably, at that time, more to defend their common faith againſt the Heathen, than to debate any ſubtilties of opinion among themſelves. But there are innumerable queſtions, in which vanity or intereſt engages mankind, which have little connection with their eternal intereſt; and yet often inflame the paſſions and produce diſlike and malevolence. Sects in philoſophy, and factions in the ſtate, eaſily excite mutual contempt, or mutual hatred. He whoſe opinions are cenſured, feels the reputation of his underſtanding injured; he, whoſe party is oppoſed, finds his influence reſiſted and perhaps his power, or his profit, in danger of diminution. It could not be the intention of St. Peter, that all men ſhould think alike, either of the operations of nature, or the tranſactions of the ſtate, but that thoſe who thought differently, ſhould live in peace; that contradiction ſhould not exaſperate the diſputants, or that the heat ſhould end with the controverſy, and that the oppoſition of party (for ſuch there muſt ſometimes be) ſhould not canker the private thoughts, or raiſe perſonal hatred or inſidious enmity. He required that they ſhould be all of one *moral* mind, that they ſhould all wiſh and promote the happineſs of each other, that the danger of a Chriſtian ſhould be a common cauſe, and that no one ſhould wiſh for advantage by the miſcarriage of another.

To ſuppoſe that there ſhould, in any community, be no difference of opinion, is to ſuppoſe all, of whom that community conſiſts, to be wiſe alike, which cannot happen; or that the underſtanding of one part is ſubmitted to that of another, which however would not produce uniformity of opinion, but only of profeſſion; and is, in important queſtions, contrary to that ſincerity and integrity, which truth requires; and an infraction of that liberty, which reaſon allows. But that men, of different opinions, ſhould live at peace, is the true effect of that humility, which makes each eſteem others better than himſelf, and of that moderation, which reaſon approves, and charity commands. Be ye therefore all of one mind; let charity be the predominant and univerſal principle that pervades your lives, and regulates your actions.

Secondly, they are directed by the Apoſtle, to live as men, which have compaſſion one of another.

The word which is rendered *having compaſſion*, ſeems to include a greater latitude of ſignification than the word compaſſion commonly obtains. Compaſſion is not uſed, but in the ſenſe of tender regard to the unhappineſs of another. But the term uſed by St. Peter may mean mutually feeling for each other, receiving the ſame impreſſions from the ſame things, and this ſenſe ſeems to be given it by one of the Tranſlators (Caſtalio.) The precept will then be connected and conſequential, *Be all of one mind, each feeling, by ſympathy, the affections of another.*

Sympathy, the quality recommended in the text, as it has been now explained, is the great ſource of ſocial happineſs. To gain affection, and to preſerve concord, it is neceſſary not only to mourn with thoſe

that

that mourn, but to rejoice with them that rejoice.

To feel ſincere and honeſt joy at the ſucceſs of another, though it is neceſſary to true friendſhip, is perhaps neither very common, nor very eaſy. There is in every mind, implanted by nature, a deſire of ſuperiority, which counteracts the pleaſure, which the ſight of ſucceſs and happineſs ought always to impart. Between men of equal condition, and therefore willingly conſulting with each other, any flow of fortune, which produces inequality, makes him who is left behind, look with leſs content on his own condition, and with leſs kindneſs on him who has reduced him to inferiority. The advancement of a ſuperior gives pain by increaſing that diſtance, by difference of ſtation, which was thought already greater than could be claimed by any difference; and the riſe of an inferior excites jealouſy, leſt he that went before ſhould be overtaken by his follower. As cruelty looks upon miſery without partaking pain, ſo envy beholds increaſe of happineſs without partaking joy.

Envy and cruelty, the moſt hateful paſſions of the human breaſt, are both counter-

acted

acted by this precept, which commanded the Christians of Asia, and now commands us, who succeed them in the profession of the same faith, and the consciousness of the same frailties, to feel one for another. He whose mind is so harmonized to the interest of his neighbour, that good and evils is common to them both, will neither obstruct his rise, nor insult his fall; but will be willing to co-operate with him through all the vicissitudes of life, and dispensations of Providence, to honour him that is exalted, to help him that is depressed. He will controul all those emotions which comparison produces; he will not consider himself as made poorer by another's wealth, or richer by another's poverty; he will look, without malignity, upon superiority, either external or intellectual; he will be willing to learn of those that excel in wisdom, and receive instruction with thankfulness; he will be willing to impart his knowledge, without fearing lest he should impair his own importance, by the improvement of his hearer.

How much this generous sympathy would conduce to the comfort and stability of life, a little consideration will convince

us.

us. Whence are all the arts of ſlander and depreciation, but from our unwillingneſs to ſee others greater, or wiſer, or happier, than ourſelves? Whence is a great part of the ſplendor, and all the oſtentation of high rank, but to receive pleaſure from the contemplation of thoſe who cannot attain dignity and riches, or to give pain to them who look with malignity on thoſe acquiſitions which they have deſired in vain? Whence is the pain which vanity ſuffers from neglect, but that it exacted painful homage, and honour which is received with more delight, as it is more unwillingly conferred? The pleaſures of comparative excellence, have commonly their ſource in the pain of others, and therefore are ſuch pleaſures as the Apoſtle warns the Chriſtians not to indulge.

Thirdly, In purſuance of his injunctions to be of one mind, and to ſympathiſe one with another, he directs them, to love as brethren, or to be lovers of the brethren. (Hammond.) He endeavours to eſtabliſh a ſpecies of fraternity among Chriſtians; that, as they have all one faith, they may have all one intereſt, and conſider themſelves as a family that muſt proſper, or ſuffer,

suffer, all together, and share whatever shail befall, either of good or evil. The highest degree of friendship is called brotherly love; and the term by which man is endeared to man, in the language of the Gospel, is the appellation of brother. We are all brethren by our common relation to the universal Father; but that relation is often forgotten amongst the contrariety of opinions, and opposition of passions, which disturb the peace of the world. Ambition has effaced all natural consanguinity, by calling nation to war against nation, and making the destruction of one half of mankind the glory of the other. Christian piety, as it revived and enforced all the original and primæval duties of humanity, so it restored, in some degree, that brotherhood, or foundation of kindness, which naturally arises from some common relation. We are brothers as we are men, we are again brothers as we are Christians; as men, we are brothers by natural necessity; but as Christians, we are brothers by voluntary choice, and are therefore under an apparent obligation to fulfil the relation; first, as it is established by our Creator, and, afterwards as it is chosen by ourselves.

selves. To have the ſame opinions naturally produces kindneſs, even when theſe opinions have no conſequence; becauſe we rejoice to find our ſentiments approved by the judgment of another. But thoſe who concur in Chriſtianity, have, by that agreement in principles, an opportunity of more than ſpeculative kindneſs; they may help forward the ſalvation of each other, by counſel or by reproof, by exortation, by example; they may recall each other from deviations, they may excite each other to good works.

Charity, or univerſal love, is named by Saint Paul, as the greateſt and moſt illuſtrious of Chriſtian virtues; and our Saviour himſelf has told us, that by this it ſhall be known that we are his diſciples, if we love one another. Every affection of the ſoul exerts itſelf moſt ſtrongly at the approach of its proper object. Chriſtians particularly love one another, becauſe they can confer and receive ſpiritual benefits. They are indeed to love all men; and how much the primitive Preachers of the Goſpel loved thoſe that differed from them, they ſufficiently ſhewed, when they incurred death by their endeavours to make them Chriſtians. This is the extent of evangelical love, to bring into the light of truth thoſe who are in darkneſs, and to keep thoſe from falling back into darkneſs to whom the light has been ſhewn.

Since life overflows with miſery, and the world is filled with evil, natural and moral, with temptation and danger, with calamity and wickedneſs, there are very frequent opportunities of ſhewing our unanimity, our ſympathy, and our brotherly love, by attempts to remove preſſures, and mitigate misfortunes. St. Peter, therefore, particularly preſſes the duty of commiſeration, by calling upon us,

Fourthly, to be pitiful, not to look negligently or ſcornfully on the miſeries of others, but to apply ſuch conſolation and aſſiſtance as Providence puts into our power.

To attempt an enumeration of all the opportunities which may occur for the exerciſe of pity, would be to form a catalogue of all the ills to which human nature is expoſed, to count over all the poſſibilities of calamity, and recount the depredations of time, the pains of diſeaſe, the blaſts

of

of caſualty, and the miſchiefs of malevo-lence.

Wherever the eye is turned, it ſees much miſery, and there is much which it ſees not; many complaints are heard, and there are many pangs without complaint. The external acts of mercy, to feed the hungry, to cloathe the naked, and to viſit the ſick, and the priſoners, we ſee daily opportunities of performing; and it may be hoped, they are not neglected by thoſe that abound with what others want.

But there are other calls upon charity. There are ſick minds as well as ſick bodies; there are underſtandings perplexed with ſcruples, there are conſciences tormented with guilt; nor can any greater benefit be conferred, than that of ſettling doubts, or comforting deſpair, and reſtoring a diſquieted ſoul to hope and tranquillity.

The duty of commiſeration is ſo ſtrongly preſſed by the Goſpel, that none deny its obligation. But as the meaſures of beneficence are left undefined, every man neceſſarily determines for himſelf, whether he has contributed his ſhare to the neceſſities of others; and amidſt the general de-

pravity

pravity of the world, it can be no wonder if there are found ſome who tax themſelves very lightly, and are ſatisfied with giving very little.

Some readily find out, that where there is diſtreſs there is vice, and eaſily diſcover the crime of feeding the lazy, or encouraging the diſſolute. To promote vice is certainly unlawful, but we do not always encourage vice when we relieve the vicious. It is ſufficient that our brother is in want; by which way he brought his want upon him let us not too curiouſly enquire. We likewiſe are ſinners. In caſes undoubted and notorious, ſome caution may be properly uſed, that charity be not perverted; but no man is ſo bad as to loſe his title to Chriſtian kindneſs. If a bad man be ſuffered to periſh, how ſhall he repent?

Not more juſtifiable is the omiſſion of duty, which proceeds from an expectation of better opportunities, or more preſſing exigencies. Of ſuch excuſes, or of ſuch purpoſes, there can be no end. Delay not till to-morrow, what thou mayeſt do to-day! A good work is now in thy power, be quick and perform it! By *thy* refuſal, *others* may be diſcouraged from aſking; or

ſo

ſo near may be the end of thy life, that thou mayeſt never do what is in thy heart. Every call to charity is a gift of God, to be received with thankfulneſs, and improved with diligence.

There are likewiſe many offices of kindneſs which cannot properly be claſſed under the duty of commiſeration, as they do not preſuppoſe either miſery or neceſſity, and yet are of great uſe for conciliating affection, and ſmoothing the paths of life; and, as it is of great importance, that goodneſs ſhould have the power of gaining the affections, the Apoſtle has not neglected thoſe ſubordinate duties, for he commands Chriſtians,

Fifthly, to be courteous.

For courteous, ſome ſubſtitute the word humble, the difference may not be conſidered as great, for pride is a quality that obſtructs courteſy.

That a precept of courteſy is by no means unworthy of the gravity and dignity of an apoſtolical mandate, may be gathered from the pernicious effects which all muſt have obſerved to have ariſen from harſh ſtrictneſs and ſour virtue, ſuch as refuſes to mingle in harmleſs gaiety, or

give

give countenance to innocent amusements, or which transacts the petty business of the day with a gloomy ferociousness that clouds existence. Goodness of this character is more formidable than lovely; it may drive away vice from its presence, but will never persuade it to stay to be amended; it may teach, it may remonstrate, but the hearer will seek for more mild instruction. To those, therefore, by whose conversation the Heathens were to be drawn away from error and wickedness; it is the Apostle's precept, that they be courteous, that they accommodate themselves, as far as innocence allows, to the will of others; that they should practise all the established modes of civility, seize all occasions of cultivating kindness, and live with the rest of the world in an amicable reciprocation of cursory civility, that Christianity might not be accused of making men less cheerful as companions, less sociable as neighbours, or less useful as friends.

Such is the system of domestic virtue, which the Apostle recommends. His words are few, but their meaning is sufficient to fill the greater part of the circle of life. Let us remember to be all of one mind, so as to grieve, and rejoice together ; to confirm, by conſtant benevolence, that brotherhood which creation and redemption have conſtituted ! Let us commiſerate and relieve affliction, and endear ourſelves by general gentleneſs and affability ; it will from hence ſoon appear how much goodneſs is to be loved, and how much human nature is meliorated by religion.

SERMON XII.

ECCLESIASTES, Chap. i. Verſe 14.

I have ſeen all the works that are done under the Sun; and behold, all is vanity and vexation of Spirit.

THAT all human actions terminate in vanity, and all human hopes will end in vexation, is a poſition, from which nature with-holds our credulity, and which our fondneſs for the preſent life, and worldly enjoyments, diſpoſes us to doubt; however forcibly it may be urged upon us by reaſon or experience.

Every man will readily enough confeſs, that his own condition diſcontents him; and that he has not yet been able, with all his labour, to make happineſs, or, with all his enquiries, to find it. But he ſtill thinks it is ſomewhere to be found, or by ſome means to be procured. His envy ſometimes perſuades him to imagine, that others poſſeſs it; and his ambition points the way by which he ſuppoſes that he ſhall reach, at laſt, the ſtation to which it is annexed. Every one wants ſomething to happineſs; and when he has gained what he firſt wanted, he wants ſomething elſe; he wears out life in efforts and purſuits, and perhaps dies, regretting that he muſt leave the world, when he is about to enjoy it.

So great is our intereſt, or ſo great we think it, to believe ourſelves able to procure our own happineſs, that experience never convinces us of our impotence; and indeed our miſcarriages might be reaſonably enough imputed by us to our own unſkilfulneſs, or ignorance, if we were able to derive intelligence from no experience but our own. But ſurely we may be content to credit the general voice of mankind, complaining inceſſantly of general infelicity; and when we ſee the reſtleſsneſs of the young, and the peeviſhneſs of the old; when we find the daring and the active combating miſery, and the calm and humble

humble lamenting it ; when the vigorous are exhaufting themfelves in ftruggles with their own condition, and the old and the wife retiring from the conteft in weari-nefs and defpondency ; we may be content at laft to conclude, that if happinefs had been to be found, fome would have found it, and that it is vain to fearch longer for what all have miffed.

But though our obftinacy fhould hold out, againft common experience and com-mon authority, it might at leaft give way to the declaration of Solomon, who has left this teftimony to fucceeding ages ; that all human purfuits and labours are va-nity. From the like conclufion made by other men, we may efcape ; by confider-ing, that *their* experience was fmall, and *their* power narrow ; that they pronounced with confidence upon that, which they could not know ; and that many pleafures might be above their reach, and many more beyond their obfervation ; *they* may be confidered, as uttering the dictates of difcontent, rather than perfuafion ; and as fpeaking not fo much of the general ftate of things, as of their own fhare, and their own fituation.

But the character of Solomon leaves no room for subterfuge; he did not judge of what he did not know. He had in his possession whatever power and riches, and what is still more, whatever wisdom and knowledge, could confer. As he understood the vegetable creation, from the Cedar of Libanus, to the Hyssop on the wall; so there is no doubt, but he had taken a survey of all the gradations of human life, from the throne of the prince, to the shepherd's cottage. He had in his hand all the instruments of happiness, and in his mind the skill to apply them. Every power of delight which others possessed, he had authority to summon, or wealth to purchase; all that royal prosperity could supply, was accumulated upon him; at home he had peace, and in foreign countries he had honour; what every nation could supply, was poured down before him. If power be grateful, he was a King; if there be pleasure in knowledge, he was the wisest of mankind; if wealth can purchase happiness, he had so much gold, that silver was little regarded. Over all these advantages, presided a mind, in the highest degree disposed to magnificence and voluptuousness,

luptuoufnefs, fo eager in purfuit of gratification, that alas! after every other price had beed bid for happinefs, Religion and virtue were brought to the fale. But after the anxiety of his enquiries, the wearinefs of his labours, and the lofs of his innocence, he obtained only this conclufion: *I have feen all the works that are done under the Sun; and behold all is vanity and vexation of Spirit.*

That this refult of Solomon's experience, thus folemnly bequeathed by him to all generations, may not be tranfmitted to us without its proper ufe; let us diligently confider,

Firft, In what fenfe we are to underftand, that all is vanity.

Secondly, How far the conviction, that all is vanity, ought to influence the conduct of life.

Thirdly, What confequences the ferious and religious mind may deduce from the pofition, that all is vanity.

When we examine, firft, in what fenfe we are to underftand, that all is vanity; we muft remember, that the Preacher is not fpeaking of religious practices, or of any actions immediately commanded by God,

God, or directly referred to him ; but of ſuch employments as we purſue by choice, and ſuch works as we perform, in hopes of a recompenſe in the preſent life; ſuch as flatter the imagination with pleaſing ſcenes, and probable increaſe of temporal felicity ; of this he determines that all is vanity, and every hour confirms his determination.

The event of all human endeavours is uncertain. He that plants, may gather no fruit ; he that ſows, may reap no harveſt. Even the moſt ſimple operations are liable to miſcarriage, from cauſes which we cannot foreſee ; and, if we could foreſee them, cannot prevent. What can be more vain, than the confidence of man, when the annual proviſion made for the ſupport of life is not only expoſed to the uncertainty of the weather, and the variation of the ſky, but lies at the mercy of the reptiles of the earth, or the inſects of the air ? The rain and the wind he cannot command ; the caterpillar he cannot deſtroy ; and the locuſt he cannot drive away.

But theſe effects, which require only the concurrence of natural cauſes, though they depend little upon human power, are yet made

made by Providence regular and certain, in comparifon with thofe extenfive and complicated undertakings which muft be brought to pafs by the agency of man, and which require the union of many underftandings, and the co-operation of many hands. The hiftory of mankind is little elfe than a narrative of defigns which have failed, and hopes that have been difappointed. In all matters of emulation and conteft, the fuccefs of one implies the defeat of another, and at leaft half the tranfaction terminates in mifery. And in defigns not directly contrary to the intereft of another, and therefore not oppofed either by artifice or violence, it frequently happens, that by negligence or miftake, or unfeafonable officioufnefs, a very hopeful project is brought to nothing.

To find examples of difappointment and uncertainty, we need not raife our thoughts to the interefts of nations, nor follow the warrior to the field, or the ftatefman to the council. The little tranfactions of private families are entangled with perplexities; and the hourly occurrences of common life are filling the world with difcontent and complaint. Every man hopes for

kindnefs

kindneſs from his friends, diligence from his ſervants, and obedience from his children; yet friends are often unfaithful, ſervants negligent, and children rebellious. Human wiſdom has, indeed exhauſted its power, in giving rules for the conduct of life, but thoſe rules are themſelves but vanities. They are difficult to be obſerved, and, though obſerved, are uncertain in the effect.

The labours of man are not only uncertain, but imperfect. If we perform what we deſigned, we yet do not obtain what we expected. What appeared great when we deſired it, ſeems little when it is attained; the wiſh is ſtill unſatisfied, and ſomething always remains behind, without which, the gratification is incomplete. He that riſes to greatneſs, finds himſelf in danger; he that obtains riches, perceives that he cannot gain eſteem. He that is careſſed, ſees intereſt lurking under kindneſs; and he that hears his own praiſes, ſuſpects that he is flattered. Diſcontent and doubt are always purſuing us. Our endeavours end without performance, and performance ends without ſatisfaction.

But, ſince this uncertainty and imperfection is the lot which our Creator has appointed for us, we are to enquire,

Secondly, How far the conviction, that all is vanity, ought to influence the conduct of life.

Human actions may be distinguished into various classes. Some are actions of duty, which can never be vain, because God will reward them. Yet these actions, considered as terminating in this world, will often produce vexation. It is our duty to admonish the vicious, to instruct the ignorant, and relieve the poor; and our admonitions will, sometimes, produce anger, instead of amendment; our instructions will be sometimes bestowed upon the perverse, the stupid, and the inattentive; and our charity will be sometimes misapplied by those that receive it, and, instead of feeding the hungry, will pamper the intemperate; but these disappointments do not make good actions vain, though they show us how much all success depends upon causes, on which we have no influence.

There are likewise actions of necessity; these are often vain and vexatious; but such is the order of the world, that they cannot be omitted. He that will eat bread muſt plow and ſow; though it is not certain, that he who plows and ſows ſhall eat bread. It is appointed, that life ſhould be ſuſtained by labour; and we muſt not ſink down in ſullen idleneſs, when our induſtry is permitted to miſcarry. We ſhall often have occaſion to remember the ſentence, denounced by the Preacher, upon all that is done under the ſun; but we muſt ſtill proſecute our buſineſs, confeſs our imbecility, and turn our eyes upon Him, whoſe mercy is over all his works, and who, though he humbles our pride, will ſuccour our neceſſities.

Works of abſolute neceſſity are few and ſimple; a very great part of human diligence is laid out in accommodations of eaſe, or refinements of pleaſure; and the further we paſs beyond the boundaries of neceſſity, the more we loſe ourſelves in the regions of vanity, and the more we expoſe ourſelves to vexation of ſpirit. As we extend our pleaſures, we multiply our wants. The pain of hunger is eaſily appeaſed; but to ſurmount the diſguſt of appetite, vitiated by indulgence, all the arts of luxury are required, and all are often vain. When to the enjoyments of ſenſe are ſuperadded the delights of fancy, we form a ſcheme of happineſs that never can be complete, for we can always imagine more than we poſſeſs. All ſocial pleaſures put us more or leſs in the power of others, who ſometimes cannot, and ſometimes will not, pleaſe us. Converſations of argument often end in bitterneſs of controverſy; and converſations of mirth, in petulance and folly. Friendſhip is violated by intereſt, or broken by paſſion; and benevolence finds its kindneſs beſtowed on the worthleſs and ungrateful.

But moſt certain is the diſappointment of him, who places his happineſs in comparative good, and conſiders, not what he himſelf wants, but what others have. The delight of eminence muſt, by its own nature, be rare, becauſe he that is eminent muſt have many below him, and therefore, if we ſuppoſe ſuch deſires general, as very general they are, *the happineſs of a few* muſt ariſe from *the miſery of many*. He that places his delight in the extent of his renown is, in ſome degree, at the mercy of every tongue; not only malevolence, but indifference, may diſturb him; and he may

be

be pained, not only by thoſe who ſpeak ill, but by thoſe likewiſe that ſay nothing.

As every engine of artificial motion, as it conſiſts of more parts, is in more danger of deficience and diſorder; ſo every effect as it requires the agency of greater numbers, is more likely to fail. Yet what pleaſure is granted to man, beyond the groſs gratifications of ſenſe, common to him with other animals, that does not demand the help of others, and the help of greater numbers, as the pleaſure is ſublimated and enlarged? And, ſince ſuch is the conſtitution of things, that whatever can give pleaſure can likewiſe cauſe uneaſineſs, there is little hope that uneaſineſs will be long eſcaped. Of them, whoſe offices are neceſſary to felicity, ſome will be perverſe, and ſome will be unſkilful; ſome will negligently with-hold their contributions, and ſome will enviouſly withdraw them. The various and oppoſite directions of the human mind, which divide men into ſo many different occupations, keep all the inhabitants of the earth perpetually buſy; but when it is conſidered, that the buſineſs of every man is to counteract the

purpoſe

purpoſe of ſome other man, it will appear, that univerſal activity cannot contribute much to univerſal happineſs. Of thoſe that contend, one muſt neceſſarily be overcome; and he that prevails never has his labour rewarded to his wiſh, but finds that he has been contending for that which cannot ſatisfy, and engaged in a conteſt where even victory is vanity.

What then is the influence which the conviction of this unwelcome truth ought to have upon our conduct? It ought to teach us humility, patience, and diffidence. When we conſider how little we know of the diſtant conſequences of our own actions, how little the greateſt perſonal qualities can protect us from misfortune, how much all our importance depends upon the favour of others, how uncertainly that favour is beſtowed, and how eaſily it is loſt; we ſhall find, that we have very little reaſon to be proud. That which is moſt apt to elate the thoughts, height of place, and greatneſs of power, is the gift of others. No man can, by any natural or intrinſick faculties, maintain himſelf in a ſtate of ſuperiority; he is exalted to his place, whatever it be, by the concurrence of

thoſe,

thoſe, who are for a time content to be counted his inferiors; he has no authority in himſelf; he is only able to controul ſome, by the help of others. If dependence be a ſtate of humiliation, every man has reaſon to be humble, for every man is dependent.

But however unpleaſing theſe conſiderations may be, however unequal our condition is to all our wiſhes or conceptions, we are not to admit impatience into our boſoms, or increaſe the evils of life, by vain throbs of diſcontent. To live in a world where all is vanity, has been decreed by our Creator to be the lot of man, a lot which we cannot alter by murmuring, but may ſoften by ſubmiſſion.

The conſideration of the vanity of all human purpoſes and projects, deeply impreſſed upon the mind, neceſſarily produces that diffidence in all worldly good, which is neceſſary to the regulation of our paſſions, and the ſecurity of our innocence. In a ſmooth courſe of proſperity, an unobſtructed progreſſion from wiſh to wiſh, while the ſucceſs of one deſign facilitates another, and the opening proſpect of life ſhews pleaſures at a diſtance, to conclude that

that the paſſage will be always clear, and that the delights which ſolicit from far will, when they are attained, fill the ſoul with enjoyments, muſt neceſſarily produce violent deſires, and eager purſuits, contempt of thoſe that are behind, and malignity to thoſe that are before. But the full perſuaſion that all earthly good is uncertain in the attainment, and unſtable in the poſſeſſion, and the frequent recollection of the ſlender ſupports on which we reſt, and the dangers which are always hanging over us, will dictate inoffenſive modeſty, and mild benevolence. *He* does not raſhly treat another with contempt, who doubts the duration of his own ſuperiority: *he* will not refuſe aſſiſtance to the diſtreſſed, who ſuppoſes that he may quickly need it himſelf. He that conſiders how imperfectly human wiſdom can judge of that, which has not been tried, will ſeldom think any poſſibilities of advantage worthy of vehement deſire. As his hopes are moderate, his endeavours will be calm. He will not fix his fond hopes upon things which he knows to be vanity, but will enjoy this world, as one who knows that he does not poſſeſs it: and that this is the diſpoſition,

which

which becomes our condition, will appear, when we consider,

Thirdly, What consequences the serious and religious mind may draw from the position, that all is vanity.

When the present state of man is considered, when an estimate is made of his hopes, his pleasures, and his possessions; when his hopes appear to be deceitful, his labours ineffectual, his pleasures unsatisfactory, and his possessions fugitive, it is natural to wish for an abiding city, for a state more constant and permanent, of which the objects may be more proportioned to our wishes, and the enjoyments to our capacities; and from this wish it is reasonable to infer, that such a state is designed for us by that Infinite Wisdom, which, as it does nothing in vain, has not created minds with comprehensions never to be filled. When Revelation is consulted, it appears that such a state is really promised, and that, by the contempt of worldly pleasures, it is to be obtained. We then find, that, instead of lamenting the imperfection of earthly things, we have reason to pour out thanks to Him who orders all for our good, that he has made

the

the world, ſuch as often deceives, and often afflicts us ; that the charms of intereſt are not ſuch, as our frailty is unable to reſiſt, but that we have ſuch interruptions of our purſuits, and ſuch languor in our enjoyments, ſuch pains of body and anxieties of mind, as repreſs deſire, and weaken temptation : and happy will it be, if we follow the gracious directions of Providence, and determine, that no degree of eathly felicity ſhall be purchaſed with a crime ; if we reſolve no longer to bear the chains of ſin, to employ all our endeavours upon tranſitory and imperfect pleaſures, or to divide our thought between the world and Heaven ; but to bid farewell to ſublunary vanities, to endure no longer an unprofitable vexation of ſpirit, but with pure heart and ſteady faith to *fear God, and to keep his commandments, and remember that this is the whole of man.*

SERMON XIII.

II. Timothy, Chap. iii. part of the 5th Verſe.

Having a form of Godlineſs, but denying the power thereof.

WHEN St. Paul, in the precepts given to Timothy for his inſtruction how to regulate and purify the converſation of the firſt Chriſtians, directed him to take care that thoſe men ſhould be avoided, as dangerous and peſtilent, who, having the form of godlineſs, denied the power; it is reaſonable to believe, that he meant, in his direct and immediate intention, to awaken his caution againſt groſs hypocrites; ſuch as may eaſily be ſuppoſed to have appeared too often in the moſt early ſeminaries of Chriſtianity; who made an appearance of righteouſneſs ſubſervient to worldly intereſt ; and whoſe converſion, real or pretended, gave them an opportunity of preying upon artleſs ſimplicity, by claiming that kindneſs which the firſt Believers ſhewed to one another ; and obtaining benefactions which they did not want ; and eating bread for which they did not labour.

To impoſtors of this kind, the peculiar ſtate of the firſt Chriſtians would naturally expoſe them. As they were ſurrounded by enemies, they were glad to find, in any man, the appearance of a friend ; as they were wearied with importunate contradiction, they were deſirous of an interval of reſpite, by conſorting with any one that profeſſed the ſame opinions ; and what was ſtill more favourable to ſuch Impoſtors, when they had, by embracing an unpopular and perſecuted religion, diveſted themſelves, in a great degree, of ſecular intereſt, they were likely often to want that vigilance and ſuſpicion which is forced, even upon honeſt minds, by much commerce with the world, and frequent tranſactions with various characters ; and which our divine Maſter teaches us to practiſe, when he commands us to join the *Wiſdom of the*

Serpent

Serpent with the harmlessness of the Dove. The first Christians must have been, in the highest degree, zealous to strengthen their faith in themselves, and propagate it in others, and zeal easily spreads the arms, and opens the bosom to an adherent, or a proselyte, as to one, that adds another suffrage to truth, and strengthens the support of a good cause. Men of this disposition, and in this state of life, would easily be enamoured of the *form* of godliness, and not soon discover, that the *power* was wanting.—Men naturally think others like themselves, and therefore a good man is easily persuaded to credit the appearance of Virtue.

Hypocrisy, however, was not confined to the Apostolic ages. All times, and all places, have produced men, that have endeavoured to gain credit by false pretensions to excellence, and have recommended themselves to kindness or esteem, by specious professions, and ostentatious displays of counterfeited virtues.—It is, however, less necessary now to obviate this kind of fraud, by exortations to caution; for that simplicity, which lay open to its operation, is not now very frequently to be found.

The

The Hypocrite, in these times, seldom boasts of much success.—He is for the most part soon discovered; and when he is once known, the world will not wait for counsel to avoid him, for the good detest, and the bad despise him. He is hated for his attempts, and scorned for his miscarriage.

It may therefore be proper to consider the danger of a *form of righteousness* without the *power*, in a different and secondary sense; and to examine whether, as there are some who by this form deceive others, there are not some, likewise, that deceive themselves; who pacify their consciences with an appearance of piety, and live and die in dangerous tranquillity and delusive confidence.

In this enquiry it will be proper to consider, First, what may be understood by the *form* of godliness, as distinct from the *power*.

Secondly, What is that power of godliness, without which the form is defective and unavailing.

Thirdly, How far it is necessary to the Christian life, that the form and power should subsist together.

Let

Let it therefore be firſt conſidered, what may be eaſily and naturally underſtood by the form of godlineſs as diſtinct from the power.

By the form of godlineſs, may be properly underſtood, not only a ſpecious practice of religious duties, exhibited to public notice, but all external acts of worſhip, all rites and ceremonies, all ſtated obſervances, and all compliance with temporary and local injunctions and regularities.

The religion of the Jews, from the time of Moſes, compriſed a great number of burthenſome ceremonies, required by God for reaſons which perhaps human wiſdom has never fully diſcovered. Of theſe ceremonies, however, ſome were typically repreſentative of the Chriſtian inſtitution; and ſome, by keeping them diſtinct, by diſſimilitude of cuſtoms from the nations that ſurrounded them, had a tendency to ſecure them from the influence of ill example, and preſerve them from the contagion of idolatry.

To the uſe of obſervances, thus important, they were confined by the ſtrongeſt obligations. They were indeed external acts, but they were inſtituted by divine authority ; they were not to be conſidered merely as inſtrumental and expedient, as means which might be omitted, if their ends were ſecured ; they were poſitively enjoined by the ſupreme legiſlator, and were not left to choice or diſcretion, or ſecular laws ; to the will of the powerful, or the judgement of the prudent.

Yet even theſe ſacred rites might be punctually performed, without making the performer acceptable to God ; the blood of bulls and of goats might be poured out in vain, if the deſires were not regulated, or the paſſions ſubdued. The ſacrifices of the oppreſſor, or extortioner, were not an atonement, but an abomination. Forgiveneſs was obtained, not by incenſe, but by repentance ; the offender was required to rend his heart, and not his garment ; a contrite and a broken heart was the oblation which the ſupreme Judge did not deſpiſe.

...ch was the moral law exalted above
...onial inſtitutions, even in that
...by which ſo many ceremonies
...ded, that thoſe two parts of
...guiſhed by the appellati-
...irit. As the body, ſepa-

rated from the ſpirit, is a maſs lifeleſs, motionleſs, and uſeleſs ; ſo the external practice of ritual obſervances was ineffectual and vain, an action without a meaning, a labour by which nothing was produced. As the ſpirit puts the limbs into motion, and directs their action to an end, ſo Juſtice and Mercy gave energy to ceremonies, made the oblation grateful, and the worſhiper accepted.

The Profeſſors of Chriſtianity have few ceremonies indiſpenſably enjoined them. Their religion teaches them to worſhip God, not with local or temporary ceremonies, but in ſpirit and in truth ; that is, with internal purity, and moral righteouſneſs. For ſpirit, in this ſenſe, ſeems to be oppoſed to the body of external rites ; and truth is known to ſignify, in the biblical language, the ſum of thoſe duties which we owe to one onother.

Yet ſuch are the temptations of intereſt and pleaſure, and ſo prevalent is the deſire of enjoying at once, the pleaſures of ſin for a ſeaſon, and the hopes of happineſs to eternity ; that even the Chriſtian religion has been depraved by artificial modes of piety, and ſuccedaneous practices of reconciliation.

thority; they were not to be confidered merely as inftrumental and expedient, as means which might be omitted, if their ends were fecured; they were pofitively enjoined by the fupreme legiflator, and were not left to choice or difcretion, or fecular laws; to the will of the powerful, or the judgement of the prudent.

Yet even thefe facred rites might be punctually performed, without making the performer acceptable to God; the blood of bulls and of goats might be poured out in vain, if the defires were not regulated, or the paffions fubdued. The facrifices of the oppreffor, or extortioner, were not an atonement, but an abomination. Forgivenefs was obtained, not by incenfe, but by repentance; the offender was required to rend his heart, and not his garment; a contrite and a broken heart was the oblation which the fupreme Judge did not defpife.

So much was the moral law exalted above all ceremonial inftitutions, even in that difpenfation by which fo many ceremonies were commanded, that thofe two parts of duty were diftinguifhed by the appellations of body and fpirit. As the body, feparated from the ſpirit, is a maſs lifeleſs, motionleſs, and uſeleſs ; ſo the external practice of ritual obſervances was ineffectual and vain, an action without a meaning, a labour by which nothing was produced. As the ſpirit puts the limbs into motion, and directs their action to an end, ſo Juſtice and Mercy gave energy to ceremonies, made the oblation grateful, and the worſhiper accepted.

The Profeſſors of Chriſtianity have few ceremonies indiſpenſably enjoined them. Their religion teaches them to worſhip God, not with local or temporary ceremonies, but in ſpirit and in truth ; that is, with internal purity, and moral righteouſneſs. For ſpirit, in this ſenſe, ſeems to be oppoſed to the body of external rites ; and truth is known to ſignify, in the biblical language, the ſum of thoſe duties which we owe to one onother.

Yet ſuch are the temptations of intereſt and pleaſure, and ſo prevalent is the deſire of enjoying at once, the pleaſures of ſin for a ſeaſon, and the hopes of happineſs to eternity ; that even the Chriſtian religion has been depraved by artificial modes of piety, and ſuccedaneous practices of reconciliation.

ciliation. Men have been ever perſuaded, that by doing ſomething, to which they think themſelves not obliged, they may purchaſe an exemption from ſuch duties as they find themſelves inclined to violate; that they may commute with Heaven for a temporal fine, and make rigour atone for relaxity.

In ages and countries, in which ignorance has produced, and nouriſhed, ſuperſtition; many artifices have been invented of practiſing piety without virtue, and repentance without amendment. The devotion of our blind fore-fathers conſiſted, for a great part, in rigorous auſterities, laborious pilgrimages, and gloomy retirement; and that which now prevails, in the darker provinces of the Popiſh world, exhauſts its power in abſurd veneration for ſome particular Saint, expreſſed too often by honours paid to his image, or in a ſtated number of prayers, uttered with very little attention, and very frequently with little underſtanding.

Some of theſe practices may be perhaps juſtly imputed to the groſſneſs of a people, ſcarcely capable of worſhip purely intellectual; to the neceſſity of complying with the

the weakneſs of men, who muſt be taught their duty by material images, and ſenſible impreſſions. This plea, however, will avail but little, in defence of abuſes not only permitted, but encouraged by pertinacious vindications, and fictitious miracles.

It is apparent that the Romiſh Clergy have attributed too much efficacy to pious donations, and charitable eſtabliſhments; and that they have made liberality to the church, and bounty to the poor, equivalent to the whole ſyſtem of our duty to God, and to our neighbour.

Yet nothing can be more repugnant to the general tenour of the Evangelical Revelation, than an opinion that pardon may be bought, and guilt effaced, by a ſtipulated expiation. We naturally catch the pleaſures of the preſent hour, and gratify the calls of the reigning paſſion: and what ſhall hinder the man of violence from outrage and miſchief, or reſtrain the purſuer of intereſt from fraud and circumvention, when they are told, that after a life paſſed in diſturbing the peace of life, and violating the ſecurity of poſſeſſion, they may die at laſt in peace, by founding by ...nſiances ...ome lauda-

ble

alms-houſe, without the agonies of deep contrition ?

But error and corruption are often to be found where there are neither Jews nor Papiſts.—Let us not look upon the depravity of others with triumph, nor cenſure it with bitterneſs.—Every ſect may find, in its own followers, thoſe who have the form of godlineſs, without the power ; every man, if he examines his own conduct, without intention to be his own flatterer, may, to a certain degree, find it in himſelf.

To give the heart to God, and to give the whole heart, is very difficult ; the laſt, the great effort of long labour, fervent prayer, and diligent meditation.—Many reſolutions are made, and many relapſes lamented ; and many conflicts with our own deſires, wit… powers of this world, and the … rkneſs, muſt be ſuf… …l of man is made … will of God.

… re willing to find … difficult and leſs … es alive by faint … conſciences by … aſily practice.

Not

ſcarc… ng an alms-

tual ; to …

Not yet resolved to live wholly to God, and yet afraid to live wholly to the world, we do something in recompense for that which we neglect, and resign something that we may keep the rest.

To be strictly religious, is difficult, but we may be zealously religious at little expence.—By expressing on all occasions our detestation of Heresy and Popery, and all other errors, we erect ourselves into champions for truth, without much hazard or trouble.—The hopes of zeal are not wholly groundless.—Indifference in questions of importance is no amiable quality.—He that is warm for truth, and fearless in its defence, performs one of the duties of a good man; he strengthens his own conviction, and guards others from delusion; but steadiness of belief, and boldness of profession, are yet only part of the form of godliness, which may be attained by those who deny the power.

As almost every man is, by nature or by accident, exposed to danger from particular temptations, and disposed to some vices more than to others; so all are, either by disposition of mind, or the circumstances of life, inclined or impelled to some lauda-

alms-houſe, without the agonies of deep contrition ?

But error and corruption are often to be found where there are neither Jews nor Papiſts.—Let us not look upon the depravity of others with triumph, nor cenſure it with bitterneſs.—Every ſect may find, in its own followers, thoſe who have the form of godlineſs, without the power ; every man, if he examines his own conduct, without intention to be his own flatterer, may, to a certain degree, find it in himſelf.

To give the heart to God, and to give the whole heart, is very difficult ; the laſt, the great effort of long labour, fervent prayer, and diligent meditation.—Many reſolutions are made, and many relapſes lamented ; and many conflicts with our own deſires, with the powers of this world, and the powers of darkneſs, muſt be ſuſtained, before the will of man is made wholly obedient to the will of God.

In the mean time, we are willing to find ſome way to Heaven, leſs difficult and leſs obſtructed, to keep our hopes alive by faint endeavours, and to lull our conſciences by ſuch expedients as we may eaſily practice.

Not

Not yet refolved to live wholly to God, and yet afraid to live wholly to the world, we do fomething in recompenfe for that which we neglect, and refign fomething that we may keep the reft.

To be ftrictly religious, is difficult, but we may be zealoufly religious, at little expence.—By expreffing on all occafions our deteftation of Herefy and Popery, and all other errors, we erect ourfelves into champions for truth, without much hazard or trouble.—The hopes of zeal are not wholly groundlefs.—Indifference in queftions of importance is no amiable quality.—He that is warm for truth, and fearlefs in its defence, performs one of the duties of a good man; he ftrengthens his own conviction, and guards others from delufion; but fteadinefs of belief, and boldnefs of profeffion, are yet only part of the form of godlinefs, which may be attained by thofe who deny the power.

As almoft every man is, by nature or by accident, expofed to danger from particular temptations, and difpofed to fome vices more than to others; fo all are, either by difpofition of mind, or the circumftances of life, inclined or impelled to fome lauda-

ble

ble practices. Of this happy tendency it is common to take advantage, by pushing the favourite, or the convenient, virtue to its utmost extent, and to lose all sense of deficiency in the perpetual contemplation of some single excellence.

Thus some please themselves with a constant regularity of life, and decency of behaviour,—they hear themselves commended, and superadd their own approbation. They know, or might know, that they have secret faults; but, as they are not open to accusation, they are not inquisitive to their own disquiet; they are satisfied that they do not corrupt others, and that the world will not be worse by their example.

Some are punctual in the attendance on public worship, and perhaps in the performance of private devotion. These they know to be great duties, and resolve not to neglect them. It is right they go so far; and with so much that is right they are satisfied. They are diligent in adoration, but defective in obedience.

Such men are often not hypocrites; the virtues which they practise arise from their principles. The man of regularity really hopes, that he shall recommend goodness

to

to thoſe that know him. The frequenter of the church really hopes to propitiate his Creator. Their religion is ſincere; what is reprehenſible is, that it is partial, that the heart is yet not purified, and that yet many inordinate deſires remain, not only unſubdued, but unſuſpected, under the ſplendid cover of ſome ſpecious practice, with which the mind delights itſelf too much, to take a rigorous ſurvey of its own motions.

In condemnation of thoſe who preſume to hope, that the performance of one duty will obtain excuſe for the violation of others, it is affirmed by St. James, that he who breaks one commandment is guilty of all; and he defends his poſition by obſerving, that they are all delivered by the ſame authority.

His meaning is not, that all crimes are equal, or that in any one crime all others are involved; but that the law of God is to be obeyed with compleat and unreſerved ſubmiſſion; and that he who violates any of its ordinances, will not be juſtified by his obſervation of all the reſt, ſince as the whole is of divine authority, every breach, wilful and unrepented, is an act of rebellion against Omnipotence.

One of the artifices, by which men, thus defectively religious, deceive themselves, is that of comparing their own behaviour with that of men openly vicious, and generally negligent; and inferring that themselves are good, because they suppose that they see others worse. The account of the Pharisee and Publican may shew us that, in rating our own merit, we are in danger of mistake. But though the estimate should be right, it is still to be remembered, that he who is not worst, may yet fall far below what will be required. Our rule of duty is not *the virtue of men*, but *the law of God*, from which alone we can learn what will be required.

Secondly, What is that power of godliness without which the form is defective and unavailing?

The power of godliness is contained in the love of God and of our neighbour; in that sum of religion, in which, as we are told by the Saviour of the world, the law and the Prophets are comprized. The love of God will engage us to trust in his protection, to acquiesce in his dispensations, to keep his laws, to meditate on his perfection, and to declare our confidence and submission by profound and frequent adoration, to impress his glory on our minds by songs of praise, to inflame our gratitude by acts of thanksgiving, to strengthen our faith, and exalt our hope, by pious meditations, and to implore his protection of our imbecillity, and his assistance of our frailty, by humble supplication: and when we love God with the whole heart, the power of godliness will be shewn by steadiness in temptation, by patience in affliction, by faith in the divine promises, by perpetual dread of sin, by continual aspirations after higher degrees of holiness, and contempt of the pains and pleasures of the world, when they obstruct the progress of religious excellence.

The power of godliness, as it is exerted in the love of our neighbour, appears in the exact and punctual discharge of all the relative and social duties. He, whom this power actuates and directs, will regulate his conduct, so as neither to do injury, nor willingly to give offence. He will neither be a tyrannical governor, nor a seditious subject; neither a cruel parent, nor a disobedient ſon; neither an oppreſſive maſter, nor an eye-ſervant. But he will not ſtop at negative goodneſs, nor reſt in the mere forbearance of evil; he will ſearch out occaſions of beneficence, and extend his care to thoſe who have no other claim to his attention than the great community of relation to the univerſal Father of mankind. To enumerate the various modes of charity, which true godlineſs may ſuggeſt, as it is difficult, would be uſeleſs. They are as extenſive as want, and as various as miſery.

We muſt however remember, that where the form of godlineſs appears, we muſt not always ſuppoſe the power to be wanting, becauſe its influence is not univerſal and compleat; nor think every man to be avoided, in whom we diſcover either defective virtues, or actual faults. The power ſubſiſts in him who is contending with corruption, though he has not yet entirely ſubdued it. He who falleth ſeven times a day may yet, by the mercy of God, be numbered among the juſt; the pureſt human virtue has much fæculence. The higheſt flights of the ſoul ſoar not beyond the clouds and vapours of the earth; the greateſt attainments are very imperfect; and he who is moſt advanced in excellence was once in a lower ſtate, and in that lower ſtate was yet worthy of love and reverence. One inſtance of the power of godlineſs is readineſs to help the weak, and comfort the fallen, to look with compaſſion upon the frail, to rekindle thoſe whoſe ardour is cooling, and to recall thoſe who, by inadvertency, or under the influence of ſtrong temptation, have wandered from the right way; and to favour all them who mean well, and wiſh to be better, though their meaning and their wiſhes have not yet fully reformed their lives.

There is likewiſe danger leſt, in the purſuit of the power of godlineſs, too little regard be paid to the form, and leſt the cenſure of hypocriſy be too haſtily paſſed, and a life apparently regular and ſerious be conſidered as an artifice to conceal bad purpoſes and ſecret views.

That this opinion, which ſome are very willing to indulge, may not prevail ſo as to diſcountenance the profeſſion of piety, we are to conſider,

Thirdly, how far it is neceſſary to the

Chriſtian life, that the form and power of godlineſs ſhould ſubſiſt together.

It may be with great reaſon affirmed, that though there may be the appearance of godlineſs without the reality, there can hardly be the reality without the appearance. Part of the duties of a Chriſtian are neceſſarily public. We are to worſhip God in the congregation; we are to make open profeſſion of our hope and faith. One of the great duties of man, as a ſocial being, is, to let his light ſhine before men, to inſtruct by the prevalence of his example, and, as far as his influence extends, to propagate goodneſs and enforce truth. No man is to boaſt of his own excellence, for this reaſon among others; that arrogance will make excellence leſs amiable, and leſs attractive of imitation. No man is to conceal his reverence of religion, or his zeal for truth and right, becauſe, by ſhrinking from the notice of mankind, he betrays diffidence of the cauſe which he wiſhes to maintain. He, whoſe piety begins and ends in zeal for opinions, and in clamour againſt thoſe who differ from him, is certainly yet without the vital energy of religion; but, if his opinions regulate his conduct,

duct, he may with great juſtice ſhew his fervour, having already ſhewn his ſincerity. He that worſhips God in public, and offends him by ſecret vices, if he means to make the good part of his conduct balance the bad, is to be cenſured and inſtructed; if he means to gain the applauſe of men, and to make outward ſanctity an inſtrument of miſchief, he is to be deteſted and avoided: but he that really endeavours to obey God in ſecret, neglects part of his duty, if he omits the ſolemnities of public worſhip. The form of godlineſs, as it conſiſts in the rites of religion, is the inſtrument given us by God for the acquiſition of the power; the means as well as the end are preſcribed; nor can he expect the help of grace, or the divine approbation, who ſeeks them by any other method than that which Infinite Wiſdom has condeſcended to appoint.

SERMON XIV.

ISAIAH, xxvi. 3.

Thou wilt keep him in perfect peace, whose mind is ſtayed on thee, becauſe he truſteth in thee.

IN order to the explication of this text, or the enforcement of the precept implied in it, there ſeems to be no neceſſity, either of proving, that all men are deſirous of happineſs, or that their deſire, for the moſt part, fails of being gratified. Every man is conſcious, that he neither performs, nor forbears any thing upon any other motive than the proſpect, either of an immediate gratification, or a diſtant reward; that whether he complies with temptation, or repels

repels it, he is ſtill influenced by the ſame general regard to his own felicity; but that when he yields to the ſolicitation of his appetite, or the impulſe of his paſſions, he is overborne by the prevalence of the object before him; and when he adheres to his duty, in oppoſition to his preſent intereſt, he is influenced by the hopes of future happineſs.

That almoſt every man is diſappointed in his ſearch after happineſs, is apparent from the clamorous complaints which are always to be heard; from the reſtleſs diſcontent, which is hourly to be obſerved, and from the inceſſant purſuit of new objects, which employ almoſt every moment of every man's life. For a deſire of change is a ſufficient proof, that we are diſſatisfied with our preſent ſtate; and evidently ſhews, that we feel ſome pain which we deſire to avoid, or miſs ſome enjoyment which we wiſh to poſſeſs.

The true cauſe of this general diſguſt, an unprejudiced and attentive ſurvey of the world will not long fail of diſcovering. It will eaſily appear, that men fail to gain what they ſo much deſire, becauſe they ſeek it where it is not to be found, becauſe they ſuffer themſelves to be dazzled by ſpecious

ſpecious appearances, reſign themſelves up to the direction of their paſſions, and, when one purſuit has failed of affording them that ſatisfaction which they expected from it, apply themſelves with the ſame ardour to another equally unprofitable, and waſte their lives in ſucceſſive deluſions, in idle ſchemes of imaginary enjoyment; in the chace of ſhadows which fleet before them, and in attempts to graſp a bubble, which, however it may attract the eye by the brightneſs of its colour, is neither ſolid nor laſting, but owes its beauty only to its diſtance, and is no ſooner touched than it diſappears.

As men differ in age or diſpoſition, they are expoſed to different deluſions in this important enquiry. The young and the gay imagine happineſs to conſiſt in ſhew, in merriment and noiſe, or in a conſtant ſucceſſion of amuſements, or in the gratification of their appetites, and the frequent repetition of ſenſual pleaſures. Inſtead of founding happineſs on the ſolid baſis of reaſon and reflection, they raiſe an airy fabrick of momentary ſatisfaction, which is perpetually decaying, and perpetually to be repaired. They pleaſe themſelves, not

with

with thinking juſtly, but with avoiding to think at all, with a ſuſpence of all the operations of their intellectual faculties, which defends them from remembrance of the paſt, or anticipation of the future. They lull themſelves in an enervate, and cowardly diſſipation, and inſtead of being happy, are only indolent.

That this ſtate is not a ſtate of happineſs, that it affords no real ſatisfaction to a reaſonable mind, thoſe who appear moſt engaged in it will, in their calmeſt moments readily confeſs. Thoſe among them, on whom Providence has beſtowed ſuch abilities as are neceſſary to the diſcovery of truth, and the diſtinction of appearance from reality (for, among the negligent and voluptuous, men of this character are ſometimes to be found,) have always owned, that their felicity is like that of a deep ſleep, from which they wake to care and ſorrow; or of a pleaſing dream, that affords them ſhort gratifications, of which the day deprives them; and that their pleaſures only differ from the phantoms of the night in this, that they leave behind them the pangs of guilt, with the vexation of diſappointment.

It may be imagined, that reaſonable beings muſt quickly diſcover how little ſuch ſatisfactions are adapted to their nature, and how neceſſary it is to change their meaſures, in order to the attainment of that happineſs which they deſire ; and in effect, it is generally found that few, except the young and unexperinced, content themſelves with ſenſual gratifications, and that men, as they advance in years, and improve their judgment by obſervation, always confeſs, by the alteration of their conduct, that mere voluptuouſneſs is not ſufficient to fill the deſires of the human mind.

They therefore ſhake off the lethargy of ſloth, forſake diverſion and amuſements, and engage in the purſuit of riches or of honours.——They employ thoſe hours, which were frequently ſuffered to paſs away unnumbered and unheeded, with the moſt ſolicitous application, and the moſt vigilant attention. They are no longer negligent of all that paſſes about them, no more careleſs of the opinions of mankind, or unconcerned with regard to cenſure or applauſe. They become anxious leſt any opportunity ſhould be loſt of improving

proving their fortunes, and lest they should give any occasion to reports which may injure their reputation, and obstruct their advancement. They constrain their words, their actions, and their looks, to obtain popularity, because they consider popularity as necessary to grandeur, and grandeur as the foundation of happiness.

But a very short experience teaches, what might indeed have been without the trial discovered by reflection, that perfect peace, that peace which is so much desired, is not to be found in wealth and greatness. He that succeeds in his first attempts is animated to new designs; new designs produce new anxieties and new opposition; and though the second attempt should be equally happy, it will be found, as soon as the transports of novelty have ceased, as soon as custom has made elevation familiar, that peace is yet to be sought, and that new measures must be taken for the attainment of that tranquillity, for which it is the nature of man to languish, and the want of which is ill supplied by hurry and confusion, by pomp and variety.

The same disposition which inclines any man to raise himself to a superiority

over

over others, will naturally excite the ſame deſires of greater elevation while he ſees any ſuperior to himſelf. There is therefore no hope that, by purſuing greatneſs, any man can be happy, or, at leaſt, this happineſs muſt be confined to one, becauſe only one can be without a ſuperior; and that one muſt ſurely feel his enjoyments very frequently diſturbed, when he remembers by how many the ſtation which he poſſeſſes is envied and coveted; when he reflects, how eaſily his poſſeſſions may be taken from him, perhaps by the ſame arts by which he attained them; how quickly the affections of the people may, by artful repreſentations of his conduct, be alienated from him; or how eaſily he may be deſtroyed by violence, and what numbers ambition or revenge may invite to deſtroy him.

There is at leaſt one conſideration, which muſt imbitter the life of him, who places his happineſs in his preſent ſtate; a conſideration that cannot be ſuppreſſed by any artful ſophiſtries, which the appetites or the ſenſes are always ready to ſuggeſt, and which it might be imagined not always poſſible to avoid in the moſt rapid

whirl

whirl of pleaſure, or the moſt inceſſant tumults of employment. As it is impoſſible for any man not to know, it may be well imagined difficult for him not to remember, that however ſurrounded by his dependents, however careſſed by his patrons, however applauded by his flatterers, or eſteemed by his friends, he muſt one day die; that though he ſhould have reaſon to imagine himſelf ſecured from any ſudden diminution of his wealth, or any violent precipitation from his rank or power, yet they muſt ſoon be taken away by a force, not to be reſiſted or eſcaped. He cannot but ſometimes think, when he ſurveys his acquiſitions, or counts his followers, *that this night his ſoul may be required of him*, and that he had applauded himſelf for the attainment of that which he cannot hope to keep long, and which, if it could make him happy while he enjoys it, is yet of very little value, becauſe the enjoyment muſt be very ſhort.

The ſtory of the great Eaſtern Monarch, who, when he ſurveyed his innumerable army from an eminence, wept at the reflection, that in leſs than a hundred years not one of all that multitude would remain, has been often mentioned ; becauſe the particular circumſtances, in which that remark occurred, naturally claim the thought, and ſtrike the imagination ; but every man that places his happineſs in external objects, may every day, with equal propriety make the ſame obſervations. Though he does not lead armies, or govern kingdoms, he may reflect, whenever he finds his heart ſwelling with any preſent advantage, that he muſt in a very ſhort time loſe what he ſo much eſteems, that in a year, a month, a day, or an hour, he may be ſtruck out from the book of life, and placed in a ſtate, where wealth or honour ſhall have no reſidence, and where all thoſe diſtinctions ſhall be for ever obliterated, which now engroſs his thoughts, and exalt his pride.

This reflection will ſurely be ſufficient to hinder that peace, which all terreſtrial enjoyments can afford, from being perfect. It ſurely will ſoon diſperſe thoſe meteors of happineſs that glitter in the eyes only of the thoughtleſs and the ſupine, and awaken him to a ſerious and rational enquiry, where real happineſs is to be found ; by what means man, whom the great Creator cannot be ſuppoſed to have formed without

out the power of obtaining happineſs, may ſet himſelf free from the ſhackles of anxiety with which he is incumbered; may throw off the load of terror which oppreſſes him, and liberate himſelf from thoſe horrors which the approach of death perpetually excites.

This he will immediately find only to be accompliſhed by ſecuring to himſelf the protection of a Being mighty to ſave; a Being whoſe aſſiſtance may be extended equally to all parts of his duration, who can equally defend him in the time of danger, and of ſecurity; in the tumults of the day, and the privacy of the night; in the time of tribulation, and in a time frequently more fatal, the time of wealth; and in the hour of death, and in the day of judgment. And when he has found the neceſſity of this ſovereign Protector, and humbled himſelf with a due conviction of his own impotence, he may at laſt find the only comfort which this life can afford him, by remembering, that this great, this unbounded Being, has informed us of the terms on which perfect peace is to be obtained, and has promiſed it to thoſe whoſe mind is ſtayed on him.

Since therefore the purſuit of perfect peace is the great, the neceſſary, the inevitable, buſineſs of human life; ſince this peace is to be attained by truſt in God, and by that only; ſince, without this, every ſtate is miſerable, and the voluptuous and the buſy are equally diſappointed; what can be more uſeful, than ſeriouſly to enquire, Firſt, what is meant, by this truſt in God, to which perfect peace is promiſed? and,

Secondly, By what means this truſt in God is to be attained?

Firſt, therefore, let us examine what is meant by this truſt in God, to which perfect peace is promiſed.

Truſt, when it is uſed on common occaſions, implies a kind of reſignation to the honeſty, or abilities of another. Thus we truſt a phyſician, when we obey his directions without knowing, or aſking, the particular reaſons for the methods which he enjoins. Thus we truſt a friend, when we commit our affairs to his management, without diſturbing ourſelves with any care concerning them. Thus we truſt a patron, when we ſerve him with diligence, without any other certainty of a reward than what our confidence in his generofity affords us. Thefe inftances may give us fome idea of that truft which we ought to repofe in God, but an idea, in the utmoft degree, grofs and inadequate. Our truft in God ought to differ from every other truft, as infinity differs from an atom. It ought to tranfcend every other degree of confidence, as its object is exalted above every degree of created excellence.

But, in our prefent ftate, it is impoffible to practife this, or any other duty, in perfection. We cannot truft God as we ought, becaufe we cannot know him as we ought. We know, however, that he is infinite in wifdom, in power, and in goodnefs ; that therefore he defigns the happinefs of all his creatures, that he cannot but know the proper means by which this end may be obtained, and that in the ufe of thefe means, as he cannot be miftaken, becaufe he is ominifcient, fo he cannot be defeated, becaufe he is almighty.

We know, therefore, that thofe whom he fhall protect cannot be in danger ; that neither the malice of wicked men, nor of wicked angels, can really injure them, but that perfecution and danger fhall only harrafs harraſs them for a time, and death ſet them free from diſappointment and from pain. He therefore that truſts in God will no longer be diſtracted in his ſearch after happineſs, for he will find it in a firm belief, that whatever evils are ſuffered to befal him will finally contribute to his felicity; and that by *ſtaying his mind upon the Lord, he will be kept in peace.*

But God has promiſed this protection, not indiſcriminately to all, but to thoſe only who endeavour to obtain it, by complying with the conditions which he has preſcribed; nor is the perfect peace, which the confidence of divine ſupport confers, to be hoped for but by thoſe who have obtained a well-grounded truſt in him; and, by the practice of his precepts, have ſtayed their minds upon him. It is therefore neceſſary to enquire,

Secondly, how this truſt is to be attained?

That there is a fallacious and precipitate truſt in God, a truſt which, as it is not founded upon God's promiſes, will in the end be diſappointed, we are informed by our Saviour himſelf. "Many will ſay unto me, in that day, Lord, Lord, have we

" not prophesied in thy name? and in thy
" name cast out devils? and in thy name
" have done many wonderful works? and
" then I will profess unto them, I never
" knew you. Depart from me, ye that
" work iniquity."

Those who contented themselves with believing, and professing Christianity, without obeying its precepts; those who while they call the great Author of our faith the Lord, their Master, and their God, and yet neglect his precepts and work iniquity, will be rejected by him at the last day, as those whom he has never known; those to whom his regard never was extended, and, notwithstanding the confidence with which they may claim his intercession, will not be distinguished by any favour from other sinners.

Trust in God, that trust to which perfect peace is promised, is to be obtained only by repentance, obedience, and supplication, not by nourishing in our own hearts a confused idea of the goodness of God, or a firm persuasion that we are in a state of grace; by which some have been deceived, as it may be feared, to their own destruction. We are not to imgaine ourselves ſafe, only becauſe we are not harraſſed with thoſe anxieties about our future ſtate with which others are tormented, but which are ſo far from being proofs of reprobation, that though they are often miſtaken by thoſe that languiſh under them, they are more frequently evidences of piety, and a ſincere and fervent deſire of pleaſing God. We are not to imagine, that God approves us becauſe he does not afflict us, nor, on the other hand, to perſuade ourſelves too haſtily that he afflicts us, becauſe he loves us. We are, without expecting any extraordinary effuſions of light, to examine our actions by the great and unchangeable rules of Revelation and Reaſon, *to do to others as we would that they ſhould do to us*, and to love God with all our heart, and expreſs that love by keeping his commandments.

He that hopes to find peace by truſting God muſt obey him; and when he has at any time failed in his obedience, which amongſt the beſt men will be very frequent, he muſt endeavour to reconcile God to him by repentance. He may then find another occaſion of exerciſing his truſt, by aſſuring himſelf, that *when the wicked for-*

ſakes

ſakes his way, and the unrighteous man his thoughts, and returns unto the Lord, he will have mercy upon him, and abundantly pardon.

This conſtant and devout practice is both the effect, and cauſe, of confidence in God. He will naturally pour out his ſupplications to the Supreme Being, who truſts in him, for aſſiſtance and protection; and he, who, with proper fervour and humility, proſtrates himſelf before God, will always riſe with an increaſe of holy confidence. By meditating on his own weakneſs, he will hourly receive new conviction of the neceſſity of ſoliciting the favour of his Creator; and by recollecting his promiſes, will confirm himſelf in the hope of obtaining what he deſires, and if, to ſecure theſe promiſes, he ſteadily practiſes the duties on which they depend, he will ſoon find his mind ſtayed on God, and be kept in perfect peace, becauſe he truſteth in him.

SERMON

SERMON XV.

JOB, xiv. 1.

Man that is born of a Woman, is of few days, and full of trouble.

THE poſition, contained in this ſentence neither requires, nor admits, proof or illuſtration; being too evident to be denied, and too clear to be miſtaken. That life is of ſhort continuance, and is diſquieted by many moleſtations, every man knows, and every man feels; andthe complaint, attributed to Job, in the hiſtory that is ſuppoſed to be the oldeſt book, of which mankind is in poſſeſſion, has been continued, and will be continued, through all human generations with endleſs repetitions.

But truth does not always operate in proportion to its reception. What has been always known, and very often ſaid, as it impreſſes the mind with no new images, excites

excites no attention, and is ſuffered to lie unheeded in the memory. Truth, poſſeſt without the labour of inveſtigation, like many of the general conveniencies of life, loſes its eſtimation by its eaſineſs of acceſs; nor is it always ſufficiently remembered, that the moſt valuable things are thoſe which are moſt plentifully beſtowed.

To conſider the ſhortneſs, or miſery, of life, is not an employment to which the mind recurs for ſolace or diverſion; or to which it is invited by any hope of immediate delight. It is one of thoſe intellectual medicines, of which the nauſeous eſſence often obſtructs the benefit, and which the faſtidiouſneſs of nature prompts us to refuſe. But we are told by Solomon, that there is *a time not only to laugh*, but *a time to weep*, and that it is good ſometimes *to enter into the houſe of mourning*. Many things which are not pleaſant may be ſalutary; and among them is the juſt eſtimate of human life, which may be made by all with advantage, though by few, very few, with delight. As it is the buſineſs of a traveller to view the way before him, whatever dangers may threaten, or difficulties obſtruct him, and however void may be the

proſpect

proſpect of elegance or pleaſure ; it is our duty, in the pilgrimage of life, to proceed with our eyes open, and to ſee our ſtate ; not as hope or fancy may delineate it, but as it has been in reality appointed by Divine Providence. From errors, to which, after moſt diligent examination, the frailty of our underſtandings may ſometimes expoſe us, we may reaſonably hope, that he, who knows whereof we are made, will ſuffer no irremediable evil to follow ; but it would be unreaſonable to expect, that the ſame indulgence ſhall be extended to voluntary ignorance ; or, that we ſhall not ſuffer by thoſe deluſions to which we reſign ourſelves by idleneſs or choice.

Nothing but daily experience could make it credible, that we ſhould ſee the daily deſcent into the grave of thoſe whom we love or fear, admire or deteſt ; that we ſhould ſee one generation paſt, and another paſſing, ſee poſſeſſions daily changing their owners, and the world, at very ſhort intervals, altering its appearance, and yet ſhould want to be reminded that life is ſhort ; or that we ſhould, wherever we turn our eyes, find misfortune and diſtreſs, and have our ears daily filled with the lamentations of miſery; that we ſhould often feel pain and ſickneſs, diſappointments and privations, and yet, at every reſpiration of momentary eaſe, or gleam of fugitive and uncertain joy, be elated beyond the true ſenſe of our condition, and need the voice of ſalutary admonition, to make us remember that life is miſerable.

But ſince the mind is always of itſelf ſhrinking from diſagreeable images, it is ſometimes neceſſary to recal them; and it may contribute to the repreſſion of many unreaſonable deſires, and the prevention of many faults and follies, if we frequently and attentively conſider,

Firſt, *That man born of a woman is of few days.* And,

Secondly, *That man born of a woman is full of trouble.*

As this changeable and uncertain life is only the paſſage to an immutable ſtate, and endleſs duration of happineſs or miſery; it ought never to be abſent from our thoughts, That *man born of a woman is of few days.*

The buſineſs of life is to work out our ſavation; and the days are few in which proviſion

proviſion muſt be made for eternity. ioy-
all ſtand upon the brink of the grave; o.
that ſtate, in which there is no repentance. He, whoſe life is extended to its utmoſt natural boundaries, can live but a little while; and that he ſhall be one of thoſe, who are comparatively ſaid to live long, no man can tell. Our days are not only few, but uncertain. The utmoſt that can be hoped, is little; and of that little, the greater part is denied to the majority of mankind.

Our time is ſhort, and our work is great, it is therefore, with the kindeſt earneſtneſs, enjoined by the Apoſtle, that we uſe all diligence to make our 'calling and election ſure.' But to an impartial ſurveyor of the ways of men, will it appear that the Apoſtle's ſummons has been heard or regarded? Let the moſt candid and charitable obſerver take cognizance of the general practice of the world; and what can be diſcovered but gay thoughtleſſneſs, or ſordid induſtry? It ſeems that to ſecure their calling and election is the care of few. Of the greater part it may be ſaid, that God is not in their thoughts. One forgets him in his buſineſs, another in his amuſe-

amuſements; one in eager enjoyment of to-day, another in ſolicitous contrivanc for to-morrow. Some die amidſt the gratifications of luxury, and ſome in the tumults of conteſts undecided, and purpoſes uncompleated. Warnings are multiplied, but without notice. *Wiſdom crieth in the ſtreets*, but is rarely heard.

Among thoſe that live thus wholly occupied by preſent things, there are ſome, in whom all ſenſe of religion ſeems extinct or dormant; who acquieſce in their own modes of life, and never look forward into futurity, but gratify themſelves within their own accuſtomed circle of amuſements, or limit their thoughts by the attainment of their preſent purſuit; and, without ſuffering themſelves to be interrupted by the unwelcome thoughts of death and judgement, congratulate themſelves on their prudence or felicity, and reſt ſatisfied with what the world can afford them; not that they doubt, but forget, a future ſtate; not that they diſbelieve their own immortality, but that they never conſider it.

To theſe men it is ſurely proper to repreſent the ſhortneſs of life, and to remind them

them that human acquiſitions and enjoyments are of few days; and that, whatever value may be aſſigned them by perverted opinions, they certainly want durability; that the fabric of terreſtrial happineſs has no foundation that can long ſupport it; that every hour, however enlivened by gaiety, or dignified by ſplendour, is a part ſubducted from the ſum of life; that age advances alike upon the negligent and anxious; and that every moment of delight makes delight the ſhorter.

If reaſon forbids us to fix our hearts upon things which we are not certain of retaining, we violate a prohibition ſtill ſtronger, when we ſuffer ourſelves to place our happineſs in that which muſt certainly be loſt; yet ſuch is all that this world affords us. Pleaſures and honours muſt quickly periſh, becauſe life itſelf muſt ſoon be at an end.

But if it be folly to delight in advantages of uncertain tenure and ſhort continuance, how great is the folly of preferring them to permanent and perpetual good! The man whoſe whole attention converges to this world, even if we ſuppoſe all his attempts proſperous, and all his wiſhes

granted,

granted, gains only empty pleaſure, which he cannot keep, at the coſt of eternal happineſs, which, if now neglected, he can never gain.

Let ſuch men therefore ſeriouſly reflect, that *man born of a woman is of few days, that he cometh forth like a flower, and is cut down; he fleeeth alſo as a ſhadow, and continueth not.*

Others there are on whom the intereſts of life have very ſtrong hold, who relax their thoughts by pleaſure, or enchain them by attention to wealth or power; and yet feel, with forcible conviction, the importance of futurity; in whoſe breaſts pious intentions are often budding, though they are quickly nipped by ſecular deſires. Such men ſuffer frequent diſturbance from the remonſtrances of reaſon, and the reproaches of conſcience, and do not ſet reaſon, or conſcience, at defiance, but endeavour to pacify them with aſſuaſive promiſes of repentance and amendment. They know that their preſent ſtate is dangerous, and therefore withdraw from it to a fancied futurity, in which whatever is crooked is to be made ſtraight; in which temptations are to be rejected, and paſſions to be conquer-

ed;

ed ; in which wiſdom and piety are to regulate the day ; in which every hour ſhall have its proper duty. The morning ſhall awake beneficence, and the evening ſtill the ſoul in gratitude and devotion.

Purpoſes like theſe are often formed, and often forgotten. When remorſe and ſolitude preſs hard upon the mind, they afford a temporary refuge, which like other ſhelters from a ſtorm, is forſaken, when the calm returns. The deſign of amendment is never diſmiſſed, but it reſts in the boſom without effect. The time convenient for ſo great a change of conduct is not yet come. There are hindrances which another year will remove ; there are helps which ſome near event will ſupply. Day riſes after day, and one year follows another, and produces nothing, but reſolutions without effect, and ſelf-reproach without reformation. The time deſtined for a new life lapſes in ſilence ; another time is fixed, and another lapſes ; but the ſame train of deluſion ſtill continues. He that ſees his danger, doubts not his power of eſcaping it ; and though he has deceived himſelf a thouſand times, loſes little of his own confidence. The indignation excited by the

paſt

paſt will, he thinks, ſecure him from any future failure. He retires to confirm his thoughts by meditation, and feels ſentiments of piety powerful within him. He ventures again into the ſtream of life, and finds himſelf again carried away by the current.

That to ſuch men, the ſenſe of their danger may not be uſeleſs; that they may no longer trifle with their own conviction; it is neceſſary to remind them, that *man is of few days*; that the life allotted to human beings is ſhort, and, while they ſtand ſtill in idle ſuſpence, is growing always ſhorter; that as this little time is ſpent well or ill, their whole future exiſtence will be happy, or miſerable; that he who begins the great work of his ſalvation early, has employment adequate to all his powers; and that he who has delayed it, can hope to accompliſh it only by delaying it no longer.

To him who turns his thoughts late to the duties of Religion, the time is not only ſhorter, but the work is greater. The more ſin has prevailed, with the more difficulty is its dominion reſiſted. Habits are formed by repeated acts, and therefore old habits are

are always ſtrongeſt. The mode of life, to which we have been accuſtomed, and which has entwined itſelf with all our thoughts and actions, is not quitted but with much difficulty. The want of thoſe vanities, which have hitherto filled the day, is not eaſily ſupplied. Accuſtomed pleaſures ruſh upon the imagination; the paſſions clamour for their uſual gratifications; and ſin, though reſolutely ſhaken off, will ſtruggle to regain its former hold.

To overcome all theſe difficulties, and overcome they muſt be, who can tell what time will be ſufficient! To diſburthen the conſcience, to reclaim the deſires, to combat ſenſuality, and repreſs vanity, is not the work of an hour, or of a day. Many conflicts muſt be endured, many falls recovered, and many temptations repelled. The arts of the enemy muſt be counteracted, and the deceitfulneſs of our own hearts detected, by ſteady and perſevering vigilance.

But how much more dreadful does the danger of delay appear, when it is conſidered, that not only life is every day ſhorter, and the work of reformation every day greater, but that ſtrength is every day leſs! It is not only comparatively leſſened by the long continuance of bad habits, but, if the greater part of our time be paſt, it is abſolutely leſs by natural decay. In the feebleneſs of declining life, reſolution is apt to languiſh; and the pains, the ſickneſs, and conſequent infirmities of age, too frequently demand ſo much care for the body, that very little care is, or can be, taken for the ſoul.

One conſideration more ought to be deeply impreſſed upon every ſluggiſh and dilatory lingerer. The penitential ſenſe of ſin, and the deſire of a new life, when they ariſe in the mind, are to be received as monitions excited by our merciful Father, as calls which it is our duty to hear, and our intereſt to follow; that to turn our thoughts away from them, is a new ſin; a ſin which, often repeated, may at laſt be puniſhed by dereliction. He that has been called often in vain, may be called no more; and when death comes upon him, he will recollect his broken reſolves with unutterable anguiſh; will wiſh for time to do what he has hitherto neglected, and lament in vain that his days are few.

The

The motives to religious vigilance, and diligence in our duties, which are afforded by ſerious meditation on the ſhortneſs of life, will receive aſſiſtance from the view of its miſery; and we are therefore to remember,

Secondly, That *man born of a woman is full of trouble.*

The immediate effect of the numerous calamities, with which human nature is threatened, or afflicted, is to direct our deſires to a better ſtate. When we know, that we are on every ſide beſet with dangers; that our condition admits many evils which cannot be remedied, but contains no good which cannot be taken from us; that pain lies in ambuſh behind pleaſure, and misfortune behind ſucceſs; that we have bodies ſubject to innumerable maladies and minds liable to endleſs perturbations; that our knowledge often gives us pain, by preſenting to our wiſhes ſuch felicity as is beyond our reach, and our ignorance is ſuch, that we often purſue, with eagerneſs, what either we cannot attain, or what, if we could attain it, diſappoints our hopes; that in the dead calm of ſolitude we are inſufficient to our own contentment, and that when wearineſs of ourſelves impels us to ſociety, we are often ill received ; when we perceive that ſmall offences may raiſe enemies, but that great benefits will not always gain us friends ; when we find ourſelves courted by intereſt, and forſaken by ingratitude ; when thoſe who love us fall daily into the grave, and we ſee ourſelves conſidered as aliens and ſtrangers by the riſing generation ; it ſeems that we muſt by neceſſity turn our thoughts to another life, where, to thoſe who are well prepared for their departure, there will no longer be pain or ſorrow.

Of the troubles incident to mankind, every one is beſt acquainted with his own ſhare. The miſeries of others may attract, but his own force, his attention ; and as man is not afflicted but for good purpoſes, that attention, if well regulated, will contribute to purify his heart.

We are taught in the hiſtory of Adam's fall, that trouble was the conſequence of ſin, and that miſery came into the world by diſobedience to the divine law. Sin and vexation are ſtill ſo cloſely united, that he who traces his troubles to their ſource will commonly find that his faults have pro-

duced

duced them ; and he is then to conſider his ſufferings as the mild admonitions of his heavenly Father, by which he is ſummoued to timely penitence. He is ſo far from having any reaſon to repine, that he may draw comfortable hopes of pardon and acceptance, and may ſay, with the higheſt reaſon, *It is good for me that I have been afflicted.*

It is, however, poſſible that trouble may, ſometime, be the conſequence of virtue. In times of perſecution this has often happened. Confeſſors of the truth have been puniſhed by exile, impriſonment, tortures, and death. The faithful have been driven from place to place, and thoſe *have wandered about in ſheep-ſkins and goat-ſkins, of whom the world was not worthy.* Heb. xi. v. 37.

Of ſuch violence Providence has now removed us from the danger ; but it is ſtill poſſible, that integrity may riſe enemies, and that a reſolute adherence to the right may not always be without danger. But evils of this kind bring their conſolation with them ; and their natural effect is to raiſe the eye and thoughts to him who certainly judges right ; and to excite ardent

dent desires of that state, where innocence and happiness shall always be united.

When we have leisure from our own cares to cast our eyes about us, and behold the whole creation groaning in misery, we must be careful that our judgement is not presumptuous, and that our charity is not regulated by external appearances. We are not to consider those on whom evil falls, as the outcasts of Providence; for though temporal prosperity was promised to the Jews, as a reward of faithful adherence to the worship of God; yet under the dispensation of the Gospel we are no where taught, that the good shall have any exemption from the common accidents of life, or that natural and civil evil shall not be equally shared by the righteous and the wicked.

The frequency of misfortunes, and universality of misery, may properly repress any tendency to discontent or murmur. We suffer only what is suffered by others, and often by those who are better than ourselves.

But the chief reason why we should send out our enquiries, to collect intelligence of

misery,

miſery, is that we may find opportunities of doing good. Many human troubles are ſuch as God has given man the power of alleviating. The wants of poverty may evidently be removed by the kindneſs of thoſe who have more than their own uſe requires. Of ſuch beneficence the time in which we live does not want examples; and ſurely that duty can never be neglected, to which ſo great rewards are ſo explicitly promiſed.

But the power of doing good is not confined to the wealthy. He that has nothing elſe to give, may often give advice. Wiſdom likewiſe has benefits in its power. A wiſe man may reclaim the vicious, and inſtruct the ignorant, may quiet the throbs of ſorrow, or diſentangle the perplexities of conſcience. He may compoſe the reſentful, encourage the timorous, and animate the hopeleſs. In the multifarious afflictions, with which every ſtate of human life is acquainted, there is place for a thouſand offices of tenderneſs; ſo that he, whoſe deſire it is to do good, can never be long without an opportunity; and every opportunity that Providence preſents, let

us

us ſeize with eagerneſs, and improve with diligence; remembering that we have no time to loſe, for *Man that is born of a Woman is of few days.*

SERMON XVI.

JOB i. 22.

In all this Job ſinned not, nor charged God fooliſhly.

SUCH is the weakneſs of human nature, that every particular ſtate, or condition, lies open to particular temptations. Different frames of conſtitution expoſe us to different paſſions, of equal danger to our virtue; and different methods of life, whether we engage in them by choice, or are forced upon them by neceſſity, have each of them their inlets to ſin, and their avenues to perdition.

The two oppoſite ſtates of proſperity and adverſity equally require our vigilance

and

and caution; each of them is a ſtate of conflict, in which nothing but unwearied reſiſtance can preſerve us from being overcome.

The vices of proſperity are well known, and generally obſerved. The haughtineſs of high rank, the luxury of affluence, and the cruelty of power, every man remarks, and no man palliates. So that they are the common ſubjects of invective.

But though compaſſion hinders men from being equally ſevere upon the faults of the unhappy and diſtreſſed, yet, as there always has been, and always will be, at leaſt an equal number in this, as in the other ſtate, it is proper that they likewiſe ſhould be warned of the crimes to which the circumſtances of their condition expoſe them, and furniſhed with ſuch reflections as may enable them to avoid them; that one miſery may not produce a greater, nor misfortune be the cauſe of wickedneſs.

There is no crime more incident to thoſe whoſe life is embittered with calamities, and whom afflictions have reduced to gloomineſs and melancholy, than that of repining at the determinations of Providence,

dence, or of *charging God foolishly.* They are often tempted to unseemly enquiries into the reason of his dispensations, and to expostulations about the justice of that sentence which condemns them to their present sufferings. They consider the lives of those whom they account happier than themselves, with an eye of malice and suspicion, and if they find them no better than their own, think themselves almost justified in murmuring at their own state.

But how widely they err from their duty, by giving way to discontent, and allowing themselves to dispute the reasonableness of those laws by which the great Creator governs the world, will appear,

First, by considering the attributes of God. And

Secondly, by reflecting on the ignorance of man.

First, by considering the attributes of God.

Many of the errors of mankind, both in opinion and practice, seem to arise originally from mistaken notions of the Divine Being, or at least from want of attention to the nature of those attributes which reason, as well as the holy scriptures, teaches

us

us to aſſign to him. A temporary forgetfulneſs has, for the time, the ſame effect as real ignorance, but has this advantage, that it is much more eaſily remedied ; ſince it is much leſs difficult to recollect our own ideas, than to obtain new ones. This is, I ſuppoſe, the ſtate of every man amongſt us who is betrayed by his impatience under afflictions to murmur at Heaven. He knows, when he reflects calmly, that the world is neither eternal, nor independent; that we neither were produced, nor are preſerved, by chance. But that Heaven and earth, and the whole ſyſtem of things, were created by an infinite and perfect Being, who ſtill continues to ſuperintend and govern them. He knows that this Great Being is infinitely wiſe, and infinitely good; ſo that the end which he propoſes muſt neceſſarily be the final happineſs of thoſe beings that depend upon him, and the means, by which he promotes that end, muſt undoubtedly be the wiſeſt and the beſt. All this he is ſufficiently convinced of, when he is awakened to recollection ; but his conviction is over-borne by the ſudden guſts of paſſion, and his impatience hurries him to wicked exclamations, before

fore he can recal to his mind thofe reafonings, which, if attended to, would ftifle every rebellious thought, and change his diftruft and difcontent into confidence and tranquillity.

It very nearly concerns every man, fince every man is expofed, by the nature of human things, to trouble and calamities, to provide againft the days of adverfity, by making fuch ideas familiar to his mind as may defend him againft any temptations to the fin of *charging God foolifhly*.

It is frequently obferved in common life, that fome favourite notion or inclination, long indulged, takes fuch an entire poffeffion of a man's mind, and fo engroffes his faculties, as to mingle thoughts perhaps he is not himfelf confcious of with almoft all his conceptions, and influence his whole behaviour. It will often operate on occafions with which it could fcarcely be imagined to have any connection, and will difcover itfelf, however it may lie concealed, either in trifling incidents, or important occurrences, when it is leaft expected or forefeen. It gives a particular direction to every fentiment and action, and carries

a man

a man ſorward, as by a kind of reſiſtleſs impulſe, or inſuperable deſtiny.

As this unbounded dominion of ideas, long entertained by the fancy, and naturalized to the mind, is a very ſtong argument againſt ſuffering ourſelves to dwell too long upon pleaſing dreams, or delightful falſehoods, or admitting any inordinate paſſion to inſinuate itſelf, and grow domeſtic; ſo it is a reaſon, of equal force, to engage us in a frequent, and intenſe meditation on thoſe important and eternal rules, which are to regulate our conduct, and rectify our minds; that the power of habit may be added to that of truth, that the moſt uſeful ideas may be the moſt familiar, and that every action of our lives may be carried on under the ſuperintendence of an over-ruling piety.

The man who has accuſtomed himſelf to conſider that he is always in the preſence of the Supreme Being, that every work of his hands is carried on, and every imagination of his heart formed, under the inſpection of his Creator, and his Judge, eaſily withſtands thoſe temptations which find a ready paſſage into a mind not guarded and ſecured by this awful ſenſe of the divine preſence.

He is not enticed by ill examples, becauſe the purity of God always occurs to his imagination ; he is not betrayed to ſecurity by ſolitude, becauſe he never conſiders himſelf as alone.

The two great attributes of our Sovereign Creator, which ſeem moſt likely to influence our lives, and, by conſequence moſt neceſſarily to claim our attention, are his juſtice and his mercy. Each of theſe may ſuggeſt conſiderations, very efficacious for the ſuppreſſion of wicked and unreaſonable murmurs.

The juſtice of God will not ſuffer him to afflict any man, without cauſe, or without retribution.——Whenever we ſuffer, therefore, we are certain, either that we have, by our wickedneſs, procured our own miſeries, or that they are ſent upon us as further trials of our virtue, in order to prepare us for greater degrees of happineſs. Whether we ſuppoſe ourſelves to ſuffer for the ſake of puniſhment or probation, it is not eaſy to diſcover with what right we repine.

If

If our pains and labours be only preparatory to unbounded ſelicity; if we are *perſecuted for righteouſneſs ſake*, or ſuffer by any conſequences of a good life; we ought to *rejoice and be exceeding glad*, and to glorify the goodneſs of God, who by uniting us in our ſufferings with Saints and Martyrs, will join us alſo in our reward.

But it is not uncharitable to believe of others, that this is not always the reaſon of their ſufferings, and certainly no man ought to believe it of himſelf, without a very ſevere and cautious examination, long continued, and often repeated; for nothing is more dangerous than ſpiritual pride. The man that eſteems himſelf a Saint will be in danger of relaxing his circumſpection, of ſtopping in his progreſs of virtue, and, if once he ſtops, of falling back into thoſe infirmities from which his imaginary exemption made him preſumptuous and ſupine. Every man therefore, when the hand of God is heavy upon him, muſt apply himſelf to an attentive, and exact retroſpection of his own life. He muſt enquire, if he has avoided all open enormities, and ſcandalous degrees of guilt; whether he is not puniſhed for ſome ſecret

crime

crime unknown to the world, and perhaps almoſt forgotten by himſelf; whether, in ſurveying himſelf, he does not overlook ſome favourite ſin, ſome criminal indulgence; or whether he has not ſatisfied himſelf with increaſing his devotions, inſtead of reforming his morals, or whether, from too much confidence in his morality, he has not been negligent of his devotions; and whether he has not contented himſelf with an imperfect and partial ſatisfaction for ſome injury done to his neighbour, when an adequate and compleat reparation was in his power.

To this enquiry he will be incited by remembering that God is juſt, that there is undoubtedly a reaſon for his miſery, which will probably be found in his own corruption. He will therefore, inſtead of murmuring at God, begin to examine himſelf; and when he has found the depravity of his own manners, it is more likely that he will admire the mercy, than complain of the ſeverity, of his Judge.

We have indeed ſo little right to complain of puniſhment, when it does not exceed the meaſure of the offence, that to bear it patiently hardly deſerves the name of virtue; but impatience under it is, in a high degree, foolish and criminal.

It is well known how partial every man is in his own cause, and therefore it is necessary to meditate much upon the justice of God, lest we be tempted to think our punishments too great for our faults; and, in the midst of our anguish and distress, *charge God foolishly.*

But we shall receive yet farther satisfaction from a frequent reflection on the *mercy* of God. We shall learn to consider him, not only as the Governor, but as the Father, of the universe; as a Being infinitely gracious, whose punishments are not inflicted to gratify any passion of anger, or revenge, but to awaken us from the lethargy of sin, and to recal us from the paths of destruction.

Every man has observed, that the greatest part of those who enjoy the pleasures of this life, without interruption or restraint, are either entirely forgetful of any other state, or at least very little solicitous about it. Men are easily intoxicated with pleasure, dazzled with magnificence, or elated with power. The most pathetic or rational discourse upon eternity has seldom

any

any laſting effect upon the gay, the young, the wealthy, and the proſperous. Even the Goſpel itſelf was firſt received by the poor.

The reaſon of this is not, becauſe Religion is beſt adapted to a gloomy and melancholy ſtate of the mind. For the truths of Religion are atteſted by evidence, which muſt be yielded to as ſoon as it is conſidered; and confirmed by proofs, which nothing but inattention can reſiſt. But to conſider, and weigh this evidence ſeriouſly and impartially, the mind muſt be abſtracted, in ſome meaſure, from the objects that ſurround us; objects that ſtrike us ſtrongly, not becauſe they are great, but becauſe they are near, while the views of futurity affect us but faintly, not becauſe they are unimportant, but becauſe they are diſtant.

A conſtant conviction of the mercy of God firmly implanted in our minds, will, upon the firſt attack of any calamity, eaſily induce us to reflect, that it is permitted by God to fall upon us, leſt we ſhould be too much enamoured of our preſent ſtate, and neglect to extend our proſpects into eternity.

Thus, by familiarizing to our minds the attributes of God, shall we, in a great measure, secure ourselves against any temptation to repine at his arrangements; but shall probably still more strengthen our resolution, and confirm our piety, by reflecting.

Secondly, On the ignorance of Man.

On egeneral method of judging, and determining upon the value, or excellence of things, is by comparing one with another. Thus it is, that we form a nation of wealth, greatness, or power. It is by comparing ourselves with others, that we often make an estimate of our own happiness, and even sometimes of our virtue. They who repine at the ways of Providence, repine often, not because they are miserable, but because they are not so happy as others; and imagine their afflictions dealt with a partial hand, not that they can conceive themselves free from guilt, but because they see, or think they see, others equally criminal, that suffer less. Should they be supposed to judge rightly of themselves and others, should it be conceived that, in rating their own excellencies, they are not misled by their self-love, or that they are not hindered by

envy

envy from difcerning the virtues of thofe whom they look upon as rivals for happinefs; yet unlefs they could prove, that the mercies which they have received, as below their merits, they have no reafon to complain. He that has more than he deferves is not to murmur merely becaufe he has lefs than another.

But when we judge thus confidently of others, we deceive ourfelves; we admit conjectures for certainties, and chimæras for realities. To determine the degrees of virtue and wickednefs in particular men, is the prerogative only of that Being that fearches the fecrets of the heart, that knows what temptations each man has refifted; how far the means of grace have been afforded him, and how he has improved or neglected them; that fees the force of every paffion, knows the power of every prejudice, attends to every conflict of the mind, and marks all the ftruggles of imperfect virtue. He only, who gave us our faculties and abilities, knows when we err by infurmountable ignorance, or when we deviate from the right by negligence or prefumption. He only, that knows every circumftance of life, and every motion of the

the mind, can tell how far the crimes, or virtues, of each man are to be puniſhed or rewarded. No man can ſay, that he is better than another, becauſe no man can tell, how far theother was enabled to reſiſt temptation, or what incidents might concur to overthrow his virtue. Nor are we able to decide, with much greater certainty, upon the happineſs of others. We ſee only the ſuperficies of men, without knowing what paſſes within. Splendour, equipage, and luxury, are not always accompanied by happineſs; but are more frequently the wretched ſolaces of a mind diſtracted with perplexities and haraſſed with terrors. Men are often driven, by reflection and remorſe, into the hurries of buſineſs, or of pleaſure, and fly from the terrifying ſuggeſtions of their own thoughts to banquets and to courts.

Proſperity and happineſs are very different, though by thoſe who undertake to judge of the ſtate of others they are always confounded. It is poſſible to know that another is proſperous, that his revenues increaſe, that his dependents grow more numerous, that his ſchemes ſucceed, and his reputation advances. But we cannot tell how much all these promote his happiness, because we cannot judge how much they may engage his care, or inflame his desires: how much he may fear his enemies, or suspect his friends. We know not how much this seeming felicity may be impaired by his folly, or his guilt; and therefore he that murmurs at the inequality of human happiness, or accuses Providence of partiality, forgets his own imperfections, and determines rashly, where he cannot judge.

Let every one then whom God shall visit with affliction humble himself before him, with steady confidence in his mercy, and unfeigned submission to his justice! Let him remember that his sins are the cause of his miseries, that his troubles are sent to awaken him to reflection, and that the evils of this life may be improved to his eternal advantage, if instead of adding sin to sin, and *charging God foolishly*, he applies himself seriously to the great work of self-examination and repentance.

For surely the frailty of this life, and the uncertainty of all human happiness, is proved by every view of the world about us, and every reflection upon ourselves.

Let not death arreſt us in a ſtate of mind unfit to ſtand the trial of eternal juſtice, or to obtain the privileges of infinite mercy! Let it not ſurpriſe us engaged in ſchemes of vanity, or wiſhes of empty pleaſure! Let death, which may ſeize us now, which will ſeize us at ſome time, equally terrible, find us, whenever it ſhall come, animated with the love of God, ſubmiſſive to his eternal will, and diffuſed in univerſal charity and benevolence to our brethren.

Let this inſtant begin a new life; and every future minute improve it! Then, in exchange for riches, honours, or ſenſual delights, we may obtain the tranquillity of a good conſcience, and that *peace of God which paſſeth all underſtanding.*

SERMON XVII.

EXODUS, xx. 16.

Thou ſhalt not bear falſe witneſs againſt thy neighbour.

NOTHING is more common than for men to make partial and abſurd diſtinctions between vices of equal enormity, and to obſerve ſome of the divine commands with great ſcrupulouſneſs; while they violate others, equally important, without any concern, or the leaſt apparent conſciouſneſs of guilt.

That to do our duty in part is better than entirely to diſregard it, cannot be denied; and he that avoids ſome crimes, from the fear of diſpleaſing God, is doubtleſs

leſs far more innocent than he that has thrown off all reſtraint, has forgotten the diſtinctions of good and evil, and complies with every temptation. But it is a very dangerous miſtake, to conceive that any man, by obeying one law, acquires the liberty of breaking another; or that all ſins, equally odious to God, or hurtful to men, are not, with equal care, to be avoided.

We may frequently obſerve, that men, who would abhor the thought of violating the property of another, by direct methods of oppreſſion or rapine, men, on all common occaſions, not only juſt, but kind and compaſſionate, willing to relieve the neceſſitous, and active in the protection of the injured, will nevertheleſs invade the characters of others with defamation and calumny, and deſtroy a reputation without remorſe.

If every day did not convince us, how little either good or bad men are conſiſtent with themſelves, it might be wondered, how men, who own their obligations to the practice of ſome duties, can overlook in themſelves the omiſſion of others equally important, and enjoined by the ſame authority; and that thoſe who avoid *theft*, because they are forbidden *to steal*, do not equally abstain from *calumny*, since they are no less forbidden *to bear false witness against their neighbour* ; a prohibition, of which I shall endeavour to explain the nature, and enforce the necessity by shewing,

First, What are the different senses, in which a man may be said *to bear false witness against his neighbour*.

Secondly, The enormity of the sin of *bearing false witness.*

Thirdly, What reflections may best enable us to avoid it.

The highest degree of guilt forbidden by this law of God, is false testimony in a literal sense, or deliberate and solemn perjury in a court of justice, by which the life of an innocent man is taken away, the rightful owner stripped of his possessions, or an oppressor supported in his usurpations. This is a crime that includes robbery and murder, sublimed to the highest state of enormity, and heightened with the most atrocious aggravations. He that robs or murders by this method, not only does it, by the nature of the action, with calmness and premeditation, but by making the name of God a ſanction to his wickedneſs. Upon this it is unneceſſary to dwell long, ſince men, arrived at this height of corruption, are ſcarcely to be reformed by argument, or perſuaſion; and indeed ſeldom ſuffer themſelves to be reaſoned with, or admoniſhed. It may be however proper to obſerve, that he who is ever ſo remotely the cauſe of any wickedneſs, if he really deſigns, and willingly promotes it, is guilty of that action in the ſame, or nearly the ſame, degree with the immediate perpetrator; and therefore he that ſuborns a falſe witneſs, or procures ſuch a one to be ſuborned, whether in his own cauſe, or in that of another, is guilty of the crime of perjury in its utmoſt extent.

Nor is that man only perjured, who delivers for truth what he certainly knows to be falſe; but he likewiſe that aſſerts what he does not know to be true. For as an oath taken implies, in the opinion of the magiſtrate who adminiſters it, a knowledge of the fact required to be proved, he that, by offering himſelf as an evidence, declares himſelf acquainted with what he is ignorant of, is guilty of bearing falſe witneſs, ſince, though what he ſwears ſhould

ſhould happen to be true, it is not true that he knew it.

Such remarks as theſe ſeem, at the firſt view, very trifling, becauſe they are obvious, and yet are made neceſſary by the conduct of mankind. Every man almoſt has had opportunities of obſerving, with what groſs and artleſs deluſions men impoſe upon themſelves; how readily they diſtinguiſh between actions, in the eye of juſtice and of reaſon, equally criminal; how often they hope to elude the vengeance of heaven, by ſubſtituting others to perpetrate the villainies they contrive; how often they mock God by groundleſs excuſes; and how often they voluntarily ſhut their eyes, to leap into deſtruction.

There is another ſenſe in which a man may be ſaid to *bear falſe witneſs againſt his neighbour*, a lower degree of the crime forbidden in the text, a degree, in which multitudes are guilty of it; or, rather, from which ſcarcely any are entirely free. He, that attacks the reputation of another by calumny, is doubtleſs, according to the malignity of the report, chargeable with the breach of this commandment.

Yet this is ſo univerſal a practice, that

it is ſcarcely accounted criminal, or numbered among thoſe ſins which require repentance. Defamation is become one of the amuſements of life, a curſory part of converſation and ſocial entertainment.— Men ſport away the reputation of others, without the leaſt reflection upon the injury which they are doing, and applaud the happineſs of their own invention, if they can increaſe the mirth of a feaſt, or animate conviviality, by ſlander and detraction.

How it comes to paſs, that men do not perceive the abſurdity of diſtinguiſhing in ſuch a manner between themſelves and others, as to conceive that conduct innocent in themſelves, which in others, they would make no difficulty of condemning, it is not eaſy to tell. Yet it is apparent, that every man is ſufficiently ſenſible, when his own character is attacked, of the cruelty and injuſtice of calumny; and it is not leſs evident, that thoſe will animadvert, with all the wantonneſs of malice, upon the moral irregularities of others, whom the leaſt reflection upon their own lives kindles into fury, and exaſperates to the utmoſt ſeverities of revenge.

To

To invent a defamatory falsehood, to rack the invention for the sake of disguising it with circumstances of probability, and propagate it industriously, till it becomes popular, and takes root in the minds of men, is such a continued act of malice, as nothing can palliate.

Nor will it be a sufficient vindication to alledge, that the report, though not wholly, yet in part is true, and that it was no unreasonable suspicion that suggested the rest. For, if suspicion be admitted for certainty, every man's happiness must be entirely in the power of those bad men, whose consciousness of guilt makes them easily judge ill of others, or whom a natural, or habitual jealousy inclines to imagine frauds or villainies, where none are intended. And if small failings may be aggravated at the pleasure of the relator, who may not, however cautious, be made infamous and detestable? A calumny, in which falsehood is complicated with truth, and malice is assisted by probability, is more dangerous, but therefore less innocent, than unmixed forgery, and groundless invectives.

Neither is the first author only of a calumny a *false witness against his neighbour*, but

but he likewiſe that diſſeminates and promotes it; ſince without his aſſiſtance, it would periſh as ſoon as it is produced, would evaporate in the air without effect, and hurt none but him that uttered it. He that blows a fire for the deſtruction of a city, is no leſs an incendiary than he that kindled it. And the man that imagines he may, without a crime, circulate a calumny which he has received from another, may, with equal reaſon, conceive, that though it be murder to prepare poiſons, it may be innocent to diſperſe them.

Many are the pleas and excuſes, with which thoſe, who cannot deny this practice, endeavour to palliate it. They frequently aſſert, in their own juſtification, that they do not know the relation, which they hand about, to be falſe. But to thoſe it may be juſtly replied, that before they ſpread a report to the prejudice of others, they ought, if not to know that it is true, at leaſt to believe it upon ſome reaſonable grounds. They ought not to aſſiſt a randum whiſper, or drive forward a flying tale; they ought not eagerly to catch at an opportunity of hurting, or add weight to a blow which may perhaps be undeſerved.

It may happen indeed, that a calumny may be ſupported by ſuch teſtimony, and connected with ſuch probabilities, as may deceive the circumſpect and juſt; and the reporter, in ſuch caſes, is by no means to be charged with bearing falſe witneſs; becauſe to believe and diſbelieve is not in our power; for there is a certain degree of evidence, to which a man cannot but yield. He, therefore, who is deceived himſelf, cannot be accuſed of deceiving others, and is only ſo far blameable, as he contributed to the diſhonour or prejudice of another, by ſpreading his faults without any juſt occaſion, or lawful cauſe. For to relate reproachful truths, only for the pleaſure of depreſſing the reputation of our neighbour, is far from being innocent. The crime indeed doth not fall under the head of calumny, but only differs from it in the falſehood, not in the malice.

There is another occaſion made uſe of, by which, if this fault could eſcape from cenſure, many others might enjoy the ſame advantage. It is urged by ſome, that they do not adopt the tale, 'till it is generally received, and only promote what they cannot hinder. But how muſt wickedneſs be controuled, if its prevalence be a reaſon for compliance ? Is it equitable and juſt to coaleſce with oppreſſors, becauſe they are already too powerful for the injured to reſiſt ? Thus any man might vindicate rebellion, by affirming that he did not join with the rebels, 'till they were already numerous enough to dethrone their prince. Thus a man may exempt himſelf from blame, for betraying his truſt, and ſelling his country, by alledging that others had already ſold it, and he only entered into the combination, that he might ſhare the reward of perfidy. But it requires few arguments to ſhew the folly of ſuch pleas as theſe. It is the duty of every man to regulate his conduct, not by the example of others, or by his own ſurmiſes, but by the invariable rules of equity and truth. Wickedneſs muſt be oppoſed by ſome, or virtue would be entirely driven out of the world. And who muſt oppoſe it in extremities, if, as it increaſes more, it be leſs criminal to yield without reſiſtance? If this excuſe will vindicate one man, it will vindicate another; and no

man

man will be found, who is obliged to maintain a poſt, from which others may fly without a crime, and to endeavour to reform the world, by which it is no reproach to be vitiated. If this reaſoning were juſt, there might be a ſtate of general depravity, in which wickedneſs might loſe its guilt, ſince every man might be led away by predominant corruption, and the univerſality of vice become its own defence.

In ſuch a ſituation indeed, there is a neceſſity for an uncommon firmneſs and reſolution to perſiſt in the right, without regard to ridicule on the one hand, or intereſt on the other. But this reſolution muſt be ſummoned; we muſt call up all our ſtrength, and awaken all our caution, and in defiance of iniquity, however warranted by faſhion, or ſupported by power, maintain an unſhaken integrity, and reproach the world by a good example, if we cannot amend it.

There is yet another way, by which we may partake, in ſo me meaſure, of the ſin of *bearing falſe witneſs.* That he, who does not hinder the commiſſion of a crime, involves himſelf in the guilt, cannot be denied ; and that his guilt is yet more flagrant, if, instead of obstructing, he encourages it, is equally evident. He therefore that receives a calumny with applause, or listens to it with a silent approbation, must be at least chargeable with conniving at wrong, which will be found no trivial accusation, when we have considered,

Secondly, the enormity of the sin of *bearing false witness.*

The malignity of an offence arises, either from the motives that prompted it, or the consequences produced by it.

If we examine the sin of calumny by this rule, we shall find both the motives and consequences of the worst kind. We shall find its causes and effects concurring to distinguish it from common wickedness, and rank it with those crimes that pollute the earth, and blacken human nature.

The most usual incitement to defamation is envy, or impatience of the merit, or success, of others ; a malice raised not by any injury received, but merely by the sight of that happiness which we cannot attain. This is a passion, of all others most hurtful and contemptible ; it is pride com-

plicated

plicated with lazineſs; pride which inclines us to wiſh ourſelves upon the level with others, and lazineſs which hinders us from purſuing our inclinations with vigour and aſſiduity. Nothing then remains but that the envious man endeavour to ſtop thoſe, by ſome artifice, whom he will not ſtrive to overtake, and reduce his ſuperiors to his own meanneſs, ſince he cannot riſe to their elevation. To this end he examines their conduct with a reſolution to condemn it; and, if he can find no remarkable defects, makes no ſcruple to aggravate ſmaller errors, 'till, by adding one vice to another, and detracting from their virtues by degrees, he has diveſted them of that reputation which obſcured his own, and left them no qualities to be admired or rewarded.

Calumnies are ſometimes the offspring of reſentment. When a man is oppoſed in a deſign which he cannot juſtify, and defeated in the perſecution of ſchemes of tyranny, extortion, or oppreſſion, he ſeldom fails to revenge his overthrow by blackening that integrity which effected it. No rage is more fierce than that of a villain diſappointed of thoſe advantages which

which he has purſued by a long train of wickedneſs. He has forfeited the eſteem of mankind, he has burthened his conſcience, and hazarded his future happineſs, to no purpoſe, and has now nothing to hope but the ſatisfaction of involving thoſe, who have broken his meaſures, in misfortunes and diſgrace. By wretches like theſe it is no wonder if the vileſt arts of detraction are practiſed without ſcruple, ſince both their reſentment and their intereſt direct them to depreſs thoſe, whoſe influence and authority will be employed againſt them.

But what can be ſaid of thoſe who, without being impelled by any violence of paſſion, without having received any injury or provocation, and without any motives of intereſt, vilify the deſerving and the worthleſs without diſtinction; and, merely to gratify the levity of temper and incontinence of tongue, throw out aſperſions equally dangerous with thoſe of virulence and enmity?

Theſe always reckon themſelves, and are commonly reckoned by thoſe whoſe gaity they promote, among the benevolent, the candid, and the humane; men without

out gall or malignity, friends to good humour, and lovers of a jeſt. But, upon a more ſerious eſtimation, will they not be, with far greater propriety, claſſed with the cruel and the ſelfiſh wretches that feel no anguiſh at ſacrificing the happineſs of mankind to the loweſt views, to the poor ambition of excelling in ſcurrility? To deſerve the exalted character of humanity and good-nature, a man muſt mean *well*; it is not ſufficient to mean *nothing*. He muſt act and think with generous views, not with a total diſregard of all the conſequences of his behaviour. Otherwiſe, with all his wit and all his laughter, what character can he deſerve, but that of *the fool, who ſcatters fire-brands, arrows, and death, and ſays, am I not in ſport?*

The conſequences of this crime, whatever be the inducements to commit it, are equally pernicious. He that attacks the reputation of another, invades the moſt valuable part of his property, and perhaps the only part which he can call his own. Calumny can take away what is out of the reach of tyranny and uſurpation, and what may enable the ſufferer to repair the injuries received from the hand of oppreſſion.

The

The perſecutions of power may injure the fortune of a good man; but thoſe of calumny muſt complete his ruin.

Nothing can ſo much obſtruct the progreſs of virtue, as the defamation of thoſe that excel in it. For praiſe is one motive, even in the beſt minds, to ſuperior and diſtinguiſhing degrees of goodneſs; and therefore he that reduces all men to the ſame ſtate of infamy, at leaſt deprives them of one reward which is due to merit, and takes away one incitement to it. But the effect does not terminate here. Calumny deſtroys that influence, and power of example, which operates much more forcibly upon the minds of men, than the ſolemnity of laws, or the fear of puniſhment. Our natural and real power is very ſmall; and it is by the aſcendant which he has gained, and the eſteem in which he is held, that any man is able to govern others, to maintain order in ſociety, or to perform any important ſervice to mankind, to which the united endeavours of numbers are required. This aſcendant, which when conferred upon bad men by ſuperiority of riches, or hereditary honour, is frequently made uſe of to corrupt and deprave the world, to juſtify debauchery, and ſhelter villainy, might be employed, if it were to be obtained only by deſert, to the nobleſt purpoſes. It might diſcountenance vanity and folly; it might make the faſhion cooperate with the laws, and reform thoſe upon whom reaſon and conviction have no force.

Calumny differs from moſt other injuries in this dreadful circumſtance. He who commits it, never can repair it. A falſe report may ſpread, where a recantation never reaches; and an accuſation muſt certainly fly faſter than a defence, while the greater part of mankind are baſe and wicked. The effects of a falſe report cannot be determined, or circumſcribed. It may check a Hero in his attempts for the promotion of the happineſs of his country, or a Saint in his endeavours for the propagation of truth.

Since therefore this ſin is ſo deſtructive to mankind, and, by conſequence, ſo deteſtable in the ſight of God, it is neceſſary that we enquire,

Thirdly, What reflections may beſt enable us to avoid it.

The

The way to avoid effects is to avoid the causes. Whoever, therefore would not be tempted *to bear false witness*, must endeavour to suppress those passions which may incite him to it. Let the envious man consider, that by detracting from the character of others, he in reality adds nothing to his own; and the malicious man, that nothing is more inconsistent with every law of God, and institution of men, than implacability and revenge.

If men would spend more time in examining their own lives, and inspecting their own characters, they would have less leisure, and less inclination, to remark with severity upon others. They would easily discover, that it will not be for their advantage to exasperate their neighbour, and that a scandalous falsehood may be easily revenged by a reproachful truth.

It was determined by our blessed Saviour in a case of open and uncontested guilt, that *he who was without fault*, should *cast the first stone*. This seems intended to teach us compassion even to the failings of bad men; and certainly that religion which extends so much indulgence to the bad, as to restrain us from the utmost ri-

gour

gour of punishment, cannot be doubted to require that the good should be exempted from calumny and reproach.

Let it be always remembered, that charity is the height of religious excellence; and that it is one of the characteristics of this virtue, that it *thinketh no ill of others!*

SERMON XVIII.

(PREACHED AT ASHBOURN.)

I CORINTHIANS, vi. 8.

Nay, you do wrong and defraud, and that your Brethren.

TO ſubdue paſſion, and regulate deſire, is the great taſk of man, as a moral agent; a taſk, for which natural reaſon, however aſſiſted and enforced by human laws, has been found inſufficient, and which cannot be performed but by the help of Religion.

The paſſions are divided by moraliſts into iraſcible and concupiſcible; the paſſions of reſentment, and the paſſions of deſire. The danger of the iraſcible paſſions, the miſchiefs of anger, envy, and revenge, every man knows, by evil which he has felt,

felt, or evil which he has perpetrated. In their lower degrees, they produce brutality, outrage, contumely, and calumny; and, when they are inflamed to the utmoſt, have too often riſen to violence and bloodſhed.

Of theſe paſſions, the miſchief is ſometimes great, but not very frequent; for we are taught to watch and oppoſe them, from our earlieſt years. Their malignity is univerſally known, and as univerſally dreaded. The occaſions; that can raiſe them high, do not often occur and when they are raiſed, if there be no immediate opportunity of gratifying them they yield to reaſon, and perſuaſion, or ſubſide by the ſoothing influence of time.

Of the iraſcible paſſions, the direct aim, and preſent purpoſe, is the hurt, or miſery of another; of the concupiſcible paſſions, the proper motive is our own good. It is therefore no reproach to human nature, that the concupiſcible paſſions are more prevalent; for, as it is more natural, it is more juſt, to deſire our own good, than another's evil.

The deſire of happineſs is inſeparable from a rational being, acquainted, by experience, with the various gradations of pain and pleaſure. The knowledge of different degrees of happineſs ſeems neceſſary to the excitement of deſire, and the ſtimulation of activity. He that had never felt pain, would not fear it, nor uſe any precaution to prevent it. He who had been always equally at eaſe, would not know, that his condition admitted any improvement, and therefore could have no end to purſue, or purpoſe to proſecute. But man, in his preſent ſtate, knowing of how much good he is capable, and to how many evils he is expoſed, has his mind perpetually employed, in defence, or in acquiſition, in ſecuring that which he has, or attaining that which, he believes, he either does, or ſhall, want.

He that deſires happineſs muſt neceſſarily deſire the means of happineſs, muſt wiſh to appropriate, and accumulate, whatever may ſatisfy his deſires. It is not ſufficient to be without want. He will try to place himſelf beyond the fear of want; and endeavour to provide future gratifications for future wiſhes, and lay up in ſtore future proviſions for future neceſſities.

It

It is by the effect of this care to provide againſt the evils, and to attain the bleſſings, of life, that human ſociety has its preſent form. For this purpoſe profeſſions are ſtudied, and trades learned; dangers are encountered, and labour endured. For this reaſon every man educates his ſon in ſome uſeful art, which, by making him neceſſary to others, may oblige others to repay him what is neceſſary to himſelf. The general employment of mankind is to increaſe pleaſure, or remove the preſſure of pain. Theſe are the vital principles of action, that fill ports with ſhips, ſhops with manufactures, and fields with buſbandmen, that keep the ſtateſman diligent in attendance, and the trader active in his buſineſs.

It is apparently the opinion of the civilized world, that he who would be happy muſt be rich. In riches the goods of life are compendiouſly contained. They do not enlarge our own perſonal powers; but they enable us to employ the powers of others for our advantage. He who cannot make what he wants, will however eaſily procure it, if he can pay an artiſt. He who ſuffers any remediable inconvenience, needs

needs not to ſuffer it long, if he can reward the labour of thoſe who are able to remove it. Riches will make an ignorant man prudent by another's wiſdom, and a weak man vigorous by another's ſtrength. It can, therefore, be no wonder, that riches are generally deſired; and that almoſt every man is buſy, through his whole life, in gaining, or in keeping them, for himſelf, or his poſterity.

As there is no deſire ſo extenſive, or ſo continual in its exertions, that poſſeſſes ſo many minds, or operates with ſuch reſtleſs activity; there is none that deviates into greater irregularity, or more frequently corrupts the heart of man, than the wiſh to enlarge poſſeſſion and accumulate wealth.

In a diſcourſe, intended for popular inſtruction, it would be of little utility to mention the ambition of Kings, and diſplay the cruelty of Conquerors. To ſlaughter thouſands in a day, to ſpread deſolation over wide and fertile regions, and to carry rapine and deſtruction indiſcriminately from one country to another, can be the crime only of thoſe few who have ſceptres in their hands; and, even among them, the wantonnefs of war is not very common in our days. But it is a fufficient evidence of the power of intereft, that fuch acts fhould ever have been perpetrated; that there could ever be any man, willing to augment his wealth, or extend his power, by flaughter and devaftation; or able to perfuade himfelf, that he might purchafe advantages, which he could enjoy only in imagination, at the expence of the lives of thoufands of his fubjects, as well as his adverfaries; of adverfaries that never had injured, or offended him, and of fubjects whom it was his duty and his engagement to preferve and to protect.

Nor is it neceffary to mention crimes, which are commonly found amongft the loweft of mankind, the crimes of robbery and theft. For, though they are too common, their enormity is fufficiently underftood by the laws which are enacted againft them, and fufficiently menaced by the terrors which thofe laws hold out. They are fo apparently deftructive of focial fecurity, their confequences are fo eafily perceived, and their perniciousnefs fo generally acknowledged, that to be fufpected of them is to be infamous; and to be detected

tected in the commiſſion of them is to be expoſed to puniſhment, and often to death.

But there is another mode of injuring the property of others, and of gaining unjuſt advantages, which, though not equally liable, at all times, to puniſhment, with theft and robbery, is, in its own nature, equally criminal, and perhaps more pernicious; therefore, equally open to the cenſures of reaſon and religion. This ſpecies of guilt is diſtinguiſhed by the appellation of *fraud*; a word which, when uttered, really excites a due degree of deteſtation, and which thoſe, who practice it, perhaps diſguiſe to their conſciences by ſtill ſofter terms.

But that ſuch diſguiſes may deceive the ſoul no longer; and that what is univerſally miſchievous may be totally abhorred; I ſhall endeavour to ſhew,

Firſt, The nature of *fraud*, and the temptations to practiſe it.

Secondly, How much it is contrary to the rules of religion, and how much it obſtructs the happineſs of the world.

The nature of fraud, as diſtinct from other violations of right or property, ſeems to conſiſt in this, that the man injured is induced to concur in the act by which the injury is done. Thus, to take away any thing valuable, without the owner's knowledge, is a *theft*; to take it away, against his consent, by threats or force, is a *robbery*; to borrow it, without intention of returning it, is a *fraud*, because the owner consents to the act, by which it passed out of his own hands.

All *fraud*, therefore, supposes deceit, either in the affirmation of what is false, or the suppression of what is true; for no man willingly wrongs himself. He must be deceived, either by false appearances of the present, or by false promises of the future, by a display of fictitious advantages, or an artful concealment of certain inconveniences.

As it often happens, that in committing a *fraud*, or persuading a man to injure himself, a considerable degree of skill and dexterity is required; the fraudulent are often considered, by themselves and others, as possessing uncommon powers of understanding, so that, though the act itself is blamed, the artifice is admired. Conscience is overpowered by vanity, and the

shame

ſhame of guilt is loſt in the pride of ſubtlety and acuteneſs.

It is to be feared, that the ſcience of over-reaching is too cloſely connected with lucrative commerce. There are claſſes of men who do little leſs than profeſs it, and who are ſcarcely aſhamed, when they are detected in impoſture. Such men live indeed without reputation. They are conſidered as exerciſing diſhonourable employments, but they are ſtill tolerated; and, however they may be deſpiſed, are very rarely puniſhed. The whole practice of buying and ſelling is indeed replete with temptation, which even a virtuous mind finds it difficult to reſiſt. * *A merchant ſhall hardly keep himſelf from doing wrong, and an huckſter ſhall not be freed from ſin.*

† *Many have ſinned for a ſmall matter; and he that ſeeketh for abundance, will turn his eyes away. As a nail ſticketh faſt between the joinings of the ſtones, ſo doth ſin ſtick cloſe between buying and ſelling.*

Such is the cenſure of the Son of Sirach, which ſurely cannot be heard without alarm and terror.

* Eccleſiaſticus, xxvi. 29.

† Eccleſiaſticus, xxvii. 1, 2.

It

It is, however, by no means to be admitted, that all trade is neceſſarily fraudulent, or that all traders are diſhoneſt. Every kind of life has its peculiar dangers, which the negligent incur, and the wiſe eſcape. The danger of a trader, like that of others may be avoided by reſolution, vigilance, and prayer, by a conſtant reference of his actions to his eternal intereſt, and by the help of God, diligently implored.

That the neceſſity of this vigilance may be more ſtrongly recommended, it is fit that we conſider,

Secondly, How much the practice of *fraud* is contrary to religion, and how much it obſtructs the happineſs of the world.

The great rule, by which religion regulates all tranſactions between one man and another, is, that every man *ſhould do to others what he would expect that others*, in the ſame caſe, *ſhould do to him.* This rule is violated in every act of fraud. For, however the *children of the world* may forgive, or applaud, themſelves, when they *practice fraud*, they complain very loudly, when they *ſuffer* it. They then can clearly diſcern its baſeneſs, and its miſchief; and

diſcover,

diſcover, that nothing deſerves praiſe but purity and goodneſs.

The crime of *fraud* has this aggravation, that it is generally an abuſe of confidence. Robberies of violence are committed commonly upon thoſe, to whom the robber is unknown. The lurking thief takes indiſcriminately what comes by chance within his reach. But deceit cannot be practiſed, unleſs by ſome previous treaty, and gradual advance, by which diſtruſt is diſſipated, and an opinion of candour and integrity excited. *Fraud*, therefore, neceſſarily diſguiſes life with ſolicitude and ſuſpicion. He that has been deceived, knows not afterwards whom he can truſt, but grows timorous, reſerved, afraid alike of enemies and friends ; and loſes, at leaſt, part of that benevolence which is neceſſary to an amiable and virtuous character.

Fraud is the more to be ſuppreſſed by univerſal deteſtation, as its effects can ſcarcely be limited. A thief ſeldom takes away what can much impoveriſh the loſer ; but by *fraud*, the opulent may at once be reduced to indigence, and the proſperous diſtreſſed ; the effects of a long courſe of induſtry may be ſuddenly annihilated, the provision made for age may be withdrawn, and the inheritance of posterity intercepted.

For the particular application of this doctrine, I am sorry, that my native place should afford an opportunity. But since this society has called me to stand here before them, I hope no man will be offended, that I do my duty with fidelity and freedom. Truth requires, that I warn you against a species of fraud, sometimes found amongst you, and that of a very shameful and oppressive kind. When any man, whose contributions have had their due part in raising the fund for occasional relief, is reduced by disease, or hurt, to want the support which he has, perhaps, for many years, supposed himself gradually accumulating against the day of distress; and for which he has denied himself many gratifications; at the time, when he expects the beneficial effects of his prudence and parsimony; at that very time, every artifice is used to defeat his claim, and elude his right. He declares himself perhaps unable to work, by which nothing more can reasonably be meant, than that he is no longer capable of labour equal to

his

his livelihood. This man is found employing the remains of his ſtrength in ſome little office. For this ſurely he deſerves to be commended. But what has been the conſequence? He has been conſidered as an impoſtor, who claims the benefit of the fund by counterfeited incapacity; and that feeble diligence, which, among reaſonable and equitable men, gives him a title to eſteem and pity, is miſapplied, and miſrepreſented into a pretence for depriving him of his right, and this done by judges, who vainly imagine they ſhall be benefited themſelves by their own wicked determination.

It is always to be remembered, that a demand of ſupport from your common fund is not a petition for charity, but a claim to juſtice. The relief thus demanded, is not a gift, but a debt. He that receives it, has firſt purchaſed it. The denial of it, therefore, is a fraud and a robbery; and fraud ſo much the more atrocious and deteſtable, as, by its nature, it muſt always be practiſed on the poor. When this ſuccour is required, there is no place for favour, or for reſentment. What is due muſt be paid, becauſe it is due. Other conſiderations have here no weight. The amiable and the perverſe, the good and the bad, have an equal right to the performance of their contract. He that has truſted the ſociety with his money, cannot, without breach of faith, be denied that payment, which, when he payed his contribution, was ſolemnly ſtipulated.

It has been always obſerved by the wiſe, that it is every man's real intereſt to be honeſt ; and he who practices *fraud*, to the injury of others, ſhews, at the ſame time, how *fraud* may be practiſed againſt himſelf. Thoſe who have been forward in watching the ſteps of others, and have objected to payment when it was required, may live to be themſelves watched, and excluded by a precedent, which their own fraudulence, or malice, has incited them to eſtabliſh. They will then feel the folly of wickedneſs, and know the neceſſity of providing againſt the day of calamity by innocence and integrity ; they will wiſh that they could claim the kindneſs of others, as a recompence for kindneſs formerly exhibited by themſelves.

Fraud is the more hurtful, becauſe the wrong is often without redreſs. As he that is wronged by fraudulent practices muſt always concur in the act that injured

him ;

him; it is not always eaſy to aſcertain the exact limits of his agency, ſo as to know preciſely how far he was deceived. This, at leaſt, is ſeldom to be done without an enquiry and diſcuſſion, liable to many legal delays, and eludible by many artifices. The redreſs, therefore, is often more pernicious than the injury; and while the robber lurks in ſecret, or flies for his life, the man of *fraud* holds up his head with confidence, enjoys the fruits of his iniquity with ſecurity, and bids defiance to detection and to puniſhment.

But this triumph, however he may eſcape human judicatures, muſt end with his life. The time will come, and will come quickly, when he that has defrauded his neighbour muſt ſtand before the Judge of all the earth, a Judge whom he cannot deceive; and before whom, whatever he has taken wrongfully, without reſtitution, and without repentance, will lie heavy on his ſoul.

"Let him, therefore, that has ſtolen, ſteal no more! let him who has gained by *fraud*, repent and reſtore, and live and die in the exercise of honeſty!

SERMON XIX

2 CORINTHIANS, ix. 7.

Every man according as he purpoſeth in his heart ſo let him give, not grudgingly, or of neceſſity, for God loveth a cheerful giver.

THE frequency with which the duty of alms-giving has of late been recommended; the perſpicuity with which it has, on many occaſions, been explained; the force of argument by which its neceſſity has been proved to the reaſon, and the ardour of zeal with which it has been impreſſed upon the paſſions; make it reaſonable to believe, that it is now generally underſtood, and that very few of thoſe, who frequent the public worſhip, and attend with proper diligence to inſtruction, can receive much

much information, with regard to the excellence and importance of this virtue.

But as moſt of the crimes and miſeries of our lives ariſe rather from negligence, than ignorance; as thoſe obligations which are beſt known, are ſometimes, from the ſecurity to which the conſciouſneſs of our knowledge naturally betrays us, moſt eaſily forgotten, and as the impreſſions which are made upon the heart, however ſtrong or durable they may at firſt appear, are eaſily weakened by time, and effaced by the perpetual ſucceſſion of other objects, which crowd the memory, and diſtract the attention; it is neceſſary that this great duty ſhould be frequently explained, that our ardour ſhould be rekindled by new motion, our conviction awakened by new perſuaſions, and our minds enlightened by frequent repetitions of the inſtructions, which, if not recollected, muſt quickly loſe their effect.

Every man, who has either applied himſelf to the examination of his own conduct with care proportioned to the importance of the enquiry, or indulged himſelf in the more frequent employment of inſpecting the behaviour of others, has had many opportu-

opportunities of obſerving, with how much difficulty the precepts of Religion are long preſerved in their full force ; how inſenſibly the ways of virtue are forſaken, and into what depravity thoſe, who truſt too much to their own ſtrength, ſometimes fall, by neglecting to preſs forward, and to confirm their reſolution, by the ſame methods as they at firſt excited it. Innumerable temptations continually ſurround us, and innumerable obſtructions oppoſe us. We are lulled with indolence, we are ſeduced by pleaſure, we are perverted by bad examples, and we are betrayed by our own hearts. No ſooner do we, in compliance either with the vanities, or the buſineſs, of life, relax our attention to the doctrines of piety, than we grow cold and indifferent, dilatory and negligent. When we are again called to our duty, we find our minds entangled with a thouſand objections ; we are ready to plead every avocation, however trifling, as an exemption from the neceſſity of holy practices ; and, becauſe we readily ſatisfy *ourſelves* with our excuſes, we are willing to imagine that we ſhall ſatisfy God, the God of infinite holineſs and juſtice, who ſees the moſt ſecret motions

motions of our minds, who penetrates through all our hypocriſy, and upon whom diſinclination can be never impoſed for inability.

With regard to the duty of Charity, it is too common for men, of avaricious and worldly diſpoſitions, to imagine that they may be ſaved without compliance with a command ſo little agreeble to their inclinations; and therefore, though perhaps they cannot always reſiſt the force of argument, or repel conviction at its firſt aſſault, yet, as they do not willingly ſuffer their minds to dwell upon reaſonings which they ſcarcely wiſh to be true, or renew, by frequent recollection, that ſenſe of their duty which they have received, they quickly relapſe into their former ſordid inſenſibility, and, by indulging every conſideration which can be applied to the juſtification of parſimony, harden their hearts, and withhold their hands; and while they ſee the anguiſh of miſery, and hear the cries of want, can paſs by without pity, and without regard; and without even feeling any reproaches from their hearts, pray to God for that mercy which they have themſelves denied to their fellow-beings.

One of the pleas, which is alledged in juſtification of the negleᶜt of Charity, is inability to practiſe it: an excuſe, when real, to which no objection can be made; for it cannot be expected, that any man ſhould give to another what he muſt himſelf want in the ſame degree. But this excuſe is too frequently offered by thoſe who are poor only in their own opinion, who have habituated themſelves to look on thoſe that are above, rather than on thoſe that are below them, and cannot account themſelves rich, while they ſee any richer; men who meaſure their revenues, not by the wants of nature, but by the demands of vanity; and who have nothing to give, only becauſe they will not diminiſh any particle of their ſplendour, nor reduce the pomp of their equipage; who, while their tables are heaped with delicacies, and their houſes crowded with feſtal aſſemblies, ſuffer the poor to languiſh in the ſtreets in miſeries and in want, complain that their fortunes are not equal to the generoſity of their minds, and applaud their own inclinations to Charity and Mercy: inclinations which are never exerted in beneficence, because they cannot ſpare any thing from their appetites and their pride.

Others there are, who frequently delight to dwell upon the excellency of Charity, and profeſs themſelves ready to comply with its precepts, whenever proper objects ſhall be propoſed, and an opportunity of proper application ſhall be found; but they pretend that they are ſo *well* informed, with regard to the perverſion of Charity, and diſcover ſo many ill effects of indiſtinguiſhing and careleſs liberality, that they are not eaſily ſatisfied with the occaſions which are offered them. They are ſometimes afraid of encouraging idleneſs, and ſometimes of countenancing impoſture, and ſo readily find objections to every method of Charity that can be mentioned to them, that their good inclinations are of very little advantage to the reſt of mankind; but however they congratulate themſelves upon their merit, and ſtill applaud that generoſity by which calamity was never ſoftened, and by which want never was relieved.

But that all theſe imaginary pleas may be once more confuted, that the opportunity of Charity, which Providence has this day put into our hands, may not be neglected, and that our alms may be given

in

in ſuch a manner as may obtain acceptance with the great Judge of all the earth, who has promiſed to ſhew mercy to the merciful, I ſhall endeavour to lay before you,

Firſt, the importance and neceſſity of the practice of Charity.

Secondly, The diſpoſition of mind, which is neceſſary to make our alms acceptable to God.

Thirdly, the reaſonableneſs of laying hold on the preſent opportunity for the exerciſe of our charity.

And, Firſt, I ſhall endeavour to ſhew the importance and neceſſity of the praetice of Charity. The importance and neceſſity of Charity is ſo evident, that as it might be hoped that no proof could be neceſſary, ſo it is difficult to produce any arguments which do not occur of themſelves to every reaſonable and attentive mind. For whither can we turn our thoughts, or direct our eyes, where we ſhall not find ſome motive to the exerciſe of Charity?

If we look up to heaven, which we have been taught to conſider as the particular reſidence of the Supreme Being, we find there our Creator, our Preſerver, and our Judge;

our Creator, whoſe infinite power gave us our exiſtence, and who has taught us, by that gift, that bounty is agreeable to his nature; our Preſerver, of whoſe aſſiſtance and protection we are, every day and every moment, in need, and whoſe favour we can hope to ſecure only by imitating his goodneſs, and endeavouring the aſſiſtance and protection of each other; and our Judge, who has already declared that the merciful ſhall obtain mercy, and that in the awful day, in which every man ſhall be recompenſed according to his works, he that *ſoweth* ſparingly ſhall *reap* alſo ſparingly.

If we caſt our eyes over the earth, and extend our obſervations through the ſyſtem of human beings, what ſhall we find but ſcenes of miſery and innumerable varieties of calamity and diſtreſs, the pains of ſickneſs, the wounds of caſualty, the gripings of hunger, and the cold of nakedneſs; wretches wandering without an habitation, expoſed to the contempt of the proud, and the inſults of the cruel, goaded forward, by the ſtings of poverty, to diſhoneſt acts, which perhaps relieve their preſent miſery, only to draw ſome more dreadful

diſtreſs

diſtreſs upon them? And what are we taught, by all theſe different ſtates of unhappineſs? what, but the neceſſity of that virtue by which they are relieved; by which the orphan may be ſupplied with a father, and the widow with a defender; by which nakedneſs may be cloathed, and ſickneſs ſet free from adventitious pains; the ſtranger ſolaced in his wanderings, and the hungry reſtored to vigour and to eaſe?

If we turn from theſe melancholy proſpects, and caſt our eyes upon ourſelves, what ſhall we find, but a precarious and frail being, ſurrounded on every ſide with danger, and beſieged with miſeries and with wants? miſeries, which we cannot avert by our own power, and wants which our own abilities cannot ſupply. We perceive ourſelves wholly unable to ſtand alone, and compelled to ſolicit, every moment, the aſſiſtance of our fellow-creatures; whom perhaps our Maker enables us at preſent to repay by mutual kindneſs, but whom we know not how ſoon we my be neceſſitated to implore, without the capacity of returning their beneficence.

This reflection ſurely ought immediately to convince us of the neceſſity of Chari-

ty.

ty. Prudence, even without Religion, ought to admonish every one to assist the helpless, and relieve the wretched, that, when the day of distress shall come upon him he may confidently ask that assistance, which he himself, in his prosperity, never did deny.

As it has pleased God to place us in a state in which we are surrounded with innumerable temptations; so it has pleased him, on many occasions, to afford us temporal incitements to virtue, as a counterbalance to the allurements of sin; and to set before us rewards which may be obtained, and punishments which may be suffered, before the final determination of our future state. As Charity is one of our most important duties, we are pressed to its practice by every principle of secular, as well as religious, wisdom; and no man can suffer himself to be distinguished for hardness of heart, without danger of feeling the consequence of his wickedness in his present state; because no man can secure to himself the continuance of riches, or of power; nor can prove, that he shall not himself *want* the assistance which he now *denies*, and perhaps be compelled to implore

it

it from thoſe whoſe petition he now rejects, and whoſe miſeries he now inſults. Such is the inſtability of human affairs, and ſo frequently does God aſſert his government of the world, by exalting the low, and depreſſing the powerful.

If we endeavour to conſult higher wiſdom than our own, with relation to this duty, and examine the opinions of the reſt of mankind, it will be found, that all the nations of the earth, however they may differ with regard to every other tenet, yet agree in the celebration of benevolence, as the moſt amiable diſpoſition of the heart, and the foundation of all happineſs. We ſhall find that, in every place, men are loved and honoured in proportion to the gifts which they have conferred upon mankind, and that nothing but Charity can recommend *one* man to the affection of *another*.

But if we appeal, as is undoubtedly reaſonable and juſt, from human wiſdom to divine, and ſearch the Holy Scriptures, to ſettle our notions of the importance of this duty, we ſhall need no further incitements to its practice; for every part of that ſacred volume is filled with *precepts* that

direct,

direct, or *examples* that inculcate it. The practice of hoſpitality among the Patriarchs, the confidence of Job, amidſt his afflictions, ariſing from the remembrance of his former Charity.

The precepts of the Prophets, and the conduct of the holy men of all times, concur to enforce the duty of attending to the cries of miſery, and endeavouring to relieve the calamities of life.

But ſurely all further proof will be ſuperſeded, when the declaration of our bleſſed Redeemer is remembered, who has condeſcended to inform us that thoſe who have ſhewn mercy ſhall find mercy from him, that the practice of Charity will be the great teſt by which we ſhall be judged, and that thoſe, and thoſe only, who have given food to the hungry, and raiment to the naked, ſhall, at the final doom, be numbered by the Son of God amongſt the Bleſſed of his Father.

There can nothing more be added to ſhow the neceſſity of the practice of Charity; for what can be expected to move him, by whom everlaſting felicity is diſregarded; and who hears, without emotion, never-ending miſeries threatened by

Omni-

Omnipotence ? It therefore now remains that we enquire,

Secondly,

How we may practice this duty, in a manner pleaſing to him who commanded it ; or what diſpoſition of mind is neceſſary to make our alms acceptable to God.

Our Saviour, as he has informed us of the neceſſity of Charity, has not omitted to teach us likewiſe how our acts of Charity are to be performed. And from his own precepts, and thoſe of his Apoſtles, may be learned all the cautions neceſſary to obviate the deceit of our own hearts, and to preſerve us from falling into follies dangerous to our ſouls, while we imagine ourſelves advancing in the favour of God.

We are commanded by Jeſus Chriſt, when we give our alms, to diveſt ourſelves of pride, vain-glory, and deſire of applauſe ; we are forbidden to give, that we may be ſeen of men, and inſtructed ſo to conduct our Charity, that it may be known to our Father which ſeeth in ſecret. By this precept it is not to be underſtood, that we are forbidden to give alms in public, or where we may be ſeen of men ; for our

Saviour

Saviour has alſo commanded, that our *light ſhould ſo ſhine before men, that they may ſee our good works, and glorify our Father which is in heaven.* The meaning therefore, of this text is not that we ſhould forbear to give alms in the ſight of men, but that we ſhould not ſuffer the preſence of men to act as the motive to our Charity, nor regard their praiſe as any object to our wiſhes; a precept ſurely reaſonable; for how can that act be virtuous, which depends not upon our *own* choice, but upon that of *others*, and which we ſhould not have performed, if we had not expected that they would have applauded it?

Of the ſame kind, though ſomewhat different in its immediate, and literal acceptation, is the inſtruction contained in the text, in which we are taught, by St. Paul, that every man ought to give according to the purpoſe of his own heart, not grudgingly, or of neceſſity; by which it is commanded, that we ſhould, as our Saviour had already taught us, lay aſide, in the diſtribution of our alms, all regard to human authority; that we ſhould give according to the purpoſe of our own hearts, without reſpect to ſolicitation or influence;

that

that we ſhould give, becauſe God has commanded, and give cheerfully, as a proof of ready and uncompelled obedience; obedience uncompelled by any other motive than a due ſenſe of our dependence upon the univerſal Lord, and the reaſonableneſs of obſerving the law of Him by whom we were created.

There are likewiſe other rules to be obſerved in the practice of Charity, which may be gathered, at leaſt conſequentially, from the Holy Scriptures; and which the common prudence of mankind at the ſame time evidently preſcribes. It is neceſſary that, in beſtowing our alms, we ſhould endeavour to promote the ſervice of God, and the general happineſs of ſociety, and, therefore, we ought not to give them, without enquiry into the ends for which they are deſired; we ought not to ſuffer our beneficence to be made inſtrumental to the encouragement of vice, or the ſupport of idleneſs; becauſe what is thus ſquandered may be wanted by others, who would uſe our kindneſs to better purpoſes, and who, without our aſſiſtance, would perhaps periſh.

Another precept, too often neglected, which yet a generous and elevated mind would naturally think highly necessary to be observed, is, that alms should be given in such a manner as may be most pleasing to the person who receives them; that our Charity should not be accompanied with insults, nor followed by reproaches; that we should, whenever it is possible, spare the wretched the unnecessary, the mortifying pain of recounting their calamities, and representing their distress; and when we have relieved them we should never upbraid them with our kindness, nor recall their afflictions to their minds by cruel and unreasonable admonitions to gratitude or industry. He only confers favours generously, who appears, when they are once conferred, to remember them no more.

Poverty is in itself sufficiently afflictive, and to most minds the pain of wanting assistance is scarcely balanced by the pleasure of receiving it. The end of Charity is to mitigate calamities; and he has little title to the reward of mercy, who afflicts with one hand, while he succours with the other. But this fault, like many others, arises from pride, and from the desire of

temporal

temporal rewards. Men either forget the common nature of humanity, and therefore, reproach others with thoſe misfortunes, to which they are themſelves equally ſubject; or they expect, from the gratitude, or applauſe, of thoſe whom they benefit, that reward which they are commanded to hope only from their Father which is in heaven.

Such are the rules of Charity, and ſuch the cautions required, to make our alms pleaſing to him, in whoſe name they ought to be given; and, that they may be *now* given not *grudgingly*, or of *neceſſity*, but with that cheerfulneſs, which the Apoſtle recommends as neceſſary to draw down the love of God upon thoſe by whom they are beſtowed, let us conſider,

Thirdly, the reaſonableneſs of laying hold on the preſent opportunity for the exerciſe of our Charity.

It is juſt that we ſhould conſider every opportunity of performing a good action as the gift of God, one of the chief gifts which God beſtows upon man, in his preſent ſtate, and endeavour to improve the bleſſing, that it may not be withdrawn from us, as a talent unemployed; for it is

not

not certain, that he, who neglects this call to his duty, will be permitted to live, till he hears another. It is likewise reasonable to seize this opportunity, because perhaps none can be afforded of more useful or beneficial Charity, none in which all the various purposes of Charity are more compendiously united.

It cannot be said, that, by this Charity, idleness is encouraged; for those who are to be benefited by it are at present incapable of labour, but hereafter designed for it. Nor can it be said, that vice is countenanced by it, for many of them cannot yet be vicious. Those who now give, cannot bestow their alms for the pleasure of hearing their Charity acknowledged, for they who shall receive it will not know their benefactors.

The immediate effect of alms given on this occasion, is not only food to the hungry, and clothes to the naked, and an habitation to the destitute, but what is of more *lasting* advantage, *instruction* to the *ignorant*.

He that *supports* an infant, enables him to live *here*; but he that *educates* him, assists him in his passage to an happier state, and

and prevents that wickedneſs which is, if not the *neceſſary*, yet the *frequent conſequence* of unenlightened infancy and vagrant poverty.

Nor does this Charity terminate in the perſons upon whom it is conferred, but extends its influence through the whole ſtate, which has very frequently experienced, how much is to be dreaded from men, bred up without principles, and without employment. He who *begs* in the ſtreet, in his *infancy*, learns only how to *rob* there in his *manhood*; and it is certainly very apparent, with how much leſs difficulty evils are prevented, than remedied.

But though we ſhould ſuppoſe, what reaſon and experience ſufficienty diſprove, that poverty and ignorance were calamities to thoſe only on whom they fall, yet ſurely the ſenſe of their miſery might be ſufficient to awaken us to compaſſion. For who can hear the cries of a naked infant, without remembering that he was himſelf once equally naked, equally helpleſs? Who can ſee the diſorders of the ignorant, without remembering that he was born as ignorant as they? and who can forbear to reflect, that he ought to bellow on others thoſe benefits which he received himſelf? Who, that ſhall ſee piety and wiſdom promoted by his beneficence, can wiſh, that what he gave for ſuch uſes had been employed in any other manner? As the Apoſtle exhorts to hoſpitality, by obſerving that ſome have entertained *Angels* unawares, let us animate ourſelves to this Charity, by the hopes of educating *Saints.* Let us endeavour to reclaim vice, and to improve innocence to holineſs; and remember that the day is not far diſtant, in which our Saviour has promiſed to conſider our gift to theſe little ones as given to himſelf; and that *they who have turned many to righteouſneſs ſhall ſhine forth as the ſun, for ever and ever.*

SERMON XX.

2 PETER iii. 3.

Knowing this firſt, that there ſhall come in the laſt days Scoffers, walking after their own luſts.

A Very little acquaintance with human nature will inform us, that there are few men who can patiently bear the imputation of being in the wrong; and that there is no action, how unreaſonable or wicked ſoever it be, which thoſe, who are guilty of it, will not attempt to vindicate, though perhaps by ſuch a defence as aggravates the crime.

It is indeed common for men to conceal their faults, and gratify their paſſions in ſecret, and eſpecially, when they are firſt

 initiated

initiated in vice, to make uſe rather of artifice and diſſimulation, than audaciouſneſs and effrontery. But the arts of hypocriſy are, in time, exhauſted, and ſome unhappy circumſtance defeats thoſe meaſures which they had laid for preventing a diſcovery. They are at length ſuſpected, and by that curioſity which ſuſpicion always excites, cloſely purſued, and openly detected. It is then too late to think of deceiving mankind by falſe appearances, nor does any thing remain, but to avow boldly what can be no longer denied. Impudence is called in to the aſſiſtance of immorality; and the cenſures which cannot be eſcaped, muſt be openly defied. Wickedneſs is in itſelf timorous, and naturally ſkulks in coverts and in darkneſs, but grows furious by deſpair, and, when it can fly no farther, turns upon the purſuer.

Such is the ſtate of a man abandoned to the indulgence of vicious inclinations. He juſtifies one crime by another; invents wicked principles to ſupport wicked practices; endeavours rather to corrupt others, than own himſelf corrupted, and, to avoid that ſhame which a confeſſion of his crimes would bring upon him, calls *evil good, and*

good

good evil, puts darkneſs for light, and light for darkneſs. He endeavours to trample upon thoſe laws which he is known not to obſerve, to ſcoff at thoſe truths which, if admitted, have an evident tendency to convict his whole behaviour of folly and abſurdity, and, from having long neglected to obey God, riſes at length into rebellion againſt him.

That no man ever became abandoned at once, is an old and common obſervation, which, like other aſſertions founded on experience receives new confirmation by length of time. A man ventures upon wickedneſs, as upon waters with which he is unacquainted. He looks upon them with horror, and ſhudders at the thought of quitting the ſhore, and committing his life to the inconſtancy of the weather; but, by degrees, the ſcene grows familiar, his averſion abates, and is ſucceeded by curioſity. He launches out with fear and caution, always anxious and apprehenſive, leſt his veſſel ſhould be daſhed againſt a rock, ſucked in by a quick-ſand, or hurried by the currents beyond ſight of ſhore. But his fears are daily leſſening, and the deep becomes leſs formidable. In time he loſes all ſenſe of danger, ventures out with full ſecurity, and roves without inclination to return ; till he is driven into the boundleſs ocean, toſſed about by the tempeſts, and at laſt ſwallowed by the waves.

Moſt men have, or once had, an eſteem and reverence for virtue, and a contempt and abhorrence of vice ; of which, whether they were impreſſed by nature, implanted by education, or deduced and ſettled by reaſon, it is at preſent of very little importance to enquire. Such theſe notions are, however they were originally received, as reaſon cannot but adopt and ſtrengthen, and every man will freely confeſs that reaſon ought to be the rule of his conduct. Whoever therefore recedes, in his practice, from rules of which he allows the obligation, and ſuffers his paſſions to prevail over his opinions, feels at firſt a ſecret reluctance, is conſcious of ſome ſort of violence done to his intellectual powers ; and though he will not deny himſelf that pleaſure which is preſent before him, or that ſingle gratification of his paſſions, he determines, or thinks he determines, that he will yield to no future temptation, that he will hereafter reject all

the

the ſolicitation of his appetites, and live in ſuch a manner as he ſhould applaud in others, and as his own conſcience ſhould approve in himſelf.

Perhaps every man may recollect, that this was the temper of his mind, when he firſt permitted himſelf to deviate from the known paths of his duty, and that he never forſook them, in the early part of his life, without a deſign to return to them, and perſevere in them; and that, when he was tempted another time, he complied, always with a tacit intention to add but this one more to his offences, and to ſpend the reſt of his life in penitence and obedience. Perhaps there are very many among the moſt profligate, who frequently ſtill their conſciences, and animate their hopes, with views of a reformation to be ſincerely entered upon in ſome diſtant period of their lives, who propoſe to dedicate, at leaſt, their laſt years to piety, and at ſome moments give way to wiſhes, that they may ſome time taſte the ſatisfaction of a good life, and *die the death of the righetous.*

But theſe, however given up to their deſires and paſſions, however ignorant of their own weakneſs, and preſumptuouſly confident

confident of their natural powers, have not yet arrived at the ſummit of impiety, 'till they have learned, not only to neglect, but to inſult, religion, not only to be vicious, but to ſcoff at virtue.

This ſeems to be the laſt effect of a long continued habit of ſin, the ſtrongeſt evidence of a mind corrupted almoſt beyond hope of a recovery. Wickedneſs in this ſtate ſeems to have extended its power from the paſſions to the underſtanding. Not only the deſire of doing well is extinguiſhed, but the diſcernment of good and evil obliterated and deſtroyed. Such is the infatuation produced by a long courſe of obſtinate guilt.

Not only our ſpeculations influence our practice, but our practice reciprocally influences our ſpeculations. We not only do what we approve, but there is danger leſt in time we come to approve what we do, though for no other reaſon but that we do it. A man is always deſirous of being at peace with himſelf; and when he cannot reconcile his paſſions to his conſcience, he will attempt to reconcile his conſcience to his paſſions; he will find reaſon for doing what he is reſolved to do, and rather than

not

not *walk after his own lusts*, will scoff at religion.

These Scoffers may be divided into two distinct classes, to be addressed in a very different manner: those whom a constant prosecution of their lusts has deluded into a real disbelief of religion, or diverted from a serious examination of it; and those who are convinced of the truth of revelation, but affect to contemn and ridicule it from motives of interest or vanity.

I shall endeavour therefore to evince,

First, The folly of scoffing at religion in those who doubt the truth of it.

And,

Secondly, The wickedness of this practice in those who believe it.

First, I shall endeavour to evince the folly of scoffing at religion in those who doubt the truth of it.

Those who in reality disbelieve, or doubt of, religion, however negligent they may be in their enquiries after truth, generally profess the highest reverence for it, the sincerest desire to discover it, and the strongest resolutions to adhere to it. They will frequently assert, and with good reason,

ſon, that every man is valuable in proportion to his love of truth; that man enjoys the power of reaſon for this great end, that he may diſtinguiſh truth from falſehood; that not to ſearch for it is the moſt criminal lazineſs, and not to declare it, in oppoſition to the frowns of power, or the prejudices of ignorance, the moſt deſpicable cowardice.

When they declaim on this darling ſubject, they ſeldom fail to take the opportunity of throwing out keen invectives againſt bigotry; bigotry, that voluntary blindneſs, that laviſh ſubmiſſion to the notions of others, which ſhackles the powers of the ſoul, and retards the progreſs of reaſon; that cloud, which intercepts our views, and throws a ſhade over the light of truth.

Such is the diſcourſe of theſe men; and who, that hears it, would not expect from them the moſt diſintereſted impartiality, the moſt unwearied aſſiduity, and the moſt candid and ſober attention to any thing propoſed as an argument upon a ſubject worthy of their ſtudy? Who would not imagine that they made it the grand buſineſs of their lives to carry the art of reaſoning

ſoning to its greateſt height, to enlighten the underſtanding of the ignorant by plain inſtructions enforced with ſolid arguments, and to eſtabliſh every important truth upon the moſt certain and unſhaken principles?

There ſeems to be nothing more inconſiſtent with ſo philoſophical a character than careleſs vivacity and airy levity. The talents which qualify a man for a diſputant and a buffoon ſeem very different; and an unprejudiced perſon would be inclined to form contrary ideas of an argument and a jeſt.

Study has been hitherto thought neceſſary to knowledge, and ſtudy cannot well be ſucceſsfully proſecuted without ſolitude and leiſure. It might therefore be conceived that this exalted ſect is above the low employments and empty amuſements of vulgar minds; that they avoid every thing which may interrupt their meditations, or perplex their ideas; and that therefore, whoever ſtands in need of their inſtructions muſt ſeek them in privacies and retirements, in deſerts or in cells.

But theſe men have diſcovered, it ſeems, a more compendious way to knowledge.

They

They decide the moſt momentous queſtions amidſt the jollity of feaſts, and the exceſſes of riot. They have found that an adverſary is more eaſily ſilenced than confuted. They inſult, inſtead of vanquiſhing, their antagoniſts, and decline the battle to haſten to the triumph.

It is an eſtabliſhed maxim among them, that he who ridicules an opinion confutes it. For this reaſon they make no ſcruple of violating every rule of decency, and treating with the utmoſt contempt whatever is accounted venerable or ſacred.

For this conduct they admire themſelves, and go on applauding their own abilities, celebrating the victories they gain over their grave opponents, and loudly boaſting their ſuperiority to the advocates for Religion.

As humility is a very neceſſary qualification for an examiner into Religion, it may not be improper to depreſs the arrogance of theſe haughty champions, by ſhewing with how little juſtice they lay claim to victory, and how much leſs they deſerve to be applauded than deſpiſed.

There are two circumſtances which, either ſingle or united, make any attainments eſtimable among men. The firſt is the uſefulneſs of it to ſociety. The other is the capacity or application neceſſary for acquiring it.

If we conſider this art of ſcoffing with regard to either of theſe, we ſhall not find great reaſon to envy or admire it. It requires no depth of knowledge, or intenſeneſs of thought. Contracted notions, and ſuperficial views, are ſufficient for a man who is ambitious only of being the author of a jeſt. That man may laugh who cannot reaſon; and he, that cannot comprehend a demonſtration, may turn the terms to ridicule.

This method of controverſy is indeed the general refuge of thoſe whoſe idleneſs or incapacity diſable them from producing any thing ſolid or convincing. They, who are certain of being confuted and expoſed in a ſober diſpute, imagine that by returning ſcurrility for reaſon, and by laughing moſt loudly, when they have leaſt to ſay, they ſhall ſhelter their ignorance from detection, and ſupply with impudence what they want in knowledge.

Nor will the poſſeſſors of this boaſted talent or ridicule appear more to deſerve reſpect on account of their uſefulneſs to mankind. Theſe gay ſallies of imagination, when confined to proper ſubjects, and reſtrained within the bounds of decency, are of no farther uſe to mankind than to divert, and can have no higher place in our eſteem than any other art that terminates in mere amuſement.

But when men treat ſerious matters ludicrouſly, when they ſtudy, not for truth, but for a jeſt, when they unite the moſt awful and moſt trifling ideas, only to tickle the imagination with the ſurprize of novelty, they no longer have the poor merit of diverting; they raiſe always either horror or contempt, and hazard their higheſt intereſt, without even the low recompence of preſent applauſe.

That they hazard their higheſt intereſt can hardly be denied, when they determine, without the moſt ſcrupulous examination, thoſe queſtions which relate to a future ſtate; and none certainly are leſs likely to diſcuſs theſe queſtions with the care which they require, than thoſe who accuſtom themſelves to continual levity.

The mind, long vitiated with trifles, and entertained with wild and unnatural combinations

binations of ideas, becomes in a ſhort time unable to ſupport the fatigue of reaſoning ; it is diſguſted with a long ſucceſſion of ſolemn images, and retires from ſerious meditation, and tireſome labour, to gayer fancies, and leſs difficult employments.

Beſides, he that has practiſed the art of ſilencing others with a jeſt, in time learns to ſatisfy himſelf in the ſame manner. It becomes unneceſſary to the tranquillity of his own mind to confute an objection ; it is ſufficient for him if he can ridicule it.

Thus he ſoon grows indifferent to truth or falſehood, and almoſt incapable of diſcerning one from the other. He conſiders eternity itſelf as a ſubject for mirth, and is equally ludicrous upon all occaſions.

What deluſions, what bigotry, is equal to this ! Men neglect to ſearch after eternal happineſs for fear of being interrupted in their mirth. If others have been miſled, they have been miſled by their reverence for great authorities, or by ſtrong prejudices of education. Such errors may be extenuated, and perhaps excuſed. They

have

have at least something plausible to plead, and their assertors act with some show of reason. But what can the most extensive charity alledge in favour of those men who, if they perish everlastingly, perish by their attachment to merriment, and their confidence in a jest?

It is astonishing that any man can forbear enquiring seriously, whether there is a GOD; whether GOD is just; whether this life is the only state of existence; whether GOD has appointed rewards and punishments in a future state; whether he has given any laws for the regulation of our conduct here; whether he has given them by revelation; and whether the religion publicly taught carries any mark of divine appointment. These are questions which every reasonable Being ought undoubtedly to consider with an attention suitable to their importance; and he, whom the consideration of eternal happiness or misery cannot awaken from his pleasing dreams, cannot prevail upon to suspend his mirth, surely ought not to despise others for dulness and stupidity.

Let it be remembered, that the nature of things is not alterable by our conduct.

We cannot make truth; it is our business only to find it. No proposition can become more or less certain or important, by being considered or neglected. It is to no purpose to wish, or to suppose, that to be false which is in itself true, and therefore to acquiesce in our own wishes and suppositions, when the matter is of eternal consequence, to believe obstinately without grounds of belief, and to determine without examination, is the last degree of folly and absurdity. It is not impossible that he who acts in this manner may obtain the approbation of madmen like himself, but he will incur the contempt of every wise man; and, what is more to be feared, amidst his security and supineness, his sallies and his flights, *He that sitteth in the heavens shall laugh him to scorn; the Lord shall have him in derision.*

Thus have I endeavoured to give a faint idea of the folly of those who scoff at Religion, because they disbelieve, and, by scoffing, harden themselves in their disbelief. But I shall be yet more unable to describe, in a proper manner, what I am to mention in the second place,

The

The wickedneſs of thoſe that believe Religion, and yet deride it from motives of intereſt or vanity.

This is a degree of guilt againſt which it might ſeem, at the firſt view, ſuperfluous to preach, becauſe it might be thought impoſſible that it ſhould ever be committed; as, in ancient ſtate, no puniſhment was decreed for the murderer of his father, becauſe it was imagined to be a crime not incident to human nature. But experience taught them, and teaches us, that wickedneſs may ſwell beyond imagination, and that there are no limits to the madneſs of impiety.

For a man to revile and inſult that God whoſe power he allows, to ridicule that revelation of which he believes the authority divine, to dare the vengeance of omnipotence, and cry, *am not I in ſport!* is an infatuation incredible, a degree of madneſs without a name. Yet there are men who, by walking after their own luſts, and indulging their paſſions, have reached this ſtupendous height of wickedneſs. They have dared to teach falſehoods which they do not themſelves believe; and to extin-

guiſh

guiſh in others that conviction which they cannot ſuppreſs in themſelves.

The motive of their proceeding is ſometimes a deſire of promoting their own pleaſures, by procuring accomplices in vice. Man is ſo far formed for ſociety, that even ſolitary wickedneſs quickly diſguſts; and debauchery requires its combinations and confederacies, which, as intemperance diminiſhes their numbers, muſt be filled up with new Proſelytes.

Let thoſe who practiſe this dreadful method of depraving the morals, and enſnaring the ſoul, conſider what they are engaged in! Let them conſider what they are promoting, and what means they are employing! Let them pauſe, and reflect a little, before they do an injury that can never be repaired, before they take away what cannot be reſtored; before they corrupt the heart of their companion by perverting his opinions, before they lead him into ſin, and by deſtroying his reverence for Religion, take away every motive to repentance, and all the means of reformation!

This is a degree of guilt, before which robbery, perjury, and murder, vaniſh into

 nothing.

nothing. No miſchief, of which the conſequences terminate in our preſent ſtate, bears any proportion to the crime of decoying our brother into the broad way of eternal miſery, and ſtopping his ears againſt that holy voice that recalls him to ſalvation.

What muſt be the anguiſh of ſuch a man, when he becomes ſenſible of his own crimes! How will he bear the thought of having promoted the damnation of multitudes by the propagation of known deluſions! What laſting contrition, what ſevere repentance, muſt be neceſſary for ſuch deep and ſuch accumulated guilt! Surely if blood be required for blood, a ſoul ſhall be required for a ſoul.

There are others who deride Religion for the ſake of diſplaying their own imaginations, of following the faſhion of a corrupt and licentious age, or gaining the friendſhip of the great, or the applauſe of the gay How mean muſt that wretch be who can be overcome by ſuch temptations as theſe! Yet there are men who ſell that ſoul which God has formed for infinite felicity, defeat the great work of their redemption, and plunge into thoſe pains

which

which ſhall never end, leſt they ſhould loſe the patronage of villains, and the praiſe of fools.

I ſuppoſe thoſe, whom I am now ſpeaking of, to be in themſelves ſufficiently convinced of the truth of the Scriptures, and may therefore, very properly, lay before them the threatnings denounced by God againſt their conduct.

It may be uſeful to them to reflect betimes on the danger of *fearing man rather than God*; to conſider that it ſhall avail a man nothing, if he *gain the whole world, and loſe his own ſoul;* and that whoever *ſhall be aſhamed of his Saviour before men, of him will his Saviour be aſhamed before his Father which is in heaven.*

That none of us may be in the number of thoſe unhappy perſons who thus ſcoff at the means of grace, and relinquiſh the hope of glory, may God, of his infinite mercy, grant, through the merits of that Saviour who hath brought life and immortality to light!

SERMON XXI.

PSALM cxlv. 9.

The Lord is good to all, and his tender mercies are over all his works.

IN this devout, maſterly, and uſeful performance, the Author appears deeply ſenſible of the divine greatneſs, and peculiarly tranſported with contemplating GOD's infinite goodneſs ; even to that degree, that he cheerfully engages in, and abſolutely devotes himſelf to, the very important ſervice of adoring and obeying this Almighty, Unbounded, and moſt Benevolent Being.

This his religion, as he intimates, was founded upon the moſt ſolid ground of reaſon ; for as the great Father and Lord of all is certainly matchleſs, and unrivalled in majeſty and in power, ſo is he diſinter-

eſted,

eſted, wonderful, and glorious, in bounty and compaſſion; averſe and ſlow to anger, but ready to receive, to favour and reward all who diligently ſeek, and faithfully ſerve him. *The Lord is good to all, and his tender mercies are over all his works.*

In diſcourſing on this ſubject, I ſhall conſider,

Firſt, Some arguments that ſupport, or prove it.

Secondly, Illuſtrate its extenſive ſignification and import in ſome remarkable inſtances, and conclude with a practical application.

Firſt, I am to conſider ſome arguments that eſtabliſh this ſentiment.

Our great Lord and Maſter has taught us, that there is none good but one, that is God. By which expreſſion we may underſtand, that there is none ſo perfectly diſintereſted, ſo diffuſively, and ſo aſtoniſhingly good as God is. For, in another place, he inſtructs us both how to comprehend, and rely on, this unchangeable and never-failing attribute of the divine nature; reſembling it to, or repreſenting it by, an human quality or virtue, namely, the affection and tender regard of parents to to their children. *If ye then, being evil, know how to give good gifts unto your children, how much more ſhall your Father, which is in Heaven, give good things to them that aſk him?* From whence it is obvious to remark, that as the humane and generous man has a peculiar tenderneſs for his more immediate deſcendants, and, proportionally to his power and influence, is willing and active to ſuccour and relieve the indigent, to divide care, leſſen miſery, and diffuſe happineſs through the world; inconceivably more affectionate is the eternal Parent unto, and regardful of, all his intelligent creatures, truly diſpoſed, according to their rank of exiſtence, to promote their welfare; and beyond comprehenſion inclined to conduct them, through the greateſt variety of circumſtances, to the nobleſt perfection, and the higheſt degree of felicity. In his righteous and benevolent nature there cannot poſſibly be the moſt diſtant tendency to caprice, ſeverity, or ſelfiſhneſs; for the multitude of ſharers, he knows, can never ſubtract from his inexhauſtible fulneſs. He created to communicate. In every evil which he prevents, he is pleaſed, and in all the good that he

beſtows,

beſtows, he glories. His goodneſs dictated the beſtowing of exiſtence, in all its forms, and with all its properties. His goodneſs diſplays itſelf in ſuſtaining and diſpoſing of all things. His goodneſs connects unnumbered worlds together, in one ſpacious, vaſt, and unbounded univerſe, and embraces every ſyſtem. *His tender mercies are over all his works.*

Without goodneſs, what apprehenſions could we entertain of all the other attributes of the Divine Being? Without the utmoſt extent of benevolence and mercy, they would hardly be perfections, or excellencies. And what would an univerſal adminiſtration produce, in the hands of an evil, or a partial, or malevolent direction, but ſcenes of horror and devaſtation? Not affliction and puniſhment for the ſake of diſcipline and correction, to prevent the offence, or reform the ſinner; but heavy judgements and dreadful vengeance, to deſtroy him; or implacable wrath and fiery indignation, to prolong his miſery, and extend the duration of his torture through the revolving periods of an endleſs eternity.

Without

Without the moſt enlarged notions of an infinite and everlaſting goodneſs in the divine nature, an impenetrable gloom muſt hang over every mind, and darkneſs overſpread the whole face of being. Neither could any other conceivable ſentiment diſperſe our ſuſpicions, or baniſh one of our guilty, or ſuperſtitious fears. For ſuppoſe he confined his goodneſs to a few, without any reaſonable cauſe or juſt ground, and we could be ſo whimſically partial to ourſelves, as to conceit that we were of this ſelect number; yet there could be no ſecurity of happineſs, not even to this little flock. He that choſe them by chance, might as accidentally abandon them; and as the former was without reaſon or goodneſs, the latter might be without righteouſneſs or mercy. Therefore it is infinitely deſirable to think, and we are confident of the truth of our idea, that *the Lord is good to all, and his tender mercies are over all his works.*

For if he be ſelf-exiſtent, omnipotent, and poſſeſſed of perfect liberty; if it be impoſſible for him ever to err, or miſtake, in what is good and fitting, and if he enjoys an infinite ability to effect, with a thought only,

only, what ſhall always be for the greateſt advantage, he muſt be originally and eſſentially, immutably and for ever good.

Holy Scripture, as if beauty and goodneſs were ſynonymous terms, or inſeparable qualities, thus deſcribes him; *How great is thy goodneſs! And let the beauty of the Lord our God be upon us.* And, as if glory and goodneſs ſignified the ſame thing, you find Exod. xxxiii. 18, 19, *And he ſaid, I beſeech thee, ſhew me thy glory.* To which the anſwer is, *I will make all my goodneſs paſs before thee.* And when, as it is written in the next chapter, the Lord deſcended, and proclaimed his name, or publiſhed the attributes in which he is peculiarly delighted, what is this diſtinguiſhing name, or what theſe divine and glorious attributes? *The Lord, the Lord God, merciful and gracious, long-ſuffering, and abundant in goodneſs and truth, keeping mercy for thouſands, forgiving iniquity, tranſgreſſion, and ſin.* The Apoſtle ſums up all theſe in one word, when he ſaith, *God is love.* Which leads me to the ſecond thing propoſed,

Namely, to illuſtrate the extenſive ſignification and import of this ſubject by ſome remarkable inſtances. *The Lord is good to all,*

all, and his tender mercies are over all his works.

No bounds can be fixed to the divine preſence, nor is any part of illimitable ſpace without his inſpection, and active influence. There is nothing remote, or obſcure to him, nor any exceptions to his favour among all the works of his hands. Far and wide then as is the vaſt range of exiſtence, ſo is the divine benevolence extended; and both in the previous trial, and final retribution, of all his rational and moral productions, *The Lord is good to all, and his tender mercies are over all his works.*

In the firſt place, to illuſtrate this, we need only to take a tranſient view of the outworks of the viſible creation, a general ſurvey of the nature and correſpondence of the various parts of this regular and grand machine, this finiſhed and ſtupendous fabrick, in which every thing is contrived and concluded for the beſt.

For do but imagine an appetite, or faculty, altered; or a change in the object prepared to gratify it, in any reſpect. Suppoſe a material alteration, or conſiderable difference in nature, and we ſhall eaſily perceive it would be a manifold diſadvan-

tage,

tage, either to individuals, or to the whole. Suppoſe the earth otherwiſe than it is, or the atmoſphere and ſurrounding air to be varied, and in any degree more rarefied or more condenſed; ſuppoſe the element of water greatly increaſed, or conſiderably diminiſhed; or the Sun's blazing orb fixed nearer, and its vertical beams therefore ſtronger, or ſuppoſe it more remote, and its heat ſenſibly abated, the alteration would be a misfortune, if the difference did not terminate in miſery and deſtruction. So that from the preſent adjuſtment, proportion, and accommodation of all matters in the wide creation, the conſequence is fairly drawn, and very evident, that *God is good to all, and his tender mercies are over all his works.*

This is certain of the *whole* of God's works, and is peculiarly apparent in *man*, the principal inhabitant of this earth. For, as his welfare, dignity, and ſatisfaction, nay his happineſs, and even the end of his being, depend on, and ariſe from, his regularity and conſtancy in virtue, what an infinite concern hath the Deity expreſſed about it? What, that can conſiſt with liberty, hath been omitted by ſupreme wiſ-

dom,

dom, in this moſt important affair? To incline him to be moderate in all his gratifications, true pleaſure proceeds from nothing elſe. To keep off intemperate indulgence, and to guard him againſt all voluptuous exceſſes, it is ſo ordained, that extravagance and inconvenience are near together, and that vice and pain are, though not immediate and inſeparable aſſociates, never far aſunder; and that it is impoſſible for that ſoul to be calm and at eaſe, which iniquity has ſtained, and which impenitent guilt corrodes.

The parts of man's body are wonderfully deſigned, and curiouſly conſtructed: regularly diſpoſed of, and moſt accurately proportioned for the ſafety and advantage of the whole. As apt as we may be to quarrel with our nature, ſuppoſe an inſtinct was ſtruck out of our frame, or a ſingle paſſion taken from us; ſuppoſe our ſenſes any ways altered, by being either ſtrengthened, or impaired; or even reaſon refined and abſtracted to ſuch a degree as to render us wholly negligent of food and raiment, neceſſary exerciſes, and ſecular concerns; in any of theſe inſtances, the imaginary emendation would be a real deficiency,

and

and a proportionable deduction from the moment and quantity of our happineſs.

It is evidently the ſame with reſpect to all the other creatures we are acquainted with. Their nature and condition, their qualities and circumſtances, are ſo adapted to one another, that, as the intellectual powers of a being of a more exalted nature would not probably ſuit an inhabitant of this lower world, ſo neither would the capacities of human nature guide the fowls of the air, or conduct the beaſts of the field, to ſo much happineſs, as they find, by following the motions and impulſes of ſenſe and inſtinct. And if reflection, enlarged ideas, and moral diſcrimination, be denied them, it is plainly becauſe they would be a burthen and a misfortune, rather than a benefit to them.

But theſe univerſal notices, and undeniable teſtimonies of divine goodneſs, throughout the animated regions of earth, ſea, and air, in the propriety and ſuitableneſs of creatures to their ſtate, and objects to their appetites, are too evident and obvious to all men to need enlargement. God's works are all wonderful; and in wiſdom, and with goodneſs, hath he made them.

Secondly, This attribute is likewiſe illuſtriouſly diſplayed in the divine providence and government of the creation, though our faculties are too limited and ſcanty, and our views too narrow and imperfect, to trace its ſecret and myſterious ways.

An omnipotent ſupport, and a perfectly wiſe direction, are evident in the laws eſtabliſhed, and regularly obſerved through all the divine productions in heaven above, or on the earth beneath. Neither have the moſt celebrated Philoſophers been able, with all their boaſted ſagacity, and after all their laborious reſearches into the volume of nature, to aſſign any other cauſe, but an inviſible agency, and an immediate energy of Providence, for mutual attraction in bodies, and the determination of all portions of matter to their centre ; for the great ſtrength of appetite, inſtinct, and ſagacity, in animals ; that the prevalence and continuance thereof ſhould be ſo preciſely and exactly commenſurate to the occaſions which require them, and that they ſhould be no longer urgent, than for the time neceſſary, as in the affection for their young. All which do greatly illuſtrate the

the wiſdom and goodneſs of God's admi-niſtration, and ſuperintending care.

Holy writ elegantly and emphatically deſcribes the excellence of goodneſs in the divine Providence in various places, parti-cularly in this Pſalm, of which my text is a part. *The eyes of all wait upon thee: thou giveſt them their meat in due ſeaſon. Thou openeſt thine hand, and ſatisfieſt the deſires of every living thing. Behold* (ſaith our bleſſed Saviour) *the fowls of the air, for they ſow not, neither do they reap, nor gather into barns; yet your heavenly Father feedeth them. Conſider the lillies of the field, how they grow; they toil not, neither do they ſpin; and yet I ſay unto you, that Solomon in all his glory was not arrayed like one of theſe.* Not one indi-vidual can be ſo minute and inconſiderable as to eſcape the notice of Heaven's all-ſur-veying eye; nor one ſo importantly large, and ſeemingly ſelf ſufficient as to ſubſiſt a moment without the divine ſupport. By him all things conſiſt: *The Lord is good to all, and his tender mercies are over all his works.*

But Man appears the diſtinguiſhed charge of the beneficent Creator; and un-leſs Providence had connected rational be-

ings

ings by the peculiar ſtrong ties of mutual obligation, perpetual dependency, and inſeparable intereſt, they would, of all creatures, be the moſt deſtitute and miſerable; for there is not one that in the firſt ſtages of its exiſtence is ſo totally helpleſs, and abſolutely inſufficient for its own preſervation, ſupport, or defence, as man. Therefore parental tenderneſs is both early and paſſionate, permanent and laſting. Our ſocial diſpoſitions and affections are enlarged to the utmoſt limits, and continue with us in the concluding decays, and laſt end of this mortal life; that we may always love one another and glorify *the Lord who is good to all, and whoſe tender mercies are over all his works.*

The conſequences in the laſt place, which reſult from the arguments you have heard, are ſo obvious, that I make no doubt but your own thoughts have already anticipated them. Ingratitude among men hath, in every age, and in every region of the earth, been an object of general deteſtation, and univerſally accounted a glaring indication of depravity of heart. If the caſe ſtand thus among mortals, whoſe common intereſts require a reciprocation of kindneſs and beneficence, how greatly is the crime aggravated, when it is committed against that Being, whoſe goodneſs towards the ſons of men is perfectly diſinterested! The exertions of Divine Providence in our behalf tend ſolely to our own welfare; nor can any thing we do in return contribute, in the ſmalleſt degree, to the augmentation of the happineſs of the Almighty Benefactor. This unqueſtionably ought to be ſufficient to exact from us the moſt profound veneration, the moſt fervent gratitude, and implicit obedience to his ſacred laws.

David, after having enumerated the tender mercies of God, is penetrated with the ſtrongeſt ſenſe of devotion. *My mouth* (he exlaims) *ſhall ſpeak the praiſe of the Lord; and let all fleſh bleſs his holy name for ever and ever.* Such was the tribute which the royal Pſalmiſt thought due to the Deity for the creation and preſervation of man. The debt is accumulated to us in an infinite proportion; for while we are bounden to the ſame return for the ſame benefits voluntarily conferred upon us, a grander obligation is ſuperadded to that for the *means of grace*, and for *the hope of glory*. Were the mercies of the Lord limited

mited to the tenure of our preſent exiſtence, great and glorious as they are, the human mind would be clouded by the conſciouſneſs that a very few years muſt exclude us for ever from the participation of them. But ſince the gracious rays of life and immortality have diſſipated the gloom that hung upon futurity, ſince, by the propitiatory ſacrifice of the Son of GOD, death is diſarmed of his ſting, and the grave deprived of its victory, divine goodneſs hath received its perfect conſummation.

If gratitude, praiſe, and adoration, therefore, be due to the Author of our being for thoſe bleſſings which we enjoy at preſent, it is no leſs our higheſt intereſt ſo to uſe them in this previous ſtate of trial, that we may finally exchange them for thoſe purer and incorruptible treaſures reſerved for the righteous in the kingdom of heaven.

Which that we may all do, may that GOD who created and preſerves us grant, through the merits and mediation of our Lord and Saviour Jeſus Chriſt!

SERMON XXII.

I CORINTHIANS xi. 29.

He that eateth and drinketh unworthily, eateh and drinketh damnation to himſelf.

THE celebration of the Sacrament is generally acknowledged, by the Chriſtian Church, to be the higheſt act of devotion, and the moſt ſolemn part of poſitive religion, and has therefore moſt engaged the attention of thoſe, who either profeſs to teach the way to happineſs, or endeavour to learn it, and, like all other ſubjects, frequently diſcuſſed by men of various interests, diſpoſitions, and capacities, has given riſe to various opinions, widely different from each other.

Such is the weakneſs of mankind, that one error, whether admitted, or detected, is is very often the cauſe of another. Thoſe who reject any opinion, however juſtly, are commonly incited by their zeal to condemn every poſition, in which they diſcover any affinity with the tenets which they oppoſe, of which they have been long accuſtomed to ſhow the falſehood and the danger, and therefore imagine themſelves nearer to truth and ſafety, in proportion as they recede from them. For this reaſon it ſometimes happens that in paſſionate conteſts, and diſputations long continued, each controvertiſt ſucceeds in the confutation of his adverſary's poſitions, and each fails in the eſtabliſhment of his own.

In this manner have writers, of different perſuaſions, treated on the worthineſs required of thoſe who partake of the Lord's Supper; a quality, not only neceſſary to procure the favour of God, and to give efficacy to the inſtitution, but ſo ſtrictly enjoined in the words of the text, that to approach the holy table without it, is to pervert the means of ſalvation, and to turn prayer into ſin.

The ardour and vehemence with which thoſe are condemned, who eat and drink unworthily, have filled the melancholy, the

the timorous, and the humble, with unnecessary terrors, which have been sometimes so much increased by the injudicious zeal of writers, erroneously pious, that they have conceived the danger of attempting to obey this precept of our Saviour more formidable than that of neglecting it, and have spent the greatest part of their lives in the omission of a duty of the highest importance; or, being equally terrified on either hand, have lived in anguish and perplexity, under a constant sense of the necessity of doing what they cannot, in their opinion, do in an acceptible manner, and which of course they shall either do, or omit, at the utmost hazard of eternal happiness.

Such exalted piety, such unshaken virtue, such an uniform ardour of divine affections, and such a constant practice of religious duties, have been represented as so indisepensably necessary to a worthy reception of this sacrament, as few men have been able to discover in those whom they most esteem for their purity of life, and which no man's conscience will perhaps suffer him to find in himself, and therefore those who know themselves not to have arrived at ſuch elevated excellence, who ſtruggle with paſſions which they cannot wholly conquer, and bewail infirmities, which yet they perceive to adhere to them, are frighted from an act of devotion, of which they have been taught to believe, that it is ſo ſcarcely to be performed worthily by an embodied ſpirit, that it requires the holineſs of angels, and the uncontaminated raptures of Paradiſe.

Thus it appeared, that, inſtead of being excited to ardent deſires of perfection, and unwearied endeavours after the utmoſt height of ſanctity, not only the ſenſual and the profligate were hardened in their wickedneſs, by conceiving a life of piety too hard to be borne, but the diffident and ſcrupulous were terrified into deſpair, conſidered vigilance and caution as unavailing fatigues, remitted their ardour, relaxed their diligence, and ceaſed to purſue what they could no longer hope to attain.

To remove theſe doubts, and diſperſe theſe apprehenſions, doctrines of very different tendency have been induſtriouſly promoted; lower degrees of piety have been declared ſufficient, and the dangers of reception have been extenuated; nor have any arts of interpretation been untried, or any conjecture, which ſagacity or learning could produce, been forgotten, to aſſign to the words of the text a ſenſe leſs to be dreaded by the unworthy communicant. But by theſe opinions, imprudently inculcated, many have been miſled to conſider the Sacrament, as little more than a curſory act of devotion; the exhortations of the Apoſtle have loſt their efficacy, and the terrors of the Lord, with which he enforces them, have no longer repreſſed the licentiouſneſs of the profligate, or diſturbed the indolence of the ſupine. Religion has ſunk into ceremony; God, has, without fear, been approached with the lips, when the heart has been far from him; and the Supper of the Lord has been frequented by thoſe, of whom it could not be perceived, that they were very ſolicitous to avoid the guilt of unworthy communication.

Thus have different interpretations of the ſame text produced errors equally dangerous, and which might have been equally obviated, by a careful attention to the nature and inſtitution of the Sacrament, an unprejudiced examination of the poſition of the Apoſtle, and the compariſon of this

this paſſage with other comminations; methods of enquiry, which, in the explication of doubtful texts of ſcripture, ought always to be obſerved, and by which it may be proved, to the comfort of the depreſſed, and the confirmation of the doubtful, that the ſin of unworthy reception, though great, is yet to be pardoned; and to the reſtraint of the preſumptuous, and confuſion of the profane, that the preparation required is ſtrict, though practicable, and the denunciation ſuch as ought to terrify the negligent, though not diſcourage the pious.

When eternal puniſhments are denounced againſt any crime, it is always evidently the intention of the writer to declare and enforce to thoſe, that are yet innocent, the duty of avoiding them, and to thoſe who have already committed them, the neceſſity of repentance, reformation, and future caution. For it is not the will of God, that any ſhould periſh, but that all ſhould repent, and be ſaved. It is not by one act of wickedneſs, that infinite mercy will be kindled to everlaſting anger, and the beneficent Father of the univerſe for ever alienated from his creatures; but by

a long

a long courſe of crimes, deliberately committed againſt the convictions of conſcience and the admonitions of grace; by a life ſpent in guilt, and concluded without repentance. *No drunkard or extortioner*, ſays the Apoſtle, *ſhall inherit eternal life.* Yet ſhall no man be excluded from future happineſs, by a ſingle inſtance, or even by long habits, of intemperance, or extortion. Repentance and new life will efface his crimes, reinſtate him in the favour of his judge, reſtore him to thoſe promiſes which he has forfeited, and open the paths to eternal happineſs.

Such is the crime of unworthy reception of the Holy Sacrament, by which *he that eateth and drinketh unworthily, eateth and drinketh damnation to himſelf;* to which no man can come unprepared, or partake of, if he is diveſted of the intentions, ſuitable to ſo ſolemn a part of divine worſhip, without adding to the number of his ſins, and, by a neceſſary conſequence, to the danger of his ſoul. But though the ſoul is, by ſuch an act of wickedneſs, endangered, it is not neceſſarily deſtroyed, or irreverſibly condemned. He that eateth and drinketh unworthily, contributes indeed, by eating

and

and drinking, to his own damnation, as he that engages in fraudulent, or unlawful commerce, may be ſaid, with great propriety, to traffic for damnation, or to ſet his ſoul to ſale; yet as it is certain, that fraud is not unpardonable, if it ſhall afterwards give way to juſtice, ſo neither is the profanation of the Sacrament a crime, which the goodneſs of God cannot forgive, if it be ſucceeded by true devotion. The whole life of man is a ſtate of probation; he is always in danger, and may be always in hope. As no ſhort fervours of piety, nor particular acts of beneficence, however exalted, can ſecure him from the poſſibility of ſinking into wickedneſs, ſo no neglect of devotion, nor the commiſſion of any crimes, can preclude the means of grace, or the hope of glory. He that has eaten and drank unworthily may enter into ſalvation, by repentance and amendment; as he that has eaten and drank worthily may, by negligence or preſumption, periſh everlaſtingly.

This account of the guilt of unworthy reception makes it neceſſary to enquire, whether by the original word in the text be meant, as it is tranſlated, *damnation*, the eternal puniſhments of a future ſtate; or, as it is more frequently interpreted, condemnation, temporary judgements, or worldly afflictions. For, from either ſenſe, the enormity of the crime, and the anger of God enkindled by it, is ſufficiently apparent. Every act of wickedneſs that is puniſhed with immediate vengeance, will, if it be aggravated by repetitions, or not expiated by repentance, incur *final* condemnation; for temporal puniſhments are the merciful admonitions of God, to avoid, by a timely change of conduct, that ſtate in which there is no repentance, and thoſe pains which can have no end. So that the confident and preſumptuous, though it ſhould be allowed that only temporal puniſhments are threatened in the text, are to remember, that, without reformation, they will be only aggravations of the crime, and that at the laſt day, thoſe who could not be awakened to a juſt reverence of this divine inſtitution, will be deprived of the benefits of that death, of which it was eſtabliſhed as a perpetual commemoration. And thoſe who are depreſſed by unneceſſary terrors, may repel any temptations to deſpondency, by conſidering, that the

crime

crime of unworthy communication is like all others, only unpardoned, where it is unrepented.

Having thus ſhewn the danger incurred by an unworthy reception of the Sacrament, it is neceſſary to enquire how it may be avoided, and to conſider,

Firſt, What it is to eat and drink unworthily.

Secondly, By what means a man may become a worthy partaker of the Lord's Supper.

Firſt, I am to conſider what it is to eat and drink unworthily.

The unworthineſs with which the Corinthians are upbraided by the Apoſtle, was, in part, ſuch, as the preſent regulated eſtabliſhment of Chriſtianity, and the aſſiſtance which religion receives from the civil power, make it unneceſſary to cenſure, ſince it is not now committed even by the moſt preſumptuous, negligent, or profane. It was a practice amongſt them to aſſemble at the Holy Table in a tumultuous manner, and to celebrate the Euchariſt with indecency and riot. But though ſuch open profanation of this ſacred ordinance is not now to be apprehended, and, therefore, no

man

man needs to be cautioned againſt it, yet the cauſe which produced it is ſuch, as we cannot too anxiouſly fear, or too diligently avoid; for its influences are various and extenſive, and often weaken the efficacy of the Sacrament, though they produce no apparent diſorders in the celebration of it.

The Corinthians fell into this enormous ſin, ſays the Apoſtle, *not diſcerning the Lord's Body*, for want of diſcerning the importance and ſanctity of the inſtitution, and of diſtinguiſhing the Lord's Body, from the common elements of bread and wine exhibited on common occaſions of feſtive jollity. It is therefore the firſt duty of every Chriſtian to diſcern the Lord's Body, or to impreſs upon his mind a juſt idea of this act of commemoration, of the commands by which it is enforced, of the great ſacrifice which it repreſents, and of the benefits which it produces. Without theſe reflections, often repeated, and made habitual by long and fervent meditation, every one will be in danger of *eating and drinking unworthily*, of receiving the Sacrament without ſufficient veneration, without that ardent gratitude for the death of Chriſt, and that ſteady confidence in his merits, by which the Sacrament is made efficacious to his ſalvation; for of what uſe can it be to commemorate the death of the Redeemer of mankind without faith, and without thankſulneſs? Such a celebration of the Sacrament is nothing leſs than a mockery of God, an act by which we *approach him with our lips, when our hearts are far from him*; and as ſuch inſincerity and negligence cannot but be, in a very high degree, criminal, as he that eateth and drinketh thus unworthily cannot but promote his own damnation, it is neceſſary to enquire,

Secondly, By what means a man may become a worthy partaker of the Lord's Supper.

The method by which we are directed by the Apoſtle to prepare ourſelves for the Sacrament, is that of ſelf-examination, which implies a careful regulation of our lives by the rules of the Goſpel; for to what purpoſe is our conduct to be examined, but that it may be amended, where it appears erroneous and defective? The duty of examination therefore is only mentioned, and repentance and reformation are ſuppoſed, with great reaſon, inſeparable from it; for nothing is more evident, than that we are to enquire into the ſtate of our ſouls, as into affairs of leſs importance, with a view to avoid danger, or to ſecure happineſs. When we enquire with regard to our faith, whether it be ſufficiently vigorous or powerful, whether it regularly influences our conduct, reſtrains our paſſions, and moderates our deſires, what is intended by this duty, but that if we find ourſelves Chriſtians only in name, if we diſcover that the example of our divine Maſter has little force upon our conſtant converſation, and that God is ſeldom in our thoughts, except in the ſolemn acts of ſtated worſhip, we muſt then endeavour to invigorate our faith by returning frequently to meditate upon the objects of it, our creation, our redemption, the means of grace, and the hope of glory; and to enlighten our underſtandings, and awaken our affections, by the peruſal of writings of piety, and, above all, of the Holy Scriptures.

If any man, in his examination of his life, diſcovers that he has been guilty of fraud, extortion, or injury to his neighbour, he is to make reparation to his utmoſt

 power.

power. If he finds malice or hatred lurking in his mind, he muſt expel them by a ſtrong reſolution never to comply with their motions, or ſuffer them to break out in any real act of revenge. If he obſerves that he is often betrayed, by paſſions, or appetites, into unlawful methods of gratifying them, he muſt reſolve to reſtrain them for the future, by watching and faſting, by a ſteady temperance and perpetual vigilance.

But let him beware of vain confidence in his own firmneſs, and implore, by fervent and ſincere prayer, the coo-peration of God's grace with his endeavours; for by grace alone can we hope to reſiſt the numberleſs temptations that perpetually ſurround us; by grace only can we reject the ſolicitations of pleaſure, repreſs the motions of anger, and turn away from the allurements of ambition. And this grace, when ſincerely implored, is always granted in a degree ſufficient for our ſalvation; and it ought, therefore, to be one of the firſt parts of our preparation for the Sacrament, to pray for that grace, without which our examination itſelf will be uſeleſs, becauſe, without it, no pious reſolution can be formed, nor any virtue be practised.

As, therefore, it is only by an habitual and unrepented unworthiness that damnation is incurred, let no man be harassed with despondency for any past irreverence or coldness! As the Sacrament was instituted for one of the means of grace, let no one, who sincerely desires the salvation of his own soul, neglect to receive it; and as eternal punishment is denounced by the Apostle against all those who receive it unworthily, let no man approach the Table of the Lord, without repentance of his former sins, steadfast purposes of a new life, and full confidence in his merits, whose death is represented by it.

[illegible]

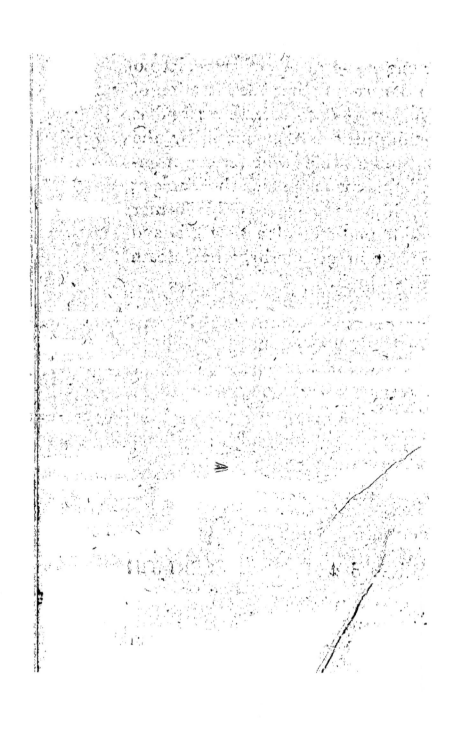

SERMON XXIII.

(Preached on the 30th of January.)

JAMES iii. 16.

Where envying and ſtrife is, there is confuſion.

THAT the life of man is unhappy, that his days are not only few, but evil, that he is ſurrounded by dangers, diſtracted by uncertainties, and oppreſſed by calamities, requires no proof. This is a truth, which every man confeſſes, or which he, that denies it, denies againſt conviction. Accordingly we find the miſeries of our preſent ſtate lamented by Writers of every claſs, from the inſpired Teachers of Religion, who admoniſh us of our frailty and infelicity, that they may incite us to labour after a better ſtate, where *there is fulneſs of joy, and pleaſures for evermore* to the vaineſt and looſeſt Author, whoſe deſign is to teach methods, not of improving, but of waſting time, and whoſe doctrine St. Paul, ſpeaking in a borrowed character, has well expreſſed in one ſhort ſentence, *Let us eat and drink, for to-morrow we die.*

When ſuch is the condition of beings, not brute and ſavage, but endowed with reaſon, and united in ſociety, who would not expect that they ſhould join in a perpetual confederacy againſt the certain, or fortuitous, troubles to which they are expoſed? that they ſhould univerſally coöperate in the promotion of univerſal felicity? that every man ſhould eaſily diſcover that his own happineſs is connected with that of every other man? that thouſands and millions ſhould continue together, as partakers of one common nature? and that every eye ſhould be vigilant, and every hand active, for the confirmation of eaſe, and the prevention of misfortune?

This expectation might be formed by ſpeculative wiſdom, but experience will ſoon diſſipate the pleaſing illuſion. A ſlight ſurvey of life will ſhew that, inſtead of hoping to be happy in the general felicity, every man purſues a private and independent intereſt, propoſes to himſelf ſome peculiar convenience, and prizes it more, as it is leſs attainable by others.

When

When the ties of ſociety are thus broken, and the general good of mankind is ſubdivided into the ſeparate advantages of individuals, it muſt neceſſarily happen, that many will deſire what few can poſſeſs, and conſequently, that ſome will be fortunate by the diſappointment, or defeat, of others, and ſince no man ſuffers diſappointment without pain, that one muſt become miſerable by another's happineſs.

This is however the natural condition of human life. As it is not poſſible for a being, neceſſitous and inſufficient as man, to act wholly without regard to his intereſt, ſo it is difficult for him to place his intereſt at ſuch a diſtance from him, as to act, with conſtant and uniform diligence, in hopes only of happineſs flowing back upon him in its circulation through a whole community, to ſeek his own good, only by ſeeking the good of all others, of many whom he cannot know, and of many whom he cannot love. Such a diffuſion of intereſt, ſuch ſublimation of ſelf-love is to all difficult, becauſe it ſo places the end at a great diſtance from the endeavour ; it is to many impoſſible, becauſe to many the end, thus removed, will be out of ſight. And

ſo

ſo great are the numbers of thoſe whoſe views either nature has bounded, or corruption has contracted, that whoever labours only for the public, will ſoon be left to labour alone, and driven from his attention to the univerſe, which his ſingle care will very little benefit, to the inſpection of his own buſineſs, and the proſecution of his private wiſhes. Every man has, in the preſent ſtate of things, wants which cannot wait for public plenty, and vexations which muſt be quieted before the days of univerſal peace. And no man can live only for others, unleſs he could perſuade others to live only for him.

The miſery of the world, therefore, ſo far as it ariſes from the inequality of conditions, is incurable. There are deſires, which almoſt all feel, but which all cannot gratify. Every man may, without a crime, ſtudy his own happineſs, if he be careful not to impede, by deſign, the happineſs of others. In the race of life, ſome muſt gain the prize, and others muſt loſe it; but the prize is honeſtly gained by him who outruns his competitor, without endeavouring to overthrow him.

In

In the profecution of private intereft, which Providence has either ordained, or permitted, there muft neceffarily be fome kind of ftrife. Where bleffings are thrown before us, as the reward of induftry, there muft be a conftant ftruggle of emulation. But this ftrife would be without confufion, if it were regulated by reafon and religion, if men would endeavour after lawful ends by lawful means.

But as there is a laudable defire of meliorating the condition of life, which communities may not only allow, but encourage, as the parent of ufeful arts, by which firft neceffity was fupplied; and conveniencies will always be multiplied; as there is likewife an honeft contention for preference and fuperiority, by which the powers of greater minds are pufhed into action, and the antient boundaries of fcience are overpaft; fo there is likewife a ftrife, of a pernicious and deftructive kind, which daily difturbs the quiet of individuals, and too frequently obftructs, or difturbs the happinefs of nations; a ftrife which always terminates in confufion, and which it is therefore every man's duty to avoid himfelf,

and

and every man's intereſt to repreſs in others.

This *ſtrife*, of which cometh *confuſion*, the Apoſtle has, in his prohibition, joined with envying. And daily experience will prove, that he has joined them with great propriety; for perhaps there has ſeldom been any great and laſting ſtrife in the world, of which envy was not either the original motive, or the moſt forcible incentive. The ravages of religious enthuſiaſts, and the wars kindled by difference of opinions, may perhaps be conſidered as calamities, which cannot properly be imputed to envy; yet even theſe may often be juſtly ſuſpected of riſing from no higher, or nobler cauſes. A man convinced of the truth of his own tenets, wiſhing the happineſs of others, and conſidering happineſs as the certain conſequence of truth, is neceſſarily prompted to extend his opinions, and to fill the world with proſelytes. But ſurely pure zeal cannot carry him beyond warm diſpute, and earneſt exhortation; becauſe by diſpute and exhortaion alone can *real* proſelytes be made. Violence may extort confeſſion from the tongue, but the mind muſt remain unchanged. Opinion, whether falſe or true, whether founded on evidence, or raiſed by prejudice, ſtands equally unſhaken in the tempeſts of commotion, and ſets at defiance the flames of hoſtility, and the ſword of perſecution.

No man, whoſe reaſon is not darkened by ſome inordinate perturbation of mind, can poſſibly judge ſo abſurdly of beings, partakers of the ſame nature with himſelf, as to imagine that any opinion can be recommended by cruelty and miſchief, or that he, who cannot perceive the force of argument, will be more efficaciouſly inſtructed by penalties and tortures. The power of puniſhment is to *ſilence*, not to *confute*. It, therefore, can never ſerve for the effectual propagation, or obſtruction, of doctrines. It may indeed ſometimes hinder the diſſemination of falſehood, and check the progreſs of error, but can never promote the reception of truth.

Whenever, therefore, we find the teacher, jealous of the honour of his ſect, and apparently more ſolicitous to ſee his opinions *eſtabliſhed* than *approved*, we may conclude, that he has added envy to his zeal; and that he feels more *pain from*

the

the want of victory, than *pleasure from the enjoyment of truth.*

It is the present mode of speculation to charge these men with total hypocrisy, as wretches who have no other design but that of temporal advancement, and consider religion only as one of the means by which power is gained, or wealth accumulated. But this charge, whatever may have been the depravity of single persons, is by no means generally true. The persecutor and enthusiast have often been superior to the desire of worldly possessions, or, at least, have been abstracted from it by stronger passions. There is a kind of mercantile speculation, which ascribes every action to interest, and considers interest as only another name for pecuniary advantage. But the boundless variety of human affections is not to be thus easily circumscribed. Causes and effects, motives and actions, are complicated and diversified without end. Many men make party subservient to personal purposes; and many likewise suffer all private considerations to be absorbed and lost in their zeal for some public cause. But envy still operates, however various in its appearance, however disguised by

specious

ſpecious pretences, or however removed from notice by intermediate cauſes. All violence, beyond the neceſſity of ſelf-defence, is incited by the deſire of humbling the opponents, and, whenever it is applied to the deciſion of religious queſtions, aims at conqueſt, rather than converſion.

Since, therefore, envy is found to operate ſo often, and ſo ſecretly, and the *ſtrife* which ariſes from it is certain to end in *confuſion*, it is ſurely the duty of every man, who deſires the proſperity of his country, as connected with a particular community, or the general happineſs of the world, as allied to general humanity,

Firſt, To conſider, by what tokens he may diſcover in himſelf, or others, that *ſtrife* which ſprings from *envy*, and ends in *confuſion*.

Secondly, What are the evils, produced by that *confuſion*, which proceeds from *ſtrife*.

Firſt, Let us conſider, by what tokens we may diſcover in ourſelves, or others, that *ſtrife* which ſprings from *envy*, and ends in *confuſion*.

That ſtrife may well be ſuppoſed to proceed from ſome corrupt paſſion, which is carried

carried on with vehemence, diſproportioned to the importance of the end openly propoſed. Men naturally value eaſe and tranquillity at a very high rate, and will not, on very ſmall cauſes, either ſuffer labour, or excite oppoſition. When, therefore, any man voluntarily engages in taſks of difficulty, and incurs danger, or ſuffers hardſhips, it muſt be imagined that he propoſes to himſelf ſome reward, more than equivalent to the comforts which he thus reſigns, and of which he ſeems to triumph in the reſignation; and if it cannot be found, that his labours tend to the advancement of ſome end, worthy of ſo much aſſiduity, he may juſtly be ſuppoſed to have formed to himſelf ſome imaginary intereſt, and to ſeek his gratification, not in that which he himſelf gains, but which another loſes.

It is a token that ſtrife proceeds from unlawful motives, when it is proſecuted by unlawful means. He that ſeeks only the right, and only for the ſake of right, will not eaſily ſuffer himſelf to be tranſported beyond the juſt and allowed methods of attaining it. To do evil that good may come, can never be the purpoſe of a man

who

who has not perverted his morality by ſome falſe principle; and falſe principles are not ſo often collected by the judgement, as ſnatched up by the paſſions. The man whoſe duty gives way to his convenience, who, when once he has fixed his eye upon a diſtant end, haſtens to it by violence over forbidden ground, or creeps on towards it through the crooked paths of fraud and ſtratagem, as he has evidently ſome other guide than the word of GOD, muſt be ſuppoſed to have likewiſe ſome other purpoſe than the glory of GOD, or the benefit of man.

The evidence of corrupt deſigns is much ſtrengthened, when unlawful means are uſed, in preference to thoſe which are recommended by reaſon, and warranted by juſtice.

When that which would have been granted to requeſt, or yielded to remonſtrance, is wantonly ſeized by ſudden violence, it is apparent that violence is choſen for its own ſake, and that the claimant pleaſes himſelf, not with the *poſſeſſion*, but the *power* by which it was gained, and the mortification of him, to whom his ſuperiority has not allowed the happineſs of choice,

but

but has at once taken from him the honour of keeping, and the credit of resigning.

There is another token that strife is produced by the predominance of some vicious passion, when it is carried on against natural or legal, superiority. This token, though perhaps it is not very frequently fallacious, is not equally certain with the former; because that superiority, which nature gives, or institutions establish, too frequently incites insolence, or oppression; such insolence as may justly be restrained, and such oppression as may be lawfully resisted. Many modes of tyranny have been practised in the world, of which it is more natural to ask, with wonder, why they were submitted to so long, than why they were at last opposed and quelled. But if history and experience inform us that power and greatness grow wanton and licentious, that wealth and prosperity elate the mind, and enslave the understanding to desire, and when men once find that no one has power to controul them, they are seldom very attentive to justice, or very careful to controul themselves: History and experience will likewise shew us, that the contrary condition has its temptations

and

and its crimes, that he who conſiders himſelf as ſubject to another, and liable to ſuffer by caprice or wickedneſs, often anticipates the evils of his ſtate, imagines himſelf to feel what he only fears, and imputes every failure of negligence, or ſtart of paſſion, to ſtudied tyranny and ſettled malevolence. To be inferior is neceſſarily unpleaſing, to be placed in a ſtate of inferiority to thoſe who have no eminent abilities, or tranſcendent merit, (which muſt happen in all political conſtitutions) increaſes the uneaſineſs; and every man finds in himſelf a ſtrong inclination to throw down from their elevated ſtate thoſe whom he obeys without approbation, whom he reverences without eſteem. When the paſſions are once in motion, they are not eaſily appeaſed, or checked. He that has once concluded it lawful to reſiſt power, when it wants merit, will ſoon find a want of merit, to juſtify his own reſiſtance of power.

Thus, if we conſider the conduct of individuals towards each other, we ſhall commonly find the labourer murmuring at him who ſeems to live by eaſier means. We ſhall hear the poor repining that others are rich, and even the rich ſpeaking with malignity of thoſe who are ſtill richer than themſelves.

And if we ſurvey the condition of kingdoms and commonwealths, it will always be obſerved, that governors are cenſured, that every miſchief of chance is imputed to ill deſigns, and that nothing can perſuade mankind, that they are not injured by an adminiſtration, either unſkilful, or corrupt. It is very difficult always to do right. To ſeem always to do right to thoſe who deſire to diſcover wrong, is ſcarcely poſſible. Every man is ready to form expectations in his own favour, ſuch as never can be gratified, and which will yet raiſe complaints, if they are diſappointed.

Such is commonly the diſpoſition, with which men look upon thoſe who are placed above them, and with ſuch diſpoſitions we cannot hope that they ſhould be often pleaſed. Life is a ſtate of imperfection, and yet every man exacts from his ſuperiors conſummate wiſdom, and unfailing virtue; and whenever he ſees, or believes himſelf to ſee, either vice or error, thinks himſelf at liberty to looſen the ties of duty, and paſs the boundaries of ſubordination, without conſidering that of ſuch *ſtrife* there muſt come *confuſion*, or without knowing, what we ſhall conſider,

Secondly, The evils and miſchiefs produced by that *confuſion* which ariſes from *ſtrife*.

That the deſtruction of order, and the abolition of ſtated regulations, muſt fill the world with uncertainty, diſtraction, and ſolicitude, is apparent, without any long deduction of argument. Yet it has too frequently happened, that thoſe who either feel their wiſhes reſtrained, ſee their fortunes wearing away, or imagine their merit neglected, and their abilities employed upon buſineſs unworthy of their attention, deſire times of tumult and diſturbance, as affording the faireſt opportunities for the active and ſagacious to diſtinguiſh themſelves, and as throwing open the avenues of wealth and honour, to be entered by thoſe who have the greateſt quickneſs of diſcernment, and celerity of diſpatch. In times of peace every thing proceeds in a train of regularity, and there is no ſudden advantage to be ſnatched, nor any unuſual change of condition to be hoped. But when ſedition and uproar have once ſilenced law, and confounded property, then is the hour

 when

when chance begins to predominate in the world, when every man may hope without bounds, and thoſe, who know how to improve the lucky moment, may gain in a day what no length of labour could have procured, without the concurrence of caſual advantage.

This is the expectation which makes ſome haſten on confuſion, and others look with concern at its approach. But what is this other than gaining by univerſal miſery, ſupplying by force the want of right, and riſing to ſudden elevation, by the ſudden downfal of others?

The great benefit of ſociety is that the weak are protected againſt the ſtrong. The great evil of confuſion is that the world is thrown into the hands, not of the beſt, but of the ſtrongeſt; that all certainty of poſſeſſion or acquiſition is deſtroyed; that every man's care is confined to his own intereſt; and that general negligence of the general good makes way for general licentiouſneſs.

Of the ſtriſe, which this day brings back to our remembrance, we may obſerve, that it had all the tokens of *ſtriſe* proceeding from *envy*. The rage of the faction, which invaded

invaded the rights of the Church and Monarchy, was diſproportionate to the provocation received. The violence, with which hoſtility was proſecuted, was more than the cauſe, that was publicly avowed, could incite or juſtify. Perſonal reſentment was apparent in the perſecution of particular men, and the bitterneſs of faction broke out in all the debates upon public queſtions. No ſecurities could quiet ſuſpicion, no conceſſions could ſatisfy exorbitance. Uſurpation was added to uſurpation; demand was accumulated on demand; and, when war had decided againſt loyalty, inſult was added to inſult, and exaction to exaction.

As the end was unjuſt, the means likewiſe were illegal. The power of the faction commenced by clamour, was promoted by rebellion, and eſtabliſhed by murder; by murder of the moſt atrocious kind, deliberate, contumelious, and cruel; by murder, not neceſſary even to the ſafety of thoſe by whom it was committed, but choſen in preference to any other expedient for ſecurity.

This war certainly did not want the third token of *ſtrife* proceeding from *envy*.

It

It was a war of the rabble againſt their ſuperiors; a war, in which the loweſt and baſeſt of the people were encouraged by men a little higher than themſelves, to lift their hands againſt their eccleſiaſtical and civil Governors, and by which thoſe who were grown impatient of obedience, endeavoured to obtain the power of commanding.

This *ſtrife*, as we all know, ended in *confuſion*. Our laws were over-ruled, our rights were aboliſhed. The ſoldier ſeized upon the property, the fanatick ruſhed into the church. The Uſurpers gave way to other Uſurpers; the Schiſmaticks were thruſt out by other Schiſmaticks; the people felt nothing from their maſters but alternatives of oppreſſion, and heard nothing from their teachers but varieties of error.

Such was the *ſtrife*, and ſuch was the *confuſion*. Such are the evils which God ſometimes permits to fall upon nations, when they ſtand ſecure in their own greatneſs, and forget their dependence on univerſal ſovereignty, depart from the laws of their Maker, corrupt the purity of his worſhip, or ſwerve from the truth of his revelation. Such evils ſurely we have too much reaſon to fear again, for we have no right to charge our Anceſtors with having provoked them by crimes greater than our own.

Let us therefore be warned by the calamities of paſt ages; and thoſe miſeries which are due to our ſins, let us avert by our penitence. *Let the wicked forſake his ways, and the unrighteous man his thoughts, and let him return unto the Lord, and he will have mercy upon him, and to our God, and he will abundantly pardon.*

SERMON XXIV.

PROVERBS, xxix. 2.

When the righteous are in authority, the people rejoice.

THAT the inſtitutions of government owe their original, like other human actions, to the deſire of happineſs, is not to be denied; nor is it leſs generally allowed, that they have been perverted to very different ends from thoſe which they were intended to promote. This is a truth, which it would be very ſuperfluous to prove by authorities, or illuſtrate by examples. Every page of hiſtory, whether ſacred or profane, will furniſh us abundantly with inſtances of Rulers that have deviated from juſtice, and ſubjects that have forgotten their allegiance; of nations ruined by the tyranny

tyranny of Governors, and of Governors overborne by the madneſs of the populace. Inſtead of a concurrence between Governor and ſubjects for their mutual advantage, they ſeem to have conſidered each other, not as allies or friends, to be aided or ſupported, but as enemies, whoſe proſperity was inconſiſtent with their own, and who were therefore to be ſubdued by open force, or ſubjected by ſecret ſtratagems.

Thus have ſlavery and licentiouſneſs ſucceeded one another, and anarchy and deſpotic power alternately prevailed. Virtue has, at one time, ſtood expoſed to the puniſhments of vice; and vice, at another time, enjoyed the ſecurity and privileges of virtue. Nor have communities ſuffered more, when they were expoſed to the paſſions and caprices of one man, however cruel, ambitious, or inſolent, than when all reſtraint has been taken off the actions of men by public confuſions, and every one left at full liberty to indulge his own deſires, and comply, without fear of puniſhment, with his wildeſt imaginations.

Man is, for the moſt part, equally unhappy, when ſubjected, without redreſs, to the paſſions of another, or left, without

controul,

controul, to the dominion of his own. This every man, however unwilling he may be to own it of himſelf, will very readily acknowledge of his neighbour. No man knows any one, except himſelf, whom he judges fit to be ſet free from the coercion of laws, and to be abandoned entirely to his own choice. By this conſideration have all civilized nations been induced to the enactions of penal laws, laws, by which every man's danger becomes every man's ſafety, and by which, though all are reſtrained, yet all are benefited.

Government is therefore neceſſary, in the opinion of every one, to the ſafety of particular men, and the happineſs ſociety; and it may be conſidered as a maxim univerſally admitted, that *the people* cannot *rejoice*, except *the righteous are in authority*; that no public proſperity, or private quiet, can be hoped for, but from the juſtice and wiſdom of thoſe, to whom the adminiſtration of affairs, and the execution of the laws, is committed. For corrupt governments operate, with equal force and efficacy, to the deſtruction of a people, as good governments to their preſervation.

But

But that authority may never ſwell into tyranny, or languiſh into ſupineneſs, and that ſubjection may never degenerate into ſlavery, nor freedom kindle into rebellion, it may be proper, both for thoſe who are intruſted with power, and thoſe from whom obedience is required, to conſider,

Firſt, How much it is the duty of thoſe in authority to promote the happineſs of the people.

Secondly, By what means the happineſs of the people may be moſt effectually promoted.

Thirdly, How the people are to aſſiſt and further the endeavours of their Governors.

Firſt, How much it is the duty of thoſe in authority to promote the happineſs of the people.

If it be true in general that no man is born merely for his own ſake, to conſult his own advantage or pleaſure, unconnected with the good of others; it is yet more evidenty true of thoſe who are exalted into high rank, dignified with honours, and inveſted with authority. Their ſuperiority is not to be conſidered as a ſanction for lazineſs, or a privilege for vice. They are not to conceive, that their paſſions are to be

allowed

allowed a wider range, or their appetites ſet more free from ſubjection to reaſon, than thoſe of others. They are not to conſult their own glory, at the expence of the lives of others, or to gratify their avarice, by plundering thoſe whom diligence and labour have entitled to affluence. They are not to conceive that power gives a right to oppreſs, and to puniſh thoſe who murmer at oppreſſion. They are to look upon their power, and their greatneſs, as inſtruments placed in their hands, to be employed for the public advantage. They are to remember they are placed upon an eminence, that their examples may be more conſpicuous, and that, therefore, they muſt take care, leſt they teach thoſe vices which they ought to ſuppreſs. They muſt reflect, that it is their duty to ſecure property from the attempts of rapine and robbery, and that thoſe whom they protect, will be very little benefited by their care, if, what they reſcue from others, they take away themſelves.

It appears from thoſe ſtruggles for dominion, which have filled the world with war, bloodſhed, and deſolation, and have torn in pieces almoſt all the ſtates and kingdoms

kingdoms of the earth, and from thoſe dai-ly conteſts for ſubordinate authority, which diſturb the quiet of ſmaller ſocieties, that there is ſomewhat in power more pleaſing than in any other enjoyment; and, conſe-quently, to beſtow upon man the happineſs of ruling others, is to beſtow upon him the greateſt benefit he is capable of receiving. Nothing then can equal the obligation of Governors to the people, and nothing but the moſt flagrant ingratitude can make them careleſs of the intereſts, or uncon-cerned at the misfortunes, of thoſe to whom they owe that, for which no danger has been thought too dreadful to be encounter-ed, no labour too tedious to be undergone, and no crime too horrible to be commit-ted.

Gratitude is a ſpecies of juſtice. He that requites a benefit may be ſaid, in ſome ſenſe, to pay a debt; and, of courſe, he that forgets favours received may be accuſed of neglecting to pay what he cannot be de-nied to owe. But this is not the only ſenſe in which juſtice may be ſaid to require from a Governor an attention to the wants and petitions of the people. He that en-gages in the management of public buſineſs, takes a truſt upon him, which it was in his power to decline, and which he is therefore bound to diſcharge with diligence and fidelity; a truſt which is of the higheſt honour, becauſe it is of the greateſt difficulty and importance, a truſt which includes, not only the care of the property, but of the morals of the people.

It is with the juſteſt reaſon, that large revenues, pompous titles, and all that contributes to the happineſs of life, are annexed to theſe high offices; for what reward can be too great for him, to whom multitudes are indebted for the ſecure enjoyment of their poſſeſſions? for him, whoſe authority checks the progreſs of vice, and aſſiſts the advancement of virtue, reſtrains the violence of the oppreſſor, and aſſerts the cauſe of the injured? Theſe are doubtleſs merits above the common rate, merits which can hardly be too loudly celebrated, or too liberally rewarded.

But it is always to be obſerved, that he only deſerves the recompenſe, who performs the work for which it is propoſed; and that he, who wears the honours, and receives the revenues, of an exalted nation, without attending to the duties of his poſt, is, in a very high degree, criminal, both in the eye of God and man.

It is, therefore, the certain and apparent duty of thofe that are in authority, to take care that the people may rejoice, and diligently to enquire, what is to be confidered,

Secondly; By what means the happinefs of the people may be moft effectually promoted.

In political, as well as natural diforders, the great error of thofe who commonly undertake, either cure or prefervation, is, that they reft in fecond caufes, without extending their fearch to the remote and original fources of evil. They therefore obviate the immediate evil, but leave the deftructive principle to operate again; and have their work for ever to begin, like the hufbandman who mows down the heads of noifome weeds, inftead of pulling up the roots.

The only uniform and perpetual caufe of public happinefs is public virtue. The effects of all other things which are confidered as advantages, will be found cafual and tranfitory. Without virtue nothing can be fecurely poffeffed, or properly enjoyed.

In

In a country like ours, the great demand, which is for ever repeated to our Governors, is for the ſecurity of property, the confirmation of liberty, and the extenſion of commerce. All this we have obtained, and all this we poſſeſs, in a degree which perhaps was never granted to any other people. Yet we ſtill find ſomething wanting to our happineſs, and turn ourſelves round on all ſides, with perpetual reſtleſſneſs, to find that remedy for our evils which neither power nor policy can afford.

That eſtabliſhed property and inviolable freedom are the greateſt of political felicities, no man can be ſuppoſed likely to deny. To depend on the will of another, to labour for that, of which arbitrary power can prohibit the enjoyment, is the ſtate to which want of reaſon has ſubjected the brute. To be happy we muſt know our own rights; and we muſt know them to be ſafe.

But though this knowledge be neceſſary to happineſs, this knowledge is not ſufficient. Liberty, if not regulated by virtue, can be only licence to do evil; and property, if not virtuouſly enjoyed, can only corrupt the poſſeſſor, and give him the

 power

power to injure others. Trade may make us rich; but riches, without goodneſs, cannot make us happy.

Let us, however, ſuppoſe that theſe external goods have that power which wiſdom cannot believe, and which experience never could confirm; let us ſuppoſe that riches and liberty could make us happy. It then remains to be conſidered, how riches and liberty can be ſecured. To this the Politician has a ready anſwer, that they are to be ſecured by laws wiſely formed, and vigorouſly executed. But, as laws can be made only by a ſmall part of an extenſive empire, and muſt be executed by a part yet far ſmaller, what ſhall protect us againſt the laws themſelves? And how ſhall we be certain, that they ſhall not be made without regard to the public good, or ſhall not be perverted to oppreſſion by the miniſters of juſtice?

But if proſperity, and laws, by which, as far as the mutability of this world permits, that proſperity is made permanent and ſafe, cannot make the people happy, what is it the Governors can do? How far is their care to be extended, and what more can ſkill and vigilance perform?

The

The wiſdom of mankind has been exerciſed in enquiries how riches may be gained and kept ; how the different claims of men may be adjuſted without violence ; and how one part of the community may be reſtrained from encroachments on the other. For this end governments have been inſtituted, in all their various forms, with much ſtudy, and too often with much bloodſhed. But what is the uſe of all this, if, when theſe ends are obtained, there is yet ſo much wanting to felicity ?

I am far from intending to inſinuate, that the ſtudies of political wiſdom, or the labours of legiſlative patriotiſm, have been vain and idle. They are uſeful, but not effectual ; they are conducive to that end, which yet they cannot fully gain. The Legiſlator, who does what human power can attain towards the felicity of his fellow-creatures, is not to be cenſured, becauſe, by the imbecillity of all human endeavours, he fails of his purpoſe ; unleſs he has become culpable, by aſcribing too much to his own powers, and arrogated to his induſtry, or his wit, that efficacy which wit and induſtry muſt always want, unleſs ſome

 higher

higher power lends them aſſiſtance, and co-operates with them.

The huſbandman may plow his fields with induſtry, and ſow them with ſkill; he may manure them copiouſly, and fence them carefully; but the harveſt muſt depend at laſt on the celeſtial influence; and all his diligence is fruſtrated, unleſs the ſun ſheds its warmth, and the clouds pour down their moiſture. Thus, in all human affairs, when prudence and induſtry have done their utmoſt, the work is left to be completed by ſuperior agency; and in the ſecurity of peace, and ſtability of poſſeſſion, our policy muſt at laſt call for help upon religion.

Human laws, however honeſtly inſtituted, or however vigorouſly enforced, muſt be limited in their effect, partly by our ignorance, and partly by our weakneſs. Daily experience may convince us, that all the avenues by which injury and oppreſſion may break in upon life, cannot be guarded by poſitive prohibitions. Every man ſees, and may feel, evils, which no law can puniſh. And not only will there always remain poſſibilities of guilt, which legiſlative foreſight cannot diſcover, but

the

the laws will be often violated by wicked men, whoſe ſubtilty eludes detection, and whom therefore vindictive juſtice cannot bring within the reach of puniſhment.

Theſe deficiencies in civil life can be ſupplied only by religion. The mere obſerver of human laws avoids only ſuch offences as the laws forbid, and thoſe only when the laws can detect his delinquency. But he who acts with the perpetual conſciouſneſs of the divine preſence, and conſiders himſelf as accountable for all his actions to the irreverſible and unerring judgment of omniſcience, has other motives of action, and other reaſons of forbearance. He is equally reſtrained from evil, in public life, and in ſecret ſolitude; and has only one rule of action, by which *he does to others what he would that others ſhould do to him*, and wants no other enforcement of his duty, than the fear of future puniſhment, and the hope of future rewards.

The firſt duty therefore of a Governor is to diffuſe through the community a ſpirit of religion, to endeavour that a ſenſe of the divine authority ſhould prevail in all orders of men, and that the laws ſhould

be

be obeyed, in ſubordination to the univerſal and unchangeable edicts of the Creator and Ruler of the world.

How religion may be moſt effectually promoted, is an enquiry which every Governor ought diligently to make; and he that enquires, with real wiſhes for reformation, will ſoon know his duty; for Providence has ſeldom made the ſame things neceſſary and abſtruſe.

That religion may be invigorated and diffuſed, it is neceſſary that the external order of religion be diligently maintained, that the ſolemnities of worſhip be duly obſerved, and a proper reverence preſerved for the times and the places appropriated to piety. The appropriations of time and place are indeed only means to the great end of holineſs; but they are means, without which the end cannot be obtained; and every man muſt have obſerved, how much corruption prevails, where the attention to public worſhip and to holy ſeaſons is broken or relaxed.

Thoſe that have in their hands the diſpoſal of riches or honours ought to beſtow them on perſons who are moſt eminent for ſanctity of life. For though no man ought to conſider temporary goods as the proper

rewards

rewards of religious duties, yet they, who have them to give, are obliged to diſtribute them in ſuch a manner as may make them moſt uſeful to the public; and they will be moſt uſeful, when they increaſe the power of beneficence, and enlarge the influence of piety.

It yet remains that Governors co-operate with their laws by their own examples, and that as, by their height of place, they are always conſpicuous, they exhibit to thoſe eyes which are turned upon them *the beauty of holineſs*.

The preſent ſtate of the world however affords us little hope, that virtue can, by any government, be ſo ſtrongly impreſſed, or ſo widely diffuſed, as to ſuperſede the neceſſity of ſuppreſſing wickedneſs. In the moſt diligent cultivation of the happieſt ſoil, weeds will ſometimes appear among fruits and flowers, and all that vigilance and labour can do is to check them as they riſe. However virtue may be encouraged or rewarded, it can never appear to all minds the ſhorteſt means of preſent good. There will always be thoſe who would rather grow rich by fraud, than by diligence, and who will provide for vicious pleaſures by violence, rather than by labour. Againſt the attempts and artifices of ſuch men, whence have ſimplicity and innocence their defence and ſecurity? Whence, but from the *Lex armata*, the vindictive law, that ſtands forth the champion of the weak, and the protectreſs of the innocent?

Nor is quiet and ſecurity in danger only from corrupt minds; for honeſt and beneficent men might often, were not the law to interpoſe, diſturb ſociety, and fill the country with violence. Two men, both of them wiſe, and both of them virtuous, may lay claim to the ſame poſſeſſion, with pretenſions, to the world ſpecious, in their own thoughts juſt. Such diſputes can be terminated only by force or law. Of force, it is apparent, that the exertion of it is an immediate evil, and that prevalence at laſt will be no proof of juſtice. Of law, the means are gentle and inoffenſive, and the concluſion not only the confirmation of property, but the eſtabliſhment of right. For this power of the law virtue itſelf will leave employment; for though crimes would hardly be committed but by predominance of paſſion, yet litigation muſt always ſubſiſt while there is difference of opinion. We can hope but faintly for the time when all men ſhall be honeſt; but the time ſeems ſtill more remote in which all men ſhall be wiſe; and until we may be able to ſettle all claims for ourſelves, let us rejoice that there is law to adjuſt them for us.

The care however of the beſt Governor may be fruſtrated by diſobedience and perverſeneſs; and the beſt laws may ſtrive in vain againſt radicated wickedneſs.

It is therefore fit to conſider,

Thirdly, How the people are to aſſiſt and further the endeavours of their Governors.

As all government is power exerted by few upon many, it is apparent, that nations cannot be governed but by their own conſent. The firſt duty therefore of ſubjects is obedience to the laws; ſuch obedience as is the effect, not of compulſion, but of reverence; ſuch as ariſes from a conviction of the inſtability of human virtue, and of the neceſſity of ſome coercive power, which may reſtrain the exorbitancies of paſſion, and check the career of natural deſires.

No man thinks laws unneceſſary for others; and no man, if he conſiders his own inherent frailty, can juſtly think them unneceſſary for himſelf. The wiſeſt man is not always wiſe, and the beſt man is not always good. We all ſometimes want the admonition of law, as ſupplemental to the dictates of reaſon, and the ſuggeſtions of conſcience. And he that encourages irreverence, in himſelf, or others, to public inſtitutions, weakens all the human ſecurities of peace, and all the corroborations of virtue.

That the proper influence of government may be preſerved, and that the liberty which a juſt diſtribution of power naturally ſupports may not operate to its deſtruction, it is always to be remembered, that even the errors and deficiencies of authority muſt be treated with reſpect. All inſtitutions are defective by their nature; and all Rulers have their imperfections, like other men. But, as not every failing makes a bad man, ſo not every error makes a bad government; and he that conſiders how few can properly adjuſt their own houſes, will not wonder that into the multiplicity of national affairs deception

or

or negligence ſhould ſometimes find their way. It is likewiſe neceſſary to remember, that as government is difficult to be adminiſtered, it is difficult to be underſtood; and that where very few have capacity to judge, very few have a right to cenſure.

The happineſs of a nation muſt ariſe from the combined endeavours of Governors and ſubjects. The duties of governing can be the lot of few, but all of us have the duties of ſubjects to perform; and every man ought to incite in himſelf, and in his neighbour, that obedience to the laws, and that reſpect to the chief Magiſtrate, which may ſecure and promote concord and quiet. Of this, as of all other virtues, the true baſis is religion. The laws will be eaſily obeyed by him who adds to human ſanctions the obligations of conſcience; and he will not eaſily be diſpoſed to cenſure his ſuperiors, whom religion has made acquainted with his own feelings.

SERMON XXV.

[Written by Dr. JOHNSON, for the Funeral of his Wife.]

JOHN xi. 25, 26 (former part.)

Jesus said unto her, I am the Resurrection, and the Life: he that believeth in me, though he were dead, yet shall he live;
And whosoever liveth, and believeth in me, shall never die.

TO afford adequate consolations to the last hour, to cheer the gloomy passage through the valley of the shadow of death, and to ease that anxiety, to which beings, prescient of their own dissolution, and conscious of their own danger, must be necessarily exposed, is the privilege only of re-

vealed

vealed religion. All thoſe, to whom the ſupernatural light of heavenly doctrine has never been imparted, however formidable ſor power, or illuſtrious for wiſdom, have wanted that knowledge of their future ſtate which alone can give comfort to miſery, or ſecurity to enjoyment; and have been forced to ruſh forwards to the grave, through the darkneſs of ignorance; or, if they happened to be more refined and inquiſitive, to ſolace their paſſage with the fallacious and uncertain glimmer of philoſophy.

There were, doubtleſs, at all times, as there are now, many who lived with very little thought concerning their end; many whoſe time was wholly filled up by public or domeſtic buſineſs, by the purſuits of ambition, or the deſire of riches; many who diſſolved themſelves in luxurious enjoyment, and, when they could lull their minds by any preſent pleaſure, had no regard to diſtant events, but withheld their imagination from ſallying out into futurity, or catching any terror that might interrupt their quiet; and there were many who roſe ſo little above animal life, that they were completely engroſſed by the objects about them, and had their views extended

tended no farther than to the next hour; in whom the ray of reaſon was half extinct, and who had neither hopes nor fears, but of ſome near advantage, of ſome preſſing danger.

But multitudes there muſt always be, and greater multitudes as arts and civility prevail, who cannot wholly withdraw their thoughts from death. All cannot be diſtracted with buſineſs, or ſtunned with the clamours of aſſemblies, or the ſhouts of armies. All cannot live in the perpetual diſſipation of ſucceſſive diverſions, nor will all enſlave their underſtandings to their ſenſes, and ſeek felicity in the groſs gratifications of appetite. Some muſt always keep their reaſon and their fancy in action, and ſeek either honour or pleaſure from intellectual operations; and from them, others, more negligent or ſluggiſh, will be in time fixed or awakened; knowledge will be perpetually diffuſed, and curioſity hourly enlarged.

But, when the faculties were once put in motion, when the mind had broken looſe from the ſhackles of ſenſe, and made excurſions to remote conſequences, the firſt conſideration that would ſtop her courſe

muſt

muſt be the inceſſant waſte of life, the approach of age, and the certainty of death; the approach of that time, in which ſtrength muſt fail, and pleaſure fly away, and the certainty of that diſſolution which ſhall put an end to all the proſpects of this world. It is impoſſible to think, and not ſometimes to think on death. Hope, indeed, has many powers of deluſion; whatever is poſſible, however unlikely, it will teach us to promiſe ourſelves; but death no man has eſcaped, and therefore no man can hope to eſcape it. From this dreadful expectation no ſhelter or refuge can be found. Whatever we ſee, forces it upon us; whatever is, new or old, flouriſhing or declining, either directly, or by a very ſhort deduction, leads man to the conſideration of his end; and accordingly we find, that the fear of death has always been conſidered as the great enemy of human quiet, the polluter of the feaſt of happineſs, and embitterer of the cup of joy. The young man who rejoiceth in his youth, amidſt his muſic and his gaiety, has always been diſturbed with the thought, that his youth will be quickly at an end. The monarch, to whom it is ſaid that he is a God, has always been reminded by his own heart, that he ſhall die like man.

This unwelcome conviction, which is thus continually preſſed upon the mind, every art has been employed to oppoſe. The general remedy, in all ages, has been to chaſe it away from the preſent moment, and to gain a ſuſpence of the pain that could not be cured. In the ancient writings, we, therefore, find the ſhortneſs of life frequently mentioned as an excitement to jollity and pleaſure; and may plainly diſcover, that the authors had no other means of relieving that gloom with which the uncertainty of human life clouded their conceptions. Some of the Philoſophers, indeed, appear to have ſought a nobler, and a more certain remedy, and to have endeavoured to overpower the force of death by arguments, and to diſpel the gloom by the light of reaſon. They enquired into the nature of the ſoul of man, and ſhewed, at leaſt probably, that it is a ſubſtance diſtinct from matter, and therefore independend on the body, and exempt from diſſolution and corruption. The arguments, whether phyſical or moral, upon which they eſtabliſhed this doctrine, it is not ne-

 ceſſary

ceſſary to recount to a Chriſtian audience, by whom it is believed upon more certain proofs, and higher authority; ſince, though they were ſuch as might determine the calm mind of a Philoſopher, inquiſitive only after truth, and uninfluenced by external objects; yet they were ſuch as required leiſure and capacity, not allowed in general to mankind; they were ſuch as many could never underſtand, and of which, therefore, the efficacy and comfort were confined to a ſmall number, without any benefit to the unenlightened multitude.

Such has been hitherto the nature of philoſophical arguments, and ſuch it muſt probably for ever remain; for, though, perhaps, the ſucceſſive induſtry of the ſtudious may encreaſe the number, or advance the probability, of arguments; and, though continual contemplation of matter will, I believe, ſhew it, at length, wholly incapable of motion, ſenſation, or order, by any powers of its own, and therefore neceſſarily eſtabliſh the immateriality, and, probably, the immortality of the ſoul; yet there never can be expected a time, in which the groſs body of mankind can attend

tend to ſuch ſpeculations, or can comprehend them; and, therefore, there never can be a time, in which this knowledge can be taught, in ſuch a manner, as to be generally conducive to virtue, or happineſs, but by a meſſenger from God, from the Creator of the World, and the Father of Spirits.

To perſuade common and uninſtructed minds to the belief of any fact, we may every day perceive, that the teſtimony of one man, whom they think worthy of credit, has more force than the arguments of a thouſand reaſoners, even when the arguments are ſuch as they may be imagined completely qualified to comprehend. Hence it is plain, that the conſtitution of mankind is ſuch, that abſtruſe and intellectual truths can be taught no otherwiſe than by poſitive aſſertion, ſupported by ſome ſenſible evidence, by which the aſſertor is ſecured from the ſuſpicion of falſehood; and that if it ſhould pleaſe God to inſpire a teacher with ſome demonſtration of the immortality of the ſoul, it would far leſs avail him for general inſtruction, than the power of working a miracle in its vindication, unleſs God ſhould, at the ſame time, inſpire all the hearers with docility and apprehenſion, and turn, at once, all the ſenſual, the giddy, the lazy, the buſy, the corrupt, and the proud, into humble, abſtracted, and diligent Philoſophers.

To bring life and immortality to light, to give ſuch proofs of our future exiſtence, as may influence the moſt narrow mind, and fill the moſt capacious intellect, to open proſpects beyond the grave, in which the thought may expatiate without obſtruction, and to ſupply a refuge and ſupport to the mind, amidſt all the miſeries of decaying nature, is the peculiar excellence of the Goſpel of Chriſt. Without this heavenly Inſtructor, he who feels himſelf ſinking under the weight of years, or melting away by the ſlow waſte of a lingering diſeaſe, has no other remedy than obdurate patience, a gloomy reſignation to that which cannot be avoided ; and he who follows his friend, or whoever there is yet dearer than a friend, to the grave, can have no other conſolation than that which he derives from the general miſery ; the reflection, that he ſuffers only what the reſt of mankind muſt ſuffer ; a poor conſideration,

deration, which rather awes us to ſilence, than ſooths us to quiet, and which does not abate the ſenſe of our calamity, though it may ſometimes make us aſhamed to complain.

But ſo much is our condition improved by the Goſpel, ſo much is the ſting of death rebated, that we may now be invited to the contemplation of our mortality, as to a pleaſing employment of the mind, to an exerciſe delightful and recreative, not only when calamity and perſecution drive us out from the aſſemblies of men, and ſorrow and woe repreſent the grave as a refuge and an aſylum, but even in the hours of the higheſt earthly proſperity, when our cup is full, and when we have laid up ſtores for ourſelves; for, in him who believes the promiſe of the Saviour of the World, it can cauſe no diſturbance to remember, that this night his ſoul may be required of him; and he who ſuffers one of the ſharpeſt evils which this life can ſhew, amidſt all its varieties of miſery; he that has lately been ſeparated from the perſon whom a long participation of good and evil had endeared to him; he who has ſeen kindneſs ſnatched from his arms, and fidelity torn from his boſom ; he whoſe ear is no more to be delighted with tender inſtruction, and whoſe virtue ſhall be no more awakened by the ſeaſonable whiſpers of mild reproof, may yet look, without horror, on the tomb which encloſes the remains of what he loved and honoured, as upon a place which, if it revives the ſenſe of his loſs, may calm him with the hope of that ſtate in which there ſhall be no more grief or ſeparation.

To Chriſtians the celebration of a funeral is by no means a ſolemnity of barren and unavailing ſorrow, but eſtabliſhed by the Church for other purpoſes.

Firſt, for the conſolation of ſorrow. Secondly, for the enforcement of piety. The mournful ſolemnity of the burial of the dead is inſtituted, firſt, for the conſolation of that grief to which the beſt minds, if not ſupported and regulated by religion, are moſt liable. They who moſt endeavour the happineſs of others, who devote their thoughts to tenderneſs and pity, and ſtudiouſly maintain the reciprocation of kindneſs, by degrees mingle their ſouls, in

ſuch

ſuch a manner, as to feel from their ſepa-ration, a total deſtitution of happineſs, a ſudden abruption of all their proſpects, a ceſſation of all their hopes, ſchemes and deſires. The whole mind becomes a gloomy vacuity, without any image or form of pleaſure, a chaos of confuſed wiſhes, directed to no particular end, or to that which, while we wiſh, we cannot hope to obtain; for the dead will not revive; thoſe whom God has called away from the preſent ſtate of exiſtence, can be ſeen no more in it; we muſt go to them; but they cannot return to us.

Yet, to ſbew that grief is vain, is to afford very little comfort; yet this is all that reaſon can afford; but religion, our only friend in the moment of diſtreſs, in the moment when the help of man is vain, when fortitude and cowardice ſink down together, and the ſage and the virgin mingle their lamentations; religion will inform us, that ſorrow and complaint are not only vain, but unreaſonble and erroneous. The voice of God, ſpeaking by his Son and his Apoſtles, will inſtruct us, that ſhe, whoſe departure we now mourn, is not dead, but

ſleepeth;

ſleepeth; that only her body is committed to the ground, but that the ſoul is returned to God, who gave it; that God, who is infinitely merciful, who hateth nothing that he has made, who deſireth not the death of a ſinner; to that God, who only can compare performance with ability, who alone knows how far the heart has been pure, or corrupted, how inadvertency has ſurpriſed, fear has betrayed, or weakneſs has impeded; to that God, who marks every aſpiration after a better ſtate, who hears the prayer which the voice cannot utter, records the purpoſe that periſhed without opportunity of action, the wiſh that vaniſhed away without attainment, who is always ready to receive the penitent, to whom ſincere contrition is never late, and who will accept the tears of a returning ſinner.

Such are the reflections to which we are called by the voice of Truth; and from theſe we ſhall find that comfort which philoſophy cannot ſupply, and that peace which the world cannot give. The contemplation of the mercy of God may juſtly afford ſome conſolation, even when the of-

fice

fice of burial is performed to thoſe who have been ſnatched away without viſible amendment of their lives; for, who ſhall preſume to determine the ſtate of departed ſouls, to lay open what God hath concealed, and to ſearch the counſels of the Moſt Higheſt?—But, with more confident hope of pardon and acceptance, may we commit thoſe to the receptacles of mortality, who have lived without any open or enormous crimes; who have endeavoured to propitiate God by repentance, and have died, at laſt, with hope and reſignation. Among theſe ſhe ſurely may be remembered whom we have followed hither to the tomb, to pay her the laſt honours, and to reſign her to the grave; ſhe, whom many, who now hear me, have known, and whom none, who were capable of diſtinguiſhing either moral or intellectual excellence, could know, without eſteem, or tenderneſs. To praiſe the extent of her knowledge, the acuteneſs of her wit, the accuracy of her judgement, the force of her ſentiments, or the elegance of her expreſſion, would ill ſuit with the occaſion.

Such praiſe would little profit the living, and as little gratify the dead, who is now

now in a place where vanity and competition are forgotten for ever; where ſhe finds a cup of water given for the relief of a poor brother, a prayer uttered for the mercy of God to thoſe whom ſhe wanted power to relieve, a word of inſtruction to ignorance, a ſmile of comfort to miſery, of more avail than all thoſe accompliſhments which confer honour and diſtinction among the ſons of Folly.—Yet, let it be remembered, that her wit was never employed to ſcoff at goodneſs, nor her reaſon to diſpute againſt truth. In this age of wild opinions, ſhe was as free from ſcepticiſm as the cloiſtered virgin. She never wiſhed to ſignalize herſelf by the ſingularity of paradox. She had a juſt diffidence of her own reaſon, and deſired to practice rather than diſpute. Her practice was ſuch as her opinions naturally produced. She was exact and regular in her devotions, full of confidence in the divine mercy, ſubmiſſive to the diſpenſations of Providence, extenſively charitable in her judgements and opinions, grateful for every kindneſs that ſhe received, and willing to impart aſſiſtance of every kind to all whom her little power enabled her

to

to benefit. She paſſed through many months languor, weakneſs, and decay, without a ſiugle murmur of impatience, and often expreſſed her adoration of that mercy which granted her ſo long time for recollection and penitence. That ſhe had no failings, cannot be ſuppoſed : but ſhe has now appeared before the Almighty Judge ; and it would ill become beings like us, weak and ſinful as herſelf, to remember thoſe faults which, we truſt, Eternal Purity has pardoned.

Let us therefore preſerve her memory for no other end but to imitate her virtues ; and let us add her example to the motives of piety which this ſolemnity was, ſecondly, inſtituted to enforce.

It would not indeed be reaſonable to expect, did we not know the inattention and perverſeneſs of mankind, that any one who had followed a funeral, could fail to return home without new reſolutions of a holy life : for, who can ſee the final period of all human ſchemes and undertakings, without conviction of the vanity of all that terminates in the preſent ſtate ? For, who can ſee the wiſe, the brave, the powerful,

or

or the beauteous, carried to the grave, without reflection on the emptiness of all those distinctions, which set us here in opposition to each other? And who, when he sees the vanity of all terrestrial advantages, can forbear to wish for a more permanent and certain happiness? Such wishes, perhaps, often arise, and such resolutions are often formed; but, before the resolution can be exerted, before the wish can regulate the conduct, new prospects open before us, new impressions are received; the temptations of the world solicit, the passions of the heart are put into commotion; we plunge again into the tumult, engage again in the contest, and forget, that what we gain cannot be kept, and that the life, for which we are thus busy to provide, must be quickly at an end.

But, let us not be thus shamefully deluded! Let us not thus idly perish in our folly, by neglecting the loudest call of Providence; nor, when we have followed our friends, and our enemies, to the tomb, suffer ourselves to be surprised by the dreadful summons, and die, at last, amazed, and unprepared! Let every one whose eye glances on this bier, examine what would

have

have been his condition, if the ſame hour had called him to judgement, and remember, that, though he is now ſpared, he may perhaps, be to-morrow among ſeparate ſpirits. The preſent moment is in our power; let us, therefore, from the preſent moment, begin our repentance! Let us not, any longer, harden our hearts, but hear, this day, the voice of our Saviour and our God, and begin to do, with all our powers, whatever we ſhall wiſh to have done, when the grave ſhall open before us! Let thoſe, who came hither weeping and lamenting, reflect, that they have not time for uſeleſs ſorrow; that their own ſalvation is to be ſecured, and that the day is far ſpent, and the night cometh, when no man can work; that tears are of no value to the dead, and that their own danger may juſtly claim their whole attention! Let thoſe who entered this place unaffected and indifferent, and whoſe only purpoſe was to behold this funeral ſpectacle, conſider, that ſhe, whom they thus behold with negligence, and paſs by, was lately partaker of the ſame nature with themſelves; and that they likewiſe are haſtening to their end, and muſt ſoon, by

others

others equally negligent, be buried and forgotten! Let all remember, that the day of life is ſhort, and that the day of grace may be much ſhorter; that this may be the laſt warning which God will grant us, and that, perhaps, he, who looks on this grave unalarmed, may ſink unreformed into his own!

Let it, therefore, be our care, when we retire from this ſolemnity, that we immediately turn from our wickedneſs, and do that which is lawful and right; that, whenever diſeaſe, or violence, ſhall diſſolve our bodies, our ſouls may be ſaved alive, and received into everlaſting habitations; where, with Angels and Archangels, and all the glorious Hoſt of Heaven, they ſhall ſing glory to God on high, and the Lamb, for ever and ever.

THE END.

Lightning Source UK Ltd.
Milton Keynes UK
UKHW020742251118
332796UK00002B/221/P

9 780483 509719